ART AS THERAPY

An introduction to the use of art as a therapeutic technique

edited by Tessa Dalley

Tavistock Publications
London and New York

First published in 1984 by
Tavistock Publications
11 New Fetter Lane, London EC4P 4EE
Reprinted 1985
Published in the USA by
Tavistock Publications
in association with Methuen, Inc.
29 West 35th Street, New York, NY 10001

© 1984 Tessa Dalley

Typeset by Tradespools Ltd, Frome, Somerset
Printed in Great Britain by Richard Clay
The Chaucer Press, Bungay, Suffolk

British Library Cataloguing in Publication Data

Art as therapy – (Social science paperback;
no. 265)
1. Art therapy
I. Dalley, Tessa   II. Series
615.8'5156   RJ505.A7

ISBN 0-422-78720-5
ISBN 0-422-78730-2 Pbk

Library of Congress Cataloging in Publication Data

Main entry under title:
Art as therapy.
Bibliography: p.
Includes index.
1. Art therapy – Addresses, essays, lectures.
I. Dalley, Tessa.
RC489.A7A74 1984   615.8"5156   84-1287
ISBN 0-422-78720-5
ISBN 0-422-78730-2 (pbk.)

A comment on art therapy by a long-term resident in a psychiatric hospital

'How strange the unconscious flow is. Painting can express it. Painting can express anything. Painting is there, even if only to tinker away an afternoon in a mental hospital. Painting is real.

Shapes and subjects. What can a farmer who has had a nervous breakdown make of them? Can he be an artist too? Does a scared, sick housewife go back to school to paint? Is the suffering too great to express? Can painting break down shyness? Is it fun! No, it isn't fun. It is soothing, however sharp and vicious the badinage of human nature in the therapy room.

Painting, art therapy is an exquisite art. It tells of people and fears. There is dynamo and dynamite in painting. It alleviates suffering and hails freedom, as if no artist was ever frightened of the misery and suffering of the world.

Just think of the universe you can paint. Just think of all you can paint. It is wonderful.'

ART THERAPY VIDEOTAPE

A videotape, ART THERAPY is also available from Tavistock Publications. Produced by Tessa Dalley (editor of this book) and Diane Waller, and directed by John Beacham, it gives a short introduction to art therapy.

Several approaches to working in different clinical situations are shown. Both individual and group sessions illustrate how different theories are put into practice. Illustrated case material and interviews with art therapists and clients in a hospital department further describe the effectiveness of the art therapy process.

Running time: 30 minutes. Colour. VHS, Beta and U-Matic. For sale only. For details please contact Caroline Lane at 11 New Fetter Lane, London EC4 Telephone: 01-583 9855.

Contents

Foreword

Peter Fuller
Writer and art critic,
author of Art and Psychoanalysis

The term 'art therapy' was not used in Britain until the 1940s, and criteria for the professional training of art therapists were not established here until as late as 1980. As the last paper in this collection explains, there are still only three colleges offering courses for would-be therapists.

Art therapy is thus a relative newcomer to the range of available therapeutic practices. The studies in this book clearly demonstrate there is no generally agreed consensus, even among its practitioners, about the scope of its applicability, its informing theories, or even its clinical objectives. Even when the discipline becomes fully 'established' it is probable, and I believe desirable, that a variety of approaches will continue to flourish.

None the less, it must be admitted that the theoretical assumptions underlying art therapy have sometimes seemed vague and ill-defined. This book is to be welcomed because it offers a wide-ranging exploration of many different aspects of both theory and practice.

Despite this variety, however, significant points of agreement can be discerned. All the papers gathered together here implicitly or explicitly reject the once fashionable idea that art therapy is primarily a diagnostic tool, or a way of providing material, sometimes for interpretation by other specialists. Whether they are discussing work with disturbed children, prisoners, anorexic, geriatric, or psychiatric patients, these art therapists have a much richer conception of the contribution they can make to the patient's well-being than that.

I believe that this growing confidence among art therapists that they have an important part to play in the therapeutic care of certain patients itself relates to a changing view about the nature and function of art, and its role in integrated, creative human living. Art therapy has roots in many longer established educational, aesthetic, and psychological disciplines. But there can be no doubt that one of its tendrils reaches back into the psychoanalytic tradition. Freud himself distinguished between the 'secondary processes' (verbal, rational, and analytic modes of thought) and the 'primary processes' (imaginative, symbolic, non-verbal, and non-discursive modes). Unfortunately, however, he tended to associate the latter, at least in so far as they manifested themselves in adults, with regression, neurosis, and ill-health. He was thus never entirely able to free himself from the view that art was on the side of illness – or, at best, an uneasy defence against it.

But recently, more and more psychoanalysts, especially in Britain, have come to regard the primary and secondary processes as being complementary rather than opposed: they argue that both are adaptive, and necessary for creative and healthy human life at every stage of development. As Marion Milner once explained, this shift of understanding came about when psychoanalysts confronted the facts of art. Until such a shift has been made, of course, art therapy remains either a diagnostic tool, or a contradiction in terms.

The late D. W. Winnicott was one British analyst who drew particular attention to the need, throughout life, for a third area of human experiencing which was concerned exclusively with neither subjective fantasy, nor objective knowledge, but involved a mingling of both. Towards the end of his life, he became increasingly interested in the relevance of these ideas to art and human creativity in general: it is gratifying to see from these papers what a profound influence his work has had on the development of so much current thinking in art therapy. One theme not touched upon in this book, however, is the way in which advanced technological societies like our own tend to marginalize the production of art, and to seal over this third area of human experiencing, which Winnicott described as 'the location of cultural experience'. Art may be necessary for human health and happiness, but it is becoming harder and harder for ordinary men, and ordinary women, to practise it. In Diane Waller's sensitive study of the similarities and differences between art teaching and therapy she suggests the distinction between the two may be institutional and professional rather than fundamental. Not only those in our society who have become ill, old, imprisoned, or mentally disturbed lack contact with creative processes and their restorative powers. In my view, there is space for two separate professions: but it would be a pity if there was not a strong interchange between them.

Introduction

Tessa Dalley

Art therapy is a relatively new discipline. Outside a small number of practitioners, its concepts and aims are not widely known or understood. This book is an attempt to change that situation. We hope to introduce the subject to people from a wide range of interests, including those in the related professions of social work, psychology, nursing, teaching, and also those who basically believe that there is more to art than paint on paper.

Our purpose is to refer specifically to the development and current practice of the profession within the British system of health and social services. The Welfare State, and the existence of the National Health Service unique to this country, have been fundamental in the development of ideas and attitudes towards the therapeutic services in general, and art therapy in particular.

This introductory chapter is divided into a number of sections that address what are believed to be the central topics for consideration. All the chapters that follow have been written by people working with art therapy. They have been chosen to reflect the ways in which art therapy can be applied in different clinical situations and represent the spectrum of ideas in contemporary practice. Chapters 1–4 are mainly theoretical; Chapters 5–12 each develop both theory and practice with different client groups, and the final chapter discusses training for the profession.

What is art therapy?

In simple terms, art therapy is the use of art and other visual media in a therapeutic or treatment setting. But as this activity ranges from the child scribbling to express him- or herself, to the mentally handicapped man working with clay to the graphic painting by a woman, deeply depressed, it is clearly very complex. Can this be called art, and if so, how and why is it therapeutic? These questions can best be answered by looking at the nature of the relationship between art and therapy. A discussion of how art therapy is derived from these two components will lead to a clearer definition.

The relationship between art and therapy

It has been suggested that art and therapy form an 'uneasy partnership' (Champernowne 1971), but it is my view that they can essentially interact as a dynamic treatment process.

The origins of using art in therapy can best be understood when considered in the context of the arts generally. Art is an indigenous feature of every society – the activity of painting is almost as ancient as man, and has symbolized both personal and cultural aspects of development. Art simultaneously reflects and predicts trends within society, and has traditionally been a forum for personal expression and creative ideas. The validity of this has long been recognized and, indeed, encouraged.

However, when used in a therapeutic setting, art is not recognized in the same way. One possible reason for this is the essential difference between 'art' in the traditional sense and art as it is used for therapeutic purposes. While it is generally understood that most art activity has some therapeutic qualities, what must be made clear is the distinct purpose of art therapy. When entered into spontaneously by an individual, the process of painting, for example, can be relaxing, satisfying, frustrating, even mildly 'therapeutic'. Although this activity is solitary, private, and contemplative, its main purpose is to produce and achieve a 'good painting' – that is, the aesthetic considerations are of prime importance. The final product is an end in itself, and is exhibited as a work of art; the process of creating it is secondary.

In contrast, art activity undertaken in a therapy setting, with clear corrective or treatment aims, in the presence of a therapist, has a different purpose and objective. In therapy, the person and process become most important, as art is used as a means of non-verbal communication. Put more elaborately, art activity provides a concrete rather than verbal medium through which a person can achieve both conscious and unconscious expression, and can be used as a valuable agent for therapeutic change.

A definition of therapy will make this clearer. Therapy involves the aim or desire to bring about change in human disorder. 'A therapeutic procedure is one designed to assist favourable changes in personality or in living that will outlast the session itself' (Ulman 1961:19). Effective therapeutic procedures are those which result in fundamental and permanent change, and so, as Ulman argues, therapy is 'distinguished from activities designed to offer only distraction from inner conflicts; activities whose benefits are therefore at best momentary' (Ulman 1961: 19).

The essence of art therapy, therefore, lies in the therapeutic outcome of the activity of creating something. A definition of art, when used in therapy, can now be formulated. For the purposes of this introduction, I would like to refer to Margaret Naumberg, a psychoanalytically orientated art therapist and the acknowledged pioneer of art therapy in the USA, although some British art therapists disagree with her approach (Maclagan 1979). She described art as a way of stating mixed, poorly understood feelings in an attempt to bring them into clarity and order. 'The process of art therapy is based on the recognition that man's most fundamental thoughts and feelings, derived from the unconscious, reach expression in images rather than words' (Naumberg 1958: 511).

It would be naive to suggest, however, that art is synonymous with therapy in the sense that all art activity is necessarily healing. This would imply an automatic fusion between art and therapy, in that the latter is a natural consequence of the former. What we must consider is what makes art therapeutic and how this is achieved.

It is widely acknowledged that the ability to communicate is an essential human characteristic. Making marks is a fundamental activity, the capacity for which is almost universal. When speech is impaired, underdeveloped, or for some reason rejected as the normal means of communication, art activity can provide a most valuable substitute. We believe that for people in these circumstances, the discovery of art as a means of communication is highly therapeutic. (This is more fully explained in Chapters 4 and 5 with specific reference to the mentally handicapped and children.) Even for the most articulate, art can be used as a type of 'symbolic speech' (Ulman 1961: 11); a means of saying something non-verbally through symbols. Images can create clarity in expression, especially with some things that are most difficult to say. Symbolizing feelings and experiences in images can be a more powerful means of expression and communication than verbal description, and at the same time, is able to render these feelings and experiences less threatening.

'The techniques of art therapy are based on the knowledge that every individual, whether trained or untrained in art, has a latent capacity to project his inner conflicts into visual form. As patients picture such inner experiences, it frequently happens that they become more verbally articulate.'   (Naumberg 1958: 511)

The drawing process itself is not the sole therapeutic agent. Like dreams, pictures have little meaning in isolation. Likewise, art therapists are not there simply to encourage people to draw and paint. When art is used for communication, as a way of expressing personal feelings and thoughts, and these are discussed afterwards with an art therapist, a person can gain insight both intellectually and emotionally by connecting the meaning of the picture to his or her own life situation. By focusing on the painting, many aspects of oneself, possibly previously hidden, may become clear. The person learns through the activity of creating something.

When analysed, various stages of art activity can be seen to contribute to this overall therapeutic effect. Art is a process in which the person is actively and physically engaged. Although perhaps initiated by a therapist, this activity is spontaneous, self-motivated, and also self-sustaining as the person becomes absorbed in what he or she is doing. At this stage, there may be a cathartic reaction; the actual process of painting can erode defences and barriers allowing powerful emotions to be expressed. (See Chapter 3 for further explanation of the therapeutic significance of art as catharsis.)

Edith Kramer, an art therapist who worked extensively with children in the USA, described the processes involved in art activity as having inherent healing properties which explain their usefulness in therapy. 'Art is a means of widening the range of human experiences by creating equivalents for such experiences. It is an area wherein experiences can be chosen, varied, repeated at will. In the creative act, conflict is re-experienced, resolved and integrated' (Kramer 1958:6). In other words, it is the rationalization of inner feelings into a comprehensible form. The actual process of creating something sets up a dialogue within the self. The conclusion of this dialogue can be seen as a concrete statement to the world. As a therapeutic tool, the art form, unique to the individual, provides the focus for discussion, analysis, and self-evaluation, and as it is concrete, acts as a record of this activity which cannot be denied, erased, or forgotten. It also survives in time and so is an index of and comparison between past and present.

If art activity is found to be beneficial or therapeutic in this way, why is it not more widely recognized and its use more widespread? One reason, already suggested, is the common misunderstanding of the way in which art is used and its purpose in therapy. There is another general point that I would like to put forward. The value of verbal communication is rated very highly in our society. This inevitably places emphasis on verbal types of therapy. The value of communication through imagery and symbols, although generally acknowledged, is seen as more obscure and even mystical. The ambiguity of art in general places it at a tangent, detached from the mainstream of communication, as people have little confidence in understanding its meaning or message. Because of this, art and artists easily generate stereotypes; in my experience, this is also true for art therapy and art therapists. Individuals tend to react to the use of art in therapy according to the way they perceive their own creativity or to their reaction to art in general. If this is valid, it may shed some light on the context in which art therapy currently operates, and this is examined in more depth in some of the chapters (Chapters 2, 6, and 13 in particular).

Generally, art therapy is little known, perhaps undervalued and its aims often misunderstood, but its practice is not so recent. There has been a long and gradual climb to achieve its present state of recognition as a profession in the UK. The historical links with art teaching, and the simultaneous development of using art for diagnosis in psychiatry have proved vital in the growth of art therapy. (This is fully explained in Chapter 1.)

The status of art therapy was well documented in 1970 by a visiting American (Betensky 1971). Betensky visited several practising art therapists who are still generally regarded as the pioneers of the profession in the UK. These included Irene Champernowne, a Jungian psychotherapist, at the Withymead Centre for Psychotherapy through the Arts; Edward Adamson at Netherne Hospital, Surrey; Professor Pickford at the Psychology Department, Glasgow University; Joyce Laing at the Ross Clinic, Aberdeen; and Dianna Halliday, artist and child psychotherapist at the Acton Child Guidance Clinic, London. She commented 'This is a generation of idealists' (Betensky 1971:85) and remarked on the dedication and true belief in their work despite almost complete professional isolation. She also described her visits to the colleges embarking on pilot training schemes for art therapists.

'The need for academic training was clearly paramount; this is the key to full recognition of art therapy as a profession, a recognition that will eventually make it possible for the art therapist to move out of his isolation and into his rightful place as a member of a team. I begin to feel that I am right in the middle of problems important for the development of British Art Therapy.'   (Betensky 1971:76)

Some theoretical approaches to art therapy

Any theoretical approach to art therapy must take account of the concept of creativity, which has its roots in all art processes. Creativity is a highly complex phenomenon and there is an extensive literature on the subject. To understand how the creative process works within the context of art therapy, Anthony Storr provides a useful general definition: 'Creativity is the ability to bring something new into existence for that person' (Storr 1972:11). It is this 'ability', similar to Naumberg's 'latent capacity', that provides the potential force for therapy.

The fact that many of the specialist approaches to art therapy in current practice are directly related to differing theories of creativity demonstrates its central importance. These, in turn, vary according to conflicting views of the derivation and origins of creativity in man. For example, a Freudian view would see the genesis of creativity in personal conflict. Unconscious defence mechanisms acting against neurosis and other symptom formation allow inner conflicts to be expressed in a creative act. Max Stern (1952), who used free painting in psychoanalysis, described how the painting by a neurotic adult is an attempt to repair, in a primitive way, the traumatic events experienced in the successive stages of Freudian development. These events are repeated in the drawings and this abreacts the neurotic conflict, as does children's play.

> 'Magic mastery through pictorial presentation is a regression to the identical stage of adaptation to reality in which the original traumata, now pressing for reparation, occurred; in most cases to the preverbal phase. The technique used in therapeutic painting is on a level with primitive, pictorial thought. It is of advantage that thus, both as to mode of thinking and of expression, it is on the same plane as the unconscious thought itself.'
>
> (Stern 1952:73)

Although Freud himself was generally regarded as having a somewhat 'philistine' attitude to formal painting (Fuller 1983) in spite of having an artist son, Ernst, he did make some reference to the role of art in psychoanalysis: 'For there is a path that leads back from phantasy to reality – the path, that is, of art' (Freud 1973:423). In this sense, Freud likens art to dreams as a starting point for interpretation, and refers to this in the following way:

> 'We experience it [a dream] predominantly in visual images; feelings may be present too, and thoughts interwoven in it as well; the other senses may also experience something, but nonetheless it is predominantly a question of images. Part of the difficulty of giving an account of dreams is due to our having to translate these images into words. "I could draw it", a dreamer often says to us, "but I don't know how to say it".'
>
> (Freud 1962:90)

One can only speculate on the impact of the development of art therapy had Freud permitted his patients to draw their dreams rather than to tell them (for a fuller discussion of his reluctance to use images in psychoanalysis see Maclagan 1983). However, art therapists who use a psychoanalytical approach, encourage this pictorial expression of inner experience. Art is recognized as a process of spontaneous imagery, released from the unconscious, using the mechanisms of repression, projection, identification, sublimation, and condensation, which are fundamental in the treatment method. Naumberg explains how this works to advantage:

> 'Objectified picturization acts then as an immediate symbolic communication which frequently circumvents the difficulties of speech. Another

advantage inherent in the making of unconscious pictured projections is that such symbolic images more easily escape repression by what Freud called the mind's "censor" than do verbal expression, which are more familiar to the patient.'   (Naumberg 1966: 2)

The Jungians, however, define creativity as finding form to express inner feelings, beliefs, and thoughts, and recognize this need to give meaningful form to experience as fundamental to art processes. Jung argued against the use of Freudian 'free association' techniques of interpretation but emphasized the general function of creative expression to restore psychological balance through symbolic meaning. (See Chapter 6 for a fuller explanation.)

In contrast, a strictly behaviourist approach uses art as a means of modifying cultural and social norms. The purpose of the activity is recognition of order and form and emphasis is placed on the acquisition of skill and learning technique. As this approach really lies within the boundaries of art teaching, it begs the question of whether it can be therapeutic. This particular issue is fully discussed in Chapter 1 which examines the similarities and differences between art therapy and art teaching.

Aesthetic considerations in art therapy

It seems that one crude distinction between teaching and therapy is that patients participating in art therapy sessions are not there to become skilled artists but to attempt to become more integrated members of society. In the same way, art therapists are not solely interested in the aesthetic quality of the work, but should be primarily concerned with the therapeutic value of producing it. The general emphasis on self-expression, rather than making a 'good' painting, means that the art work produced in therapy sessions tends to be diagrammatical, even simplistic, in terms of representational imagery.

But, however clearly this distinction is made, or indeed whatever theoretical approach is adopted, such is the nature of art that some therapeutic objectives may become duplicated or overlap. For example, it has happened that patients who are introduced to art in therapy sessions discover considerable natural talent or continue to pursue it actively as a hobby in their own leisure time. Although perhaps incidental to the original reason for participating in art, a discovery of this nature can be beneficial and 'therapeutic'. It can strengthen self-confidence and improve self-esteem when a painting becomes the focus of praise and enthusiasm. Learning any skill helps co-ordination, concentration, awareness of immediate surroundings and results in a sense of achievement, satisfaction, and self-improvement generally. Art activity offers this opportunity; it may even create a meaning or purpose to life. A former 'client' may become 'artist' in his or her own right.

Aesthetic considerations must not therefore be completely discounted, as some of the art work produced is of outstanding quality. Art collections such as the Guttman Maclay, comprised entirely of 'psychiatric art', and several major exhibitions of art arising from therapy have encouraged the viewer or critic to consider this work in terms of its aesthetic value alone – that is as a 'work of art'. A notable example is the work of Jimmy Boyle (see Chapter 10), whose sculpture is permanently exhibited in Glasgow. Exhibiting work produced in therapy has long been the subject of debate within the profession. While some therapists feel that to exhibit work creates a misplaced assessment of the aims of the activity (see Chapter 3), others feel that aesthetic aspects of art are highly important within the art therapy process and emphasis should be placed on their contribution to the art world generally (Byrne 1978).

Client groups

A wide variety of patients are referred to art therapy which forms an integral part of their treatment programme (see Chapters 5, 6, and 7). But there are a number of people who come to art therapy who realistically have no hope of 'getting better'; for example, those people with severe mental or physical handicap, psychogeriatrics, and the long-term institutionalized. As they must be approached with a less curative emphasis, a more appropriate therapeutic objective is to use art for enjoyment, exploration, and stimulation. Different media provide an enormous variety of sensory and tactile experiences; making things with others helps interaction, communication, and awareness of other people. The long-term or 'chronic' patient population are without doubt the silent majority of the people, frequently forgotten, who fill most hospitals and institutions. Art therapy is probably their only outlet and opportunity for individual expression, stimulation, and creative occupation. Several chapters (Chapters 8 and 12 for example) fully demonstrate how art is not just important but often central to the lives of many of these people.

Connected with this, Chapter 10 examines the role of art in prisons and how it can operate within the restrictions inevitably imposed on a client group sentenced to institutional life. Chapter 9 illustrates how the arts generally have been used to deal with mortality. Art is able to cut through and transcend the taboos that surround the acceptance of death, and this can be of great therapeutic value for those who are coming to the end of their life and face the imminence of death.

From this it can be seen that art has unique, universal, and ubiquitous properties for its application in therapy. Having concentrated mostly on these properties, attention must now be turned to the role of the therapist, the other essential participant in the art therapy process. Art has little therapeutic significance without the intervention or presence of a therapist, who basically provides the 'human factor' in establishing a therapeutic relationship through an art form. So if art is used as a therapeutic tool, how do art therapists work? What in fact do they do?

Art therapy in practice

Art therapists work in their own departments or studios, or on hospital wards as part of a multi-disciplinary team. They can work in a one-to-one situation or in different types of groups using various art therapy techniques. Working conditions vary enormously according to the place of work, theoretical standpoints, therapeutic objectives, client groups, working environment, staff co-operation, and so on.

On the whole, art therapy sessions are divided into two stages. The first involves a period of painting or other creative activity, during which there is a sense of isolation and alienation as the participants begin to think, self-reflect, and withdraw into themselves. This is followed by a period of discussion which tends to focus on the actual production of the art form, how it makes the clients feel, how it reflects their feelings, and generally how the process of creating an image relates to the individual's situation.

Using this kind of format, the art therapist must first decide on therapeutic approach; in particular whether to be directive or non-directive. Some art therapists work entirely non-directively. The choice of subject is left to the patient, who is encouraged to express him- or herself freely, however and with whatever he or she chooses. This is a type of 'free association' through art, and this approach is more fully discussed in Chapters 5, 7, and 8. Whether the session is directive or non-directive, the therapist usually explains, at the outset, the aim of the session and how this might be achieved using the materials available. The session can be directed by concentrating on a specific theme which may be useful in resolving particular conflict areas. The themes range from the deeply personal and troubling to the relatively superficial and light-hearted, but must be chosen according to therapeutic objectives.

Art therapy in groups can take various forms, but each sets up powerful group dynamics, using the art work in the group as a focus. In projective art groups, themes are introduced to provide a common framework to which each individual in the group relates his or her own personal meaning. This encourages both self- and group exploration in the sharing of a common theme.

The groups are self-sustaining since many members identify with each other's contributions. The group process is very powerful, as everyone participates to some degree. There may be a sense of regression, and also inhibition, as adults faced with the prospect of painting link this with childhood and generally failure in art at school. Initial resistance is usually expressed in responses such as 'Are we back in kindergarten?', 'I can't draw a straight line', and 'You won't make an artist out of me'. If other group members offer reassurance to dispel these anxieties, participating in a group of this nature can strengthen self-confidence.

Group art involves working together as a group, rather than each person offering an individual contribution, and this helps to elucidate interpersonal relationships within the group. Many of these group techniques are described in more depth in Chapter 11, which looks at a variety of approaches which can be used with a wide range of client and community groups.

A more specialized form of art therapy is working with the family. Art is used as a means of communication which provides an unusual opportunity to observe how the family unit functions in a situation less formal and less subject to the established mechanisms of control and behaviour pattern. An individual's painting portrays a personal insight into the dynamics of the family unit – a group of people who are not linked by general maladjustment or common symptoms, but who have simply lived together as a unit for many years – and illustrates the person's perception of his or her position within it.

Whether working with individuals or groups, art therapists are participants as well as observers in this therapeutic process. By working together and discussing the art work produced in the sessions, the therapist must help the client make sense of his or her own painting. This does not imply direct analysis or interpretation, but mutual suggestion and exploration, by both client and therapist, of the meaning of the images. The solidity and concrete nature of the art form provides a clear visual arena for therapeutic work and some obvious starting points for interpretation. Interpretation should be approached with caution, however, for, despite the apparent advantages in having such a tangible focus, art forms are statements on many different levels, and this tends to exacerbate the risk of error or misunderstanding.

For example, a black blob which appears in the corner of a painting may be mistaken for an evil symbol when it was only spilt paint or simply a lack of drawing skill. Even the most experienced art therapist cannot be totally confident about correct interpretation without active participation and cooperation from the client within the therapeutic encounter. As the painting is unique to the 'artist', it is only he or she who can ultimately come to understand its full significance. The therapist must therefore first ask the client to attempt an explanation of the content and meaning of his or her work, which can then be further explored and understood through interaction with and possible interpretation by the therapist.

The amount of interpretation must obviously depend on the individual therapist's style. For those inexperienced or unskilled in therapy, or unfamiliar with the use of art in this way, there may be a temptation to make premature interpretations when it seems that the meaning of a symbol is clear and obvious. Champernowne (1971) makes the following point:

'Logical analysis and translation of pictured ideas into words can be dangerous and destructive in the hands of inexperienced therapists. This is why a good analysis for any therapist is a great advantage. He should then know how not to interfere. The art form has its own validity and to translate from one language to another is bound to bring loss or error.'

(Champernowne 1971:141)

Winnicott (1971) also refers to the essential dangers of the need of the inexperienced therapist to make interpretations:

'If only we can wait, the patient arrives at understanding creatively and with immense joy, and I now enjoy this more than I used to enjoy the sense of having been clever. I think I interpret mainly to let the patient know the limits of my understanding. The principle is that it is the patient and only the patient who has the answers. We may or may not enable him or her to encompass what is known or become aware of it with acceptance.'   (Winnicott 1971:102)

The skill and effectiveness of an art therapist does not only lie in the ability to intervene or aid interpretation of the painting or product. The art therapist's choice of materials is also of great importance. Both two- and three-dimensional art materials have enormous potential and flexibility for therapy. The therapist has many options available in the appropriate choice of different media, which may include paint, clay, sand, crayon, collage, or 'junk', each of which contains particular therapeutic properties. The versatility of these materials offers immense scope, and the choice made in planning depends on the type of client, the stage that has been reached in therapy, and the main presenting therapeutic problems. The session must thus be carefully planned and thought out beforehand.

The outcome of a session is directly linked to correct and careful planning. This is partly due to the crucial nature of the first stage of an art therapy session. It is the point at which, after explanation by the therapist, the person begins to work by putting paint to paper. In therapeutic terms, this is most significant as each mark is a unique, personal commitment of the self to the blank sheet. This is further explained by Laing:

'Every original art production by the patient is in some degree an aspect of that person. No-one else can create the same result on paper or canvas. Art therapy offers an area where the patient can proclaim his identity and it offers an atmosphere where he can be himself.... Art offers a medium which can give both communication with others and confrontation with the self.'   (Laing 1974:17)

As with any therapeutic endeavour, the relationship between therapist and client is of central importance. Art is used as a medium through which this relationship develops. Although the art production becomes the focus of the relationship, the strong feelings that develop between patient and therapist are usually concerned with transference. Transference occurs when the patient transfers strong, often infantile feelings that originate from childhood experiences or early relationships on to the therapist. This transference is central to any psychotherapeutic relationship, and is most important in unfolding early history and experiences, which in turn can be related to the present-day circumstances.

The dynamics of transference and counter-transference are complex, and it could be argued that these are more wholly based in psychoanalysis. In fact, it is sometimes considered that focusing on an art production essentially detracts from the real work of a psychoanalytic relationship. However, whereas transference is the main 'tool' of a psychoanalyst, art is the central therapeutic agent for an art therapist, even though transference develops and is a powerful phenomenon within an art therapy relationship. 'The art therapist should remain, more fully than the psychotherapist or psychiatrist, related to and within the creative pattern, participating primarily at the level of the symbols and images used' (Champernowne 1971:141). The transference relation in art therapy is therefore modified by images through which the patient, by means of free association, begins to understand more clearly the origins of his or her conflicts, which may have begun in very early family relationships. (Chapters 1, 3, and 5 explain the workings of transference in more depth.)

Equally important is the therapeutic environment or atmosphere in which this relationship between client and therapist can develop and grow. Rogers (1976), in his client-centred approach to psychotherapy, lists three factors – warmth, empathy, and genuineness – that he regards as essential to ensure the development of openness and trust in the relationship and so facilitate therapeutic progress. I would also consider the presence of these to be fundamental to the successful development of any relationship in art therapy, whatever theoretical stance is adopted. In addition to this I think it is essential that the art therapist fully understands the potency of communication through symbols and images and should have a personal familiarity with this process.

What art therapy is not

By now I hope that some common misconceptions generally held about art therapy have been dispelled. First, that art therapy is not only for potential artists or those who show an interest or natural talent in the subject. It happens all too often that referrals are made to art therapists on this basis.

More contact between the different disciplines would help solve this particular misunderstanding. The majority of patients treated successfully in art therapy have neither drawn nor painted before. Those inexperienced in creative expression must be helped to gain confidence in their capacity to express thoughts and feelings through images. The approach for somebody already skilled in art is quite different, as there is a tendency for the 'artist' to use these specialized skills to distort or repress unconscious material when attempts are made to work with inner conflicts in therapy. As Naumberg explains:

> 'It is especially difficult to free an artist from the tyranny of his technical knowledge. When archaic forms begin to break through from his unconscious, during treatment, the artist becomes eager to capitalize, immediately, on this new content for his professional work. He must then be persuaded to postpone the application of such unconscious imagery to conscious work until therapy is completed.'   (Naumberg 1958:514)

It is certainly my experience, when working with trained artists in art therapy workshops, that they have found it necessary to abandon their technique in favour of spontaneity and self-revelation. Group pressure tends to have the effect of 'de-skilling' the artist by removing these technical barriers as other members feel a sense of inadequacy in not having this skill to hide behind. What is interesting is that this experience has, in many cases, caused a radical and permanent change in the artist's work.

Second, art therapists are not art teachers. They may be artists but they must also be trained in the awareness of their actions within the therapeutic process. Ideally, they should have some experience of personal therapy to increase insight and self-knowledge. Art is too 'powerful' to play with in that it is not a trivial or menial activity. Its potential effect in therapy necessitates rigorous training and professional standards from which art therapists work in practice.

Third, art therapy is not just a form of occupational therapy. This confusion was compounded by administrative organization, which until recently meant that art therapists worked under the auspices of the occupational therapy department. Traditionally, occupational therapy is concerned with working on a conscious level, with the aim of developing technique in making products, using methods which are really more compatible with those of teaching. Certainly, the activity of art has some occupational aspects which are therapeutic, but other qualities, peculiar to art, particularly in relation to working with the unconscious, have contributed to its development as a separate specialism. As a result, art therapy is really more closely allied to psychoanalytic therapy procedures, as its methods are based on the encouragement of free association and spontaneous expression. However, both art therapists and occupational therapists can offer their own expertise in working together within a treatment programme, particularly as the more progressive ways of working in occupational therapy now concentrate more fully on creativity.

In British practice, most people consider that art therapists cannot, indeed should not, 'read' or interpret any painting. However experienced or well-qualified an art therapist, the only person able or 'qualified' to interpret correctly is the 'artist', as the meaning of the painting has relevance only to his or her personal situation. The therapist may speculate, suggest, and connect aspects of the picture, but this occurs within the therapeutic relationship in an environment of trust, openness, and safety, and should not occur outside this context. It has been my experience that art therapists are asked to analyse or make sense of paintings about which they know nothing. This stems from the notion that art therapists possess the ability to make complete objective assessments of people from their art work.

Finally, art therapy is not diagnosis through art. There is a popular conception that a disturbed, fragmented type of painting is connected with a disturbed personality: Van Gogh and Edward Munch are prime examples. While this is a very interesting idea, at the present time we believe it is a matter only for speculation, as there is no way of testing its validity. Whereas it is easy to make the connection between a disturbed mental state and 'disturbance' in art forms, it is not so easy to determine whether we are seeing a valid connection or, forearmed with knowledge of the disturbance, we look for indicators of this in the artist's work.

Of more immediate concern for our clinical purposes in art therapy is the evidence that certain images and symbols do recur in paintings by similar client groups, particularly by those with similar symptoms. But this is not the same as making the assumption that these symbols reflect the particular symptoms or mental states in general. For example, a depressed person will express feelings of blackness, hopelessness, emptiness, which are similar to those of another depressed person. These same two people will, independently of each other, communicate these depressive feelings in paintings that have similar features in terms of form, content, and colour. This does not imply, however, that because a person draws a certain image, he or she is depressed. Our present knowledge does not allow this particular leap and so makes the idea untenable. However, those experienced in working with specific client groups can recognize recurring features in their paintings, and would probably say that some people can be crudely categorized according to what and how they paint. But these ideas are based solely on observational accounts of individual practitioners.

Of course this does not mean that art therapists do not already make clinical assessments, but decisions are made by taking an overall account of art work and of how the art work has developed and changed during the course of therapy (see Chapter 8, for example). Paintings act as a record as well as an accurate monitor of change since they can be compared over time. They are therefore invaluable in the assessment of therapeutic change for both therapist and client. We are not yet at the stage, however, of reaching the same conclusions from the objective analysis of the content of paintings. It is often argued that if art therapy is to become methodologically sound and accountable, scientific study must investigate the validity of diagnosis from painting, which is certainly an enormous area for enquiry. There is more research being undertaken into art therapy generally, and in particular into the efficacy of diagnosis through art, in the USA, where I understand its use in practice is also more widespread.

Research and the future

One of the major criticisms levelled at art therapy by those unconvinced of its effectiveness is the lack of conclusive evidence of results. Research into art therapy in Britain has admittedly been rather sporadic and unsystematic. Far more work has been done in the USA, particularly in the areas of clinical effectiveness and diagnosis (see Serban 1972, Wadeson 1971, Anastasi and Foley 1944, for example). Extensive psychological research into subjects related to art therapy, such as studies in the drawing of the human figure, has also contributed to our present body of knowledge (Machover 1949, Holzberg and Wexler 1950, Swensen 1968), but it is very hard to find conclusive statistical results in art therapy research which are anyway notoriously difficult to achieve (Dalley 1978).

Some studies are based on descriptive case material that looks at the working of the art therapy process in detail (Rosenberg 1965, Dalley 1980 and 1981). Given the difficulties surrounding other methods of assessment, a practicable way of obtaining research information is actually to ask the patient concerned, who is after all the 'consumer'. Feedback from patients has been found to provide material that, although subjective, is useful in establishing how art therapy operates and for whom it is most effective (Dalley 1978). For example, the following explanation was obtained from one patient:

> 'Most of my paintings consist of only two or three colours – red, black and occasionally yellow. When I am depressed, black represents total despair and a great sense of personal worthlessness: red represents anger of an almost suffocating kind – anger directed mainly at myself because of this sense of worthlessness: the occasional use of yellow suggests feeble and rare glimmers of hope for a future. Where I have drawn a figure, it is usually a black silhouette, I think that the figure is a silhouette because I don't want to acknowledge that the figure bombarded by despair and anger is myself.

When I was in hospital I found art therapy very valuable, with an almost cathartic element. Frequently I went to the art sessions in a very anxious, depressed frame of mind, not really wanting to make any effort – which I was allowed to do in my own time – I found that my hostile and even aggressive feelings were quickly translated onto paper.'

(Dalley 1978)

This type of comment can give some indication as to how and even why art therapy is effective. However, it is essential that the effectiveness of art therapy be evaluated by specific data in the future, in order that the field may develop more productively and so that we may determine how much emphasis should be placed on it in treatment.

What of the future of art therapy? As a profession, art therapy has become established within the British National Health Service, although many anomalies still exist. There are now three training centres that offer a variety of postgraduate courses. Bearing in mind the professional origins of art therapy and its evolution from separate 'camps', there is still a current debate about whether an art therapist must be primarily trained in art or in psychology and psychotherapy. Accordingly, although they are well standardized, each of the training courses offers slightly different orientations in their approach to art therapy. Training issues and details of the courses available in the UK are fully discussed in Chapter 13, which provides a thorough analysis of all the relevant questions surrounding the subject. However, most of the chapters stress that actual participation in art therapy is fundamental to the learning process.

It has been, and still remains, a hard struggle to establish art therapy as a valid and accepted discipline in Britain. Gradually attitudes are changing, but much remains to be done. The ultimate goal must be to establish art therapy as an integral and valued part of every treatment programme. We hope that this book will go some way towards achieving that end.

All the chapters in this book are written by practitioners and teachers of art therapy, but the book is not designed as a manual for practice; nor should the reader expect to find consensus amongst all the writers. Art therapy in Britain is a young and fast-growing discipline, and this is reflected in the lively discourse contained in current thinking. It is greatly to the advantage of the profession that this should continue, and it is this exciting exchange of ideas that we hope will stimulate the interest of general readers, and perhaps encourage them to enquire further into the vast field to which this book can only be an introduction.

References

Anastasi, A. and Foley, J. P. (1944) An Experimental Study of the Drawing Behaviour of Adult Psychotics in Comparison with that of a Normal Control Group. *Journal of Experimental Psychology* 34(3): 170–94.

Betensky, M. (1971) Impressions of Art Therapy in Britain: A Diary. *American Journal of Art Therapy* 10 (Jan.): 75–86.

Byrne, P. (1978) The Meaning of Art in Art and Psychopathology. *Inscape* 3(1): 13–20.

Champernowne, I. (1971) Art and Therapy: An Uneasy Partnership. *American Journal of Art Therapy* 10(3) (April): 131–43.

Dalley, T. (1978) 'An Investigation of the Efficacy of Art Therapy in Psychiatric Treatment.' Unpublished thesis, Hertfordshire College of Art and Design, St Albans.

— (1978) Drawing out Tensions with Art Therapy. *Therapy* 5(20/21): 4.

— (1980) Art Therapy in Psychiatric Treatment: An Illustrated Case Study. *Art Psychotherapy* 6(4): 257–65.

— (1981) Assessing the Therapeutic Effects of Art: An Illustrated Case Study. *Art Psychotherapy* 7(1): 11–17.

Freud, S. (1962) Part II: Dreams. In *New Introductory Lectures in Psychoanalysis*, vol. 15. London: Hogarth Press.

— (1973) *Introductory Lectures on Psychoanalysis.* Harmondsworth: Penguin.

Fuller, P. (1983) Does Therapy Disrupt the Creative Process? *Inscape* (April): 5–7.

Holzberg, J. D. and Wexler, M. (1950) Validity of Human Drawings of Personality Deviation. *Journal of Projective Techniques* 14: 344–61.

Kramer, E. (1958) *Art Therapy in a Children's Community.* Springfield, Ill.: C. C. Thomas.

Laing, J. (1974) Art Therapy: Painting Out the Puzzle of the Inner Mind. *New Psychiatry* 6 (Nov. 28): 16–18.

Machover, K. (1949) *Personality Projection in the Drawing of the Human Figure.* Springfield, Ill.: C. C. Thomas.

Maclagan, D. (1979) Missing, Presumed Lost. *Artscribe* 17: 22–6.

— (1983) Freud and the Figurative. *Inscape* (October): 10–12.

Naumberg, M. (1958) Art Therapy: Its Scope and Function. In E. F. Hammer (ed.) *Clinical Applications of Projective Drawings.* Springfield, Ill.: C. C. Thomas.

— (1966) *Dynamically Orientated Art Therapy: Its Principles and Practice.* New York: Grune & Stratton.

Rosenberg, L. (1965) Rapid Changes in Overt Behaviour Reflected in the 'Draw a Person': A Case Report. *Journal of Projective Techniques and Personality Assessment* 29(3): 349–51.

Rogers, C. (1976) *Client-Centred Therapy.* London: Constable.

Serban, G. (1972) A Critical Study of Art Therapy in Treating Psychotic Patients. *Behavioural Neuropsychiatry* 3(1–2): 2–20.

Stern, M. (1952) Free Painting as an Auxiliary Technique in Psychoanalysis. In G. Bychowski and J. L. Despert *Specialized Techniques in Psychotherapy.* New York: Basic Books.

Storr, A. (1972) *The Dynamics of Creation.* Harmondsworth: Penguin.

Swenson, C. H. (1968) Empirical Evaluations of Human Figure Drawings. *Psychological Bulletin* 70(1): 20–40.

Ulman, E. (1961) Art Therapy: Problems of Definition. *Bulletin of Art Therapy* 1(2): 10–20.

Wadeson, H. (1971) Characteristics of Art Expression in Depression. *Journal of Nervous and Mental Disease* 153(3): 197–204.

Winnicott, D. (1971) *Playing and Reality*. Harmondsworth: Penguin.

Biographical note

Tessa Dalley Having always been interested in painting, I 'discovered' art therapy by meeting some artists working in a large mental hospital where I was temporarily employed during my university vacations (BA Hons, Leeds University 1974). I went on to do the Postgraduate Diploma in Art Therapy (Hertfordshire College of Art and Design, St Albans 1976), after which I was awarded the Rank Xerox Research Fellowship, through Herts College of Art and Design, to undertake clinically based research at Fulbourn Hospital, Cambridge. Since then, I have worked in a variety of settings, most recently in a psychiatric day centre in Leeds. An increasing interest in the combination of art and psychotherapy led to the Diploma in Psychotherapy (Leeds University 1981). I have also been involved in setting up exhibitions, teaching sessions, and running workshops for many different professional groups. I have regularly contributed to administration and teaching in the annual Art Therapy Spring School run by Leeds Polytechnic. Currently I work as an art therapist in a primary school on a part-time basis and am involved in child psychotherapy training at the Tavistock Clinic.

A consideration of the similarities and differences between art teaching and art therapy

1

Diane Waller

Introduction

Before I began to work on this chapter, I asked myself, how did it happen that I came to write on the similarities and differences between art teaching and art therapy in the first place? What aspects of these two professional activities can usefully be subjected to a comparison? Furthermore, why should it even be necessary to compare them – is it just because they include the word 'art', or is it that they have often been confused? Do they have common ground, and if so, what and why is this? If there are differences, do they arise because of the environment in which they are practised – that is to say, teachers work in schools with 'normal' children and therapists work in hospitals with 'sick' people? But what about the teachers who work in hospitals and the therapists in schools? By changing their title, would they be doing the same thing?

For my part, I was made acutely aware of how British, or possibly American, these questions appear when I visited Bulgaria, a country where art therapy is beginning to be used and where it has no connection whatsoever with art teaching. Art therapists in Bulgaria are doctors and psychologists and they work within the medical model of psychiatry. Art teachers are concerned with imparting skills and with teaching the history of art. It would not occur to a Bulgarian art student to think of training as an art therapist. Nor would it occur to the student to explore the similarities and differences between art teaching and art therapy. There would be no real point in it, for there is no obvious link to be made and no stand to be taken.

I tried to free myself from the unquestioning attitude I must have adopted in seeing this issue as quite a logical one to explore. Such an attitude was no doubt formed as a result of my own education and experience as an art student, art therapist, and psychotherapist who has been involved with the training of art teachers, art therapists, and teachers who wish to become art therapists. Some of these teachers wish to use their art skills and the insights from art therapy to be more effective as art teachers or to teach children with special needs. More often than not, though, they feel daunted by this prospect and prefer to work in the health service where there is now a structure in which art therapists can confidently use their professional skills. As yet, there is no such structure within education.

This presupposes that there is such a difference of approach between teaching and therapy that it is necessary for a teacher to take another course of professional training. My contention is that there is, and indeed the most recent report, by the Calouste Gulbenkian Foundation, makes the following observation:

'In any school there are children, who, for a variety of reasons require some form of remedial activities or therapy.... All may need the attention of specialist teachers and/or therapists.

We approach our comments here with caution because of the emphatic differences between general education and therapy. We only want to note the growing body of experience and opinion which points to the particular value of the arts – especially music, art, dance and drama – in these two areas of remedial education and therapy.... In drawing attention to these specialized uses of the arts in education, we emphasize that they are the province of trained and qualified specialists in art, drama and music therapy and not of the general classroom teacher. Nevertheless, the existence and value of this work should be recognized in schools and by local education authorities.'

(Calouste Gulbenkian Foundation 1982:105)

The task of the Educational Mode of the Diploma in Art Therapy[1] has been to address itself to the needs of art teachers who wish to re-orientate themselves as art therapists. This has proved both exciting and difficult and I would not wish to minimize the problems these teachers face, which are of a professional and emotional nature. By carefully monitoring their processes of change, we have been able to see a little more clearly where the similarities and differences in practice actually lie between art teaching and art therapy. This does not explain, however, why it is that art teachers should come onto a course of training in art therapy in the first place, nor why art therapy has been intimately linked with art education in Britain, to the point where two of the three art therapy courses have grown out of art education departments in art colleges or faculties, and one of these

(Birmingham Polytechnic) still remains within. Was this an accident of fate, or expediency, or were there good reasons for the link?

I have to say that I owe a particular debt to Eisner (1974), whose article 'The Mythology of Art Education' stimulated me to examine the myth of the 'hothouse' approach to art education, which I suspect frequently gets confused with art therapy. I have referred to the 'hothouse', for a central element of this myth is that the child is like a budding plant and the teacher is the gardener. If left to his own resources, the child will develop 'naturally' – that is, he will develop his potential to be a certain kind of person and to produce a certain kind of art. The assumption here is that the child develops from the inside out, and that the teacher's job is to provide a rich environment and emotional support.

I went on to read Eisner's 'Educating Artistic Vision' in which he quotes a passage from the American art therapist, Naumberg (Eisner 1972: 253–54). He contrasts Naumberg's psychoanalytic language with that of Staats (1968) – an author who writes in terms of perceptual development and behaviour modification, thus indicating a totally different orientation to the problem of understanding behaviour and art education. As Naumberg (1966) was one of the first persons to use the term 'art therapy' and her work has been highly influential both in the USA and in Britain, it is fair to suppose that her language and methods will have been extensively absorbed and incorporated into art therapy theory and practice.

It would seem useful, then, to select 'dynamically orientated art therapy' as described by Naumberg and which is allied to the 'non-directive' method so popular in Britain for comparison with the 'child-centred' approach in art education, which puts emphasis on the child's personal expression through art. We could also refer to child-centred as person-centred, for obviously art teaching and art therapy are not confined to children. To fail to select specific areas for comparison would suggest that there is only one approach to art teaching and art therapy, which is clearly not the case.

The present chapter, then, will explore some of the questions I have asked in this introduction, with reference to the history of art education and art therapy in Britain and to the current practice of both.

Historical links between art education and art therapy

In order to tackle the task of comparison, it is necessary to look at the historical background of art education, for, in Britain, art therapy has evolved in part from these roots. MacDonald writes of the state of art at the end of the nineteenth century:

'The downfall of academic High Art at the end of the 19th century and the rise of the colourful post Impressionist work shortly afterwards, made possible for the first time a comparison between child and adult art. Child art, primitive art, tribal art and Western Asiatic art were no longer regarded as crude, but rather as sensitive and expressive forms of art.'

(MacDonald 1970:329)

No doubt the acceptance of other forms of art led to the art work of the 'insane' being considered worthy of attention and the romantic view that insanity and genius were closely related was once more of great interest. Such art was still however considered to be outside the mainstream, although the margins were becoming less clearly defined. This attempt to link primitive and child art is evident throughout the early decades of this century when there was a growth of interest in expression and imagination among art educators (Viola 1944). Tomlinson, a man of great influence as Senior Art Adviser and Inspector for the London County Council and Chairman of the Board of Examiners for the Art Teacher's Certificate, observed the following:

'The teacher's attitude towards the child has changed. Instead of impressing upon the child pre-conceived ideas of his own, relating to technical attainment and adult standards, the teacher encourages him to express fearlessly his own creative and imaginative impulses. Efforts are made by some to release the subconscious mind by letting the child draw and paint patterns and colours which he sees in his mind's eye. It is believed that morbid fears and fancies are thus released.'

(Tomlinson 1934:37)

John Iveson, Director of a Yorkshire psychiatric hospital, also referred indirectly to this approach (and alluded to the dangers inherent within it when a patient's 'morbid fancies' get out of control) (Iveson 1938:73). Therefore a comparison was made, perhaps unintentionally, between psychiatric patients and children – and also to 'primitive' people. As we shall see, such ideas predated that form of art therapy which stresses the spontaneous expression of the patient and assumes that there is a stage when the art work reaches a 'primitive' or 'pre-verbal' level which is somehow culture and value free.

The theories of art education prevalent in the 1930s continued in modified forms well into the 1960s under the influence of authors like Herbert Read (*Education Through Art*, 1943) and Viktor Lowenfeld (*Creative and Mental Growth*, 1947). Art was a means for developing a seeing, thinking, feeling and creative human being, a logical development of the ideas of the early twentieth-century American educational philosopher John Dewey and an ideal well suited to a world war and immediately post-war period: let the children, at least, have their freedom. There does not now seem to be a single, overall pattern, although the 'child-centred' concept of earlier decades still exists in some schools and colleges. Where these ideas do seem to continue, in modified form, is in some aspects of art therapy, for a parallel development seems to have taken place.

Interest in the art of the mentally disturbed was apparent at the turn of the nineteenth century under the same impetus as the interest in child art. Tardieu (1872), Simon (1876), Lombroso (1891) wrote about the art of the insane and Prinzhorn produced his major work *Bildernei der Geisteskranken (Artistry of the Mentally Ill)* in 1922, referring to a collection of paintings from his Heidelberg clinic. Jung, who was an artist himself, was a great influence on the art educator and philosopher Herbert Read, and through Read, had a strong influence on the movement in art education termed 'Child Art'. There is evidence that Jung had begun to use the art work of his patients therapeutically before 1920 at his clinic in Zurich.[2]

Freud wrote about art in 1917 and described the artist as:

'an introvert, not far removed from neurosis. He desires to win honour, power, wealth, fame and the love of women; but he lacks the means for achieving these satisfactions. Consequently, like any other unsatisfied man, he turns away from reality and transfers all his interest and his libido too, to the wishful constructions of his life in phantasy, whence the path might lead to neurosis.' (Freud 1971:376)

Such views were not without criticism. Roger Fry (1924) wrote a scathing critique of Freud and Jung's views of art; but if according to Roger Fry, Jung's patients, whom he encouraged to draw and paint, were not making art, what were they doing? Were they, like children in a way, using art to 'grow through' neurosis? Or were they, in the sense of Melanie Klein and the Object Relations psychologists, using it to move from one stage of development to another with the painting as transitional object, being the means of achieving change? It is tempting to believe that an adult is capable of regression to a pre-verbal stage of development through making art, but unless one holds firmly to the view that mental disorder is created solely from the failure to negotiate certain developmental stages in life, then it may be unhelpful to view the art therapy process as having only this aim. On the other hand, early childhood traumas do account for many disturbances later on in life and if an art therapist can provide a safe environment and herself as a 'good enough' parent, then perhaps such trauma may be relived and worked through by the process of making art, rather than, say, through free association in a verbal mode.

However there is a weakness in a theory of art as development which stresses 'natural' development and which seems to pay scant attention to the fact that a child or adult may be positively as well as negatively influenced by social and cultural factors. It is not simply a matter of biology and internal growth. There can be no such thing as a 'culture-free' environment.

My contention is that interest in 'child art', like in 'naive' and 'primitive' art was initially a progressive move, but now has strong elements of the sophisticated adult's nostalgic vision of an innocent state of grace.

Early days of art therapy

It seems as if 'art' as therapy in hospitals began almost by chance. Adrian Hill, an artist convalescing in a sanatorium during the Second World War, turned to his own paintings as a release from stultifying boredom and shared with other patients the sustaining effects of creative activity in times of stress. By accident, it seems, some of the patients began to draw and paint horrifying scenes from the war, or used their painting as a vehicle to talk about their pain and their fears of illness and death. Adrian Hill found himself unwittingly an 'art therapist'. His long campaign to promote the availability of art and artists is well documented in his books *Painting out Illness* and *Art Versus Illness*[3] and, although his work began in sanatoria for tuberculosis patients, it was in a state psychiatric hospital, Netherne, that the first 'art therapist' was employed in 1946.

It is at this point that mention should be made of the conflict in art education between the relative value of the art process as opposed to the art object[4] for this division also appears in art therapy.

If we are concerned with significant art objects, is it then the role of the teacher or therapist to facilitate the production of art objects? Some influential art therapists have been quite definite about this being the case in the past and the idea still lingers that they do not interpret the paintings – that is for the analysts. Thus, as in education, there can be conflicting views of what happens at different levels in the hierarchy in an institution.

Reitman and Cunningham-Dax, who were instrumental in appointing Edward Adamson as the first art therapist at Netherne Hospital, had quite clear views as to how they saw his role. These two doctors believed that creative activity was useful in treatment, but their main aim was the production of 'objects', i.e. paintings, for diagnostic purposes. These paintings were to be produced under standard conditions with minimum intervention by Adamson. It seems that the doctors were anxious for Adamson to be 'more than an occupational therapist' but they did not want him to be an analyst, they stressed that he was not to attempt to interpret pictures or to show any special interest in the psychological problems of the patients (Cunningham-Dax 1953). Both Cunningham-Dax and Reitman held critical views on the interpretations of symbols made by Jungian and Freudian analysts (Reitman 1950, Cunningham-Dax 1953) and implied that by interpreting a picture the therapist predetermined the content of the next picture, thus assigning a very powerful role to the therapist.

Why Reitman should have thought Adamson's activities to be an 'occupational therapy' rather than a form of art teaching is puzzling, since Adamson was adopting the recommended approach of Dewey (1934), Tomlinson (1944; Senior Inspector of Art in the London County Council in the 1940s), and other advocates of the 'child-centred' approach. For, although he was working with adults who happened to be in hospital, he provided an environment with materials and himself as a concerned other who did not intervene with his own suggestions but facilitated the creative process.

Reitman also made the assumption that the art products are a pure representation of an individual's state of mind, which is questionable since they were actually produced in a studio containing many other people including Adamson. This view ignores the possible effects of transference in a group. It is interesting that, although Adamson's 'passive role' is stressed time and time again by the artist himself and by Cunningham-Dax, the latter observed that when Adamson was absent, attendances at the studio declined and those who painted did poor work of little psychiatric value (Cunningham-Dax 1953).[5]

Looking back over the history so far, it is possible to see how art therapy and art education came to be linked, despite the confusion which prevailed over the meaning of what was generally termed 'art'. Indeed, if we take writers such as Herbert Read and John Dewey, we may ask if there was any difference inherent in the two disciplines during the 1940s, or if art therapy as we know it even existed then. Art was seen as vital in developing the 'whole' personality, the teacher's role was to stimulate that development by holding back and not influencing, by providing suitable materials and a stimulating environment. Does this not sound quite familiar to many art therapists growing up in the 1950s and even later?

There was however, still considerable confusion in the state sector about the role of artists in hospitals. Did they become art therapists by virtue of the fact that they worked in hospitals whereas if they worked in schools they would, in the eyes of the adherents to the Dewey school, be progressive art teachers? It appeared that in medical circles they were considered to be 'occupational therapists'. This frustrating position led artists and art teachers working in hospitals to form a central association in 1964, with a view to clarifying the role of the would-be art therapist in hospitals in order to arrive at a suitable training and a structure for employment. The British Association of Art Therapists allied with the National Union of Teachers in 1967, and for some time full members of BAAT were required to have a teaching qualification.

The optimistic 1960s, when psychiatry was jolted by writers such as R. D. Laing, David Cooper, Ervin Goffman, Thomas Szasz and the anti-psychiatry movement, the Californian growth movement, Gestalt, and encounter groups, gave a boost to those artists and art teachers who rejected the view of themselves as primarily passive providers of art materials. They had a more radical view of the possibilities of using art in the treatment of patients, and they wanted to be centrally involved in such treatment. As there was no specific training for the job, they turned to art education as the nearest model. There seemed more common ground between these two professions than between, say, being an artist in a hospital and an occupational therapist. Yet until 1980, the Department of Health and Social Security (DHSS) official view was of art therapy as an *ad hoc* grade subsumed under occupational therapy. It seemed as if the view of art merely as a pleasant hobby or form of recreation and relaxation on the one hand, or as merely an aid to the diagnosis of psychological symptoms on the other, was a very difficult one to dispel.

Current considerations of the relationship between art therapy and art teaching

Nevertheless the differences between the teacher's role and that of the therapist began to emerge as art therapy theory and practice developed gradually in the direction of psychotherapy throughout the 1970s, and as teaching moved away from the 'child-centred' approach. I think it fair to say that most training nowadays encourages art teachers to be active in the classroom, to take ideas in with them, and to have prepared their lessons beforehand with a clear idea of their aims and objectives. The school, too, has its own culture as well as its expectations. There may be a tradition of 'good art' and teachers have to fulfil the expectations such a tradition raises, or they disappoint. Or, art may be reserved for the 'non-academic' child, and the art room be a refuge for the rejects of the mainstream. Especially in the inner-city schools I have visited, teachers comment that the art room regularly contains more than its share of bored, disillusioned, unhappy children. They find a niche within the often less structured, colourful environment of the art department (Calouste Gulbenkian Foundation 1982). We have yet to discover exactly why it is that the art room should provide such a positive experience for these children. Perhaps it has something to do with the fact that there is more room for establishing personal criteria, of making, chancing, and experimenting – and less fear of going wrong in the face of a well-established academic discipline?

It is not within the scope of this chapter to examine all the reasons why art therapy and art teaching definitely separated during the 1970s, to the point where there is now a specialist training for art therapy. It could be in part to do with a return to a form of art education in the 1960s and 1970s which, having been influenced by 'basic design' movement in art education (de Sausmarez 1964), did not appear to be a fertile ground for art therapy to develop in. It may also be to do with the recognition that art therapy could make a contribution similar to that of psychotherapy, and that, therefore, a training specifically orientated towards this was necessary. There is, though, still much in common between art therapy and art teaching and this can be used for the benefit of both, provided that the boundaries of each are understood.

These could be seen to exist on a continuum: at one end is that aspect of art therapy which is really a specialized, alternative form of psychotherapy and which is used mainly in psychiatric clinics, child guidance, day hospitals, and so on. At the other end of the line is that aspect of art education which deals with formal, 'objective', and aesthetic values in art and does not pay attention to the psychological development of the child or adult and especially not to his unconscious mind. There seems to be a point around the middle where art therapy and art education overlap. That is, within special schools, where the teacher is expected to use therapeutic insights to teach the children and where there may be more emphasis on the formation of positive relationships between teacher and pupil and in a group than would usually be the case in an ordinary school.

It may be helpful to look at an art therapist actually working with an individual child in a school, to help clarify the boundaries between teaching and therapy. First, the art therapist needs to be acknowledged as such, by the staff and the child. This is difficult, as 'therapy' has many connotations, several of them negative. It appears to be easier to avoid the problem of the label by calling the therapist a teacher, but this sets up all kinds of expectations in the child, and in the staff, which are difficult to expel. The child will have been selected and referred by the head or a class-teacher. It is important that he knows what to expect and that he does not feel he is being punished for bad behaviour, or rewarded by avoiding a lesson he dislikes. The child must be willing to meet the therapist.

There are many reasons why a child could be referred to a therapist, ranging from anxiety and difficulty in learning, distress brought on by breakdown of family life or death of a parent, to disruptive behaviour, stealing, violence which persists and which isolates the child from his peers, and so on.

When the therapist meets the child, she introduces him to herself, the room, the materials, and the boundaries and basic limitations. Boundaries such as meeting at the same time each week for about an hour, not physically damaging the therapist, the room, or the furniture within could be stated. Within these boundaries and limitations, the child is free to use the materials as he likes. One of the problems experienced in using art therapy in schools is that the staff fear the loss of control they imagine will result if children are allowed free use of materials and get in touch with angry feelings; they are afraid the children will 'act out' throughout the school. In practice this rarely happens if the therapist sets the basic boundaries and if the other staff are aware of the process which takes place in the therapy room.

The therapist avoids praising or criticizing the work but encourages without judging its technical merit or aesthetic value. The child often demands such a response and is hypercritical of his own performance. He tries to turn the therapist into a teacher and gets angry with her when she does not perform this function. He blames the therapist for not 'helping' him. On the other hand, he may be self-sufficient to the point where he ignores the therapist and absorbs himself in his work. The way that the child relates to the therapist tells her much about his habitual way of relating to adults and to boundaries and limitations. By sharing her observations with teachers, who see the child in his peer group, she can perhaps help to promote greater understanding and acceptance on both sides.

As most teachers are required to work with groups of children, it may be useful to look at an art therapist working with a group of adolescents, for there are more similarities to be found in the approach here, I would suggest, than in the case of an individual child. It is unlikely, though, that an art therapist working in, say, a psychiatric adolescent unit would have more than eight adolescents in a group, whereas in a school there could be up to twenty-five or even more, which constitutes a 'large group' in clinical terms.

The art therapist, appreciating the difficulty that adolescents have in knowing what they feel, for they are usually ambivalent about themselves at this time, would probably try to introduce a theme designed to elicit some sharing of feelings on a level with which the adolescents could cope. To give an example, in an adolescent group, the therapist sets a theme 'Myself as I am now and as I would ideally like to be'. This was perceived by the group as a good laugh, and quite a few caricatures resulted. Yet underlying the hilarity was a serious point, as the adolescents struggled with their conflicting feelings about their bodies, their sexuality, their anxieties about making relationships. By talking about the paintings, which contained these mixed-up feelings, they were able to share some of these anxieties in a 'safe' way. The therapist focused on the feelings and the relationships between group members and pointed out the similarities in the work.

An art teacher, working in a school and having responsibilities for the art curriculum, including probably O level, A level, and CSE art, would usually not be trained to work in this way and would feel that it was not appropriate to do so, given that very strong feelings are likely to emerge and need to be contained within a group art therapy session such as the one described above. It would be a problem for a teacher, who has the primary task of improving the child's art skills for possible external assessment, to be involved at such a level. Not only that, the teacher would not be in a position to deal with elements which are present in all therapy groups, namely transference, counter-transference, projective identification. In other words, the teacher may be stuck with very powerful feelings projected from the group and have no means of coping with these. The teacher would be emotionally endangered as much as, if not more than, the children, for, although the relationship between teacher and pupil is important, it is not seen as crucial to the process of teaching, as it is in art therapy, nor is the transference usually acknowledged or understood. It is not helpful to teachers, children, or therapists if the processes involved in art teaching and art therapy are continually misunderstood.

If an art teacher trains as an art therapist, he may still concentrate on the art work of the children rather than on their unconscious feelings and intergroup relationships, but he would also be aware of the processes that take place in a group and how they affect himself as well as the children. Here is a simple example of how valuable such training could be: a child constantly misbehaves, is rude to the teachers, irritates his peers, gets sent to the head time and again. The art therapist/teacher asks: 'Why is this? What is happening in that class room? What role is that child playing and why does he make me so angry, and the other children too?' This child is twelve years old, but he seems to be acting in a way more appropriate to a much younger boy. His pattern of behaviour is to interfere with others' work and to abuse the materials. The therapist observes that he is being subtly encouraged by several others. His own pathology (occasioned in part in this instance by the fact that his mother had just had a new baby boy) was utilized by the class, unconsciously, to play out their own disruptive behaviour and displaced feelings. The therapist linked this to the fact that a much-loved female teacher was pregnant and about to go on maternity leave. Instead of punishing the boy and dismissing him from the group, she was able to deal with the situation in a way which proved to be positive for the whole class, and avoided 'scapegoating'. In this case, she devised a task which involved the class dividing into small groups and co-operating on a mutually agreed project. Small 'family' groups formed and the art work was produced with the therapist being able to observe clearly the interactions within the groups.

This example might seem obvious to many teachers who deal with such situations every day of their lives, sometimes consciously, sometimes intuitively. How useful such understanding could be to all teachers, not only art teachers.

On a pessimistic note, given the present structure of our education system at all levels, it would seem difficult to establish the kind of environment and support where art therapy could take place and where it was seen as valuable not only for 'disturbed and handicapped' children but for all children. Having said that, are the ultimate aims of the art teacher and art therapist so very different or are the external factors, such as economic expediency, institutional constraints, professional ambitions, myth, and mutual suspicion which surround the practice of art teaching and art therapy, the ones to divide them?

I would like to suggest that a training in art therapy and group dynamics would be a valuable component in all art education courses, and contend that this could well replace some more marginally important educational theory. Perhaps if some understanding of art therapy processes could be introduced during school days and at art college, we would not be in the position we are now of having to deal with the fear, misconceptions, and even sabotage which so often occurs when art therapists attempt to work within the education system. (That is not to say that the situation is so very different within the health service, even though there is now a recognition of the profession of art therapy.)

Since art therapy, which is so deeply rooted in art education, now exists as a separate profession, why not take advantage of the situation and employ an art teacher who is trained as an art therapist in every school? It might just be the tip of the iceberg in dispelling the myths surrounding 'therapy'; it could bring together different insights from art education, art therapy, and psychotherapy and make a positive contribution to the life of the school (or art college!).

Surely greater knowledge and understanding of who we are and how and why we do what we do can only be valuable and prevent us from making dangerous assumptions about ourselves and others?

Notes

1 There are two modes of the postgraduate Diploma in Art Therapy at the University of London, Goldsmiths' College: Mode I – Clinical – for students wishing to work in the Health and Social Services. Mode II – Educational – for qualified teachers wishing to work within the Education Service.
2 Letter from Aniela Jaffé to the author, 23 November, 1970.
3 Detailed accounts of the campaign to introduce 'art therapy' to hospitals all over Britain, are given by Hill (1945 and 1951).
4 See Eisner (1974) for elaboration.
5 A detailed history of the development of art therapy at Netherne Hospital is given by Rona Rumney (art therapist) in her Postgraduate Diploma Art Therapy thesis 'Art Therapy at Netherne Hospital', Goldsmiths' College, University of London, 1980.

References

Calouste Gulbenkian Foundation (1982) *The Arts in Schools – Principles, Practice and Provisions*. 98 Portland Place, London, W1N 4ET.

Cunningham-Dax, E. (1953) *Experimental Studies in Psychiatric Art*. London: Faber.

Dewey, J. (1934) *Art as Experience*. New York: Minter, Balch.

Eisner, E. W. (1972) *Educating Artistic Vision*. New York: Macmillan.

— (1975) The Mythology of Art Education. *Inscape* 1(11): 14–25 (Journal of the British Association of Art Therapists).

Freud, S. (1971) *The Complete Introductory Lectures on Psychoanalysis*. London: Allen & Unwin.

Fry, R. (1924) *The Artist and Psychoanalysis*. London: Hogarth.

Hill, A. (1945) *Art Versus Illness*. London: Allen & Unwin.

— (1951) *Painting out Illness*. London: Williams & Northgate.

Iveson, J. (1938) *The Occupational Treatment of Mental Illness*. London: Balliere, Tindall & Cox.

Lowenfeld, V. (1947) *Creative and Mental Growth*. New York: Macmillan.

Lombroso, C. (1891) *Man of Genius*. London: Scott.

MacDonald, S. (1970) *The History and Philosophy of Art Education*. London: University of London Press.

Naumberg, M. (1966) *Dynamically Oriented Art Therapy*. New York: Grune & Stratton.

Prinzhorn, H. (1922) *Bildernei der Geisteskranken*. Berlin: Springer.

Read, H. (1938) *Collected Essays in Literary Criticism*. London: Faber.

— (1943) *Education Through Art*. New York: Pantheon.

Reitman, F. (1950) *Psychotic Art*. London: Routledge & Kegan Paul.

Rosseau, J. J. (1961) *Emile*. London: Dent.

Sausmarez, M., de (1964) *Basic Design: the Dynamics of Visual Form*. London: Studio Vista.

Simon, M. (1876) L'Imagination dans la folie. In *Anales Medico Psychologiques* 16, Paris.

— (1888) Les Escrits et les dessins des aliénés. In *Archives Anthropologique de Criminologie*, Paris.

Staats, A. W. (1968) Categories and Underlying Mental Processes for Representative Behaviour Samples and S–R Analyses: Opposing Heuristic Strategies. *Ontario Journal of Education Research* 10(3) (Spring): 195.

Tardieu, A. (1872) *Etudes medico et légales sur la folie*. Paris.

Tomlinson, R. R. (1934) *Picture and Pattern Making for Children*. London: Studio.

— (1944) *Children as Artists*. London: Penguin.

Viola, W. (1944) *Child Art*. London: University of London Press.

Acknowledgements

I would like to thank Dan Lumley and Joan Woddis for their invaluable advice.

Biographical note

Diane Waller   Graduated in Fine Art from the Ruskin School of Drawing and Fine Art of the University of Oxford in 1968. Worked as part-time Art Therapist in the

Adolescent Unit of Longrove Hospital from 1969 to 1970 when she was accepted by the Royal College of Art for a two-year research project on art therapy leading to an MA. Was employed as part-time Art Therapist at Paddington Centre for Psychotherapy between 1970 and 1977 and as a Lecturer in Art Therapy at Goldsmiths' College, University of London from 1974 to 1978, when she was appointed Head of the new postgraduate Art Therapy Unit.

Held offices as Hon. Secretary and Vice-Chairman of British Association of Art Therapists (BAAT) from 1971 to 1975 and was Chairman from 1975 to 1981. Trained as a psychotherapist specializing in group analytic psychotherapy at London Centre for Psychotherapy from 1976 to 1981. Is now registered for a D.Phil. at the University of Sussex. Research concerns the history and development of art therapy as a profession in Britain. Has held Leverhulme and British Council research scholarships and has studied and worked extensively in Bulgaria and Yugoslavia.

2 | Art, psychotherapy, and symbol systems

John Henzell

This chapter will consist of a discussion of some theoretical reasons for directing pictorial image-making to psychotherapeutic ends; in effect to try to supply a number of justifications for such an apparently specialized technique. If a procedure is to be thought of as therapeutic then there is an ethical requirement that its efficacy can be clearly demonstrated and the reasons for this pointed to. I do not think it unfair to claim that the literature that exists at present is less convincing than it might be in this respect. If art therapy is conceived of as a psychotherapy however, that is using the term psychotherapy generically to embrace the class of psychological therapies as a whole, then the idea of efficacy and the reasons behind it may be more complex, subtle, and extended than has been usually imagined. Indeed psychotherapy is beset by many of the same problems of evaluation as bear upon art therapy. It has been said of psychoanalysis, for example, that it is a speculative explanation of human behaviour offered in advance of the empirical evidence that might justify it. Some of these problems of justification may, however, arise from false conceptions concerning scientific approaches to human action and experience. The view is increasingly gaining ground that appropriate methodologies in the social sciences might have no recourse but to be rooted in the real life situations which are in fact being examined, rather than in artificially contrived experimental conditions (Harré and Secord 1975, Glymour 1982). This is certainly true of traditional sciences such as astronomy and modern ones such as ethology, both of which investigate phenomena in their naturally occurring context. Other disciplines concerned with knowledge of human action, for example anthropology and linguistics, as well as many of the classical humanities like history, law, criticism, and aesthetics, depend upon methods naturally fitted to the phenomena with which they are occupied.

I will not therefore attempt to demonstrate the clinical currency of the practice which forms the subject matter of this volume by means of the 'double-blind trial', by controlling variables, or by statistical correlations, valuable as these techniques may be in certain circumstances. By way of analogy how could one clearly demonstrate the efficacy of knowledge? Rather I will attempt to clarify where pictorial expression lies within a range of symbolic activities and show how some of these are connected together systematically. In order to do this I will draw on areas of knowledge which may seem removed from the mainstream of clinical literature as such, for example aesthetics and semiotics, but which nevertheless are centrally concerned with the expression of meaning. By so doing the role of art in furthering certain goals of psychotherapy, greater self-understanding, insight, and knowledge of the mind, should become clearer.

I will first turn my attention to psychotherapy and the expressive modalities in which it has most often operated. Psychotherapy I take to consist of a collection of related techniques that attempt to impinge on human awareness, including awareness of the self, in order to increase and alter its range of operation. Such psychotherapies take consciousness and its possible impairment, choice, responsibility, and subjective experience into account. I exclude therapeutic procedures of a more technological kind which at one point or another may bypass the subject as a responsible agent potentially able to give an account of his feelings and actions.

There can be little doubt that the most pervasive and powerful model underlying psychotherapy in its many forms is that of psychoanalysis. Over the past ninety years the original postulates and therapeutic techniques in which psychoanalysis originated have undergone many changes and informed countless aspects of our thinking generally. It has become almost impossible to imagine a world devoid of insights derived from psychoanalysis. Psychoanalytic ideas have passed into popular and colloquial usage and its theories have been brought to bear on many fields other than its original concerns. Within psychotherapeutic practice it has been reformulated and modified in a number of alternative versions, Jungian, Adlerian, and Kleinian being some of the major schools, as well as in practices and therapeutic beliefs that have arisen in reaction to it, for example bioenergetics, Gestalt therapy, and humanistic psychology.

From the outset psychoanalysis and most of its derivatives have made use of the spoken word as their principal medium of expression. In the 1890s Freud referred to a form of therapy, that in fact replaced his use of hypnosis in the treatment of hysteria, as the 'talking cure'; later he was to say

'Nothing takes place in a psychoanalytic treatment but an interchange of words between the patient and the analyst' (Freud 1951b: 17). That this reliance on verbal language should be the case in psychoanalysis should not really surprise us if we consider that most of our social life, both public and intimate, is mediated and effected through speech. A person's identity, place in a society, birth, life and death are marked by words spoken, written, and inscribed. Not only is a person known by his or her name, identifying their status, family position and often occupation, but their use of language itself, their literacy, dialect and accent, place them, frequently rigidly, in a social position and role. It has been asserted that we are, in a distinctively human sense, what we are capable of uttering and what can be uttered of us. Our range of utterances constitute the final range of our imagination, the scope and limits of our world. According to Wittgenstein, 'What we cannot speak of we must pass over in silence' (Wittgenstein 1961: 74).

This being the case, or even if it is only partly the case, we can see that many mental disorders, or disorders of the imagination as they were once known, will have their origins in social, family, and personal situations encompassed by language. At both overt and covert levels a person's psychopathology will be manifest in his or her words. Consider, for example, Lacan's view of a person as an 'utterance' and his idea of giving the patient back the 'word' which has become a hidden or denied aspect of the self (Lacan 1977). Clearly then, given that psychoanalysis and kindred methods are concerned with a re-evaluation of experience, language is a principal and appropriate means by which to examine a psyche determined in such large part by the self-same language; for how else could the matter be approached?

Reflection on our everyday experience, however, might lead us to want to first soften and then fill out this account of the embodiment of a person's identity, meaning, and experience in verbal language. Such reflection informs us of the place of such language in a whole context of expressive, symbolic, and significative modalities. While words are the necessary and everyday accompaniment of our relationships to others in our private and public life (this chapter for example), our life is also mediated by countless gestures and artifacts of a non-verbal kind; the gestures that accompany and qualify speech, writing, diagrams, images, pictures, dials and gauges, graphs, maps, colours, lights, photographs, television, bells, music, tastes, odours, elaborately prepared and coded foodstuffs, clothes, rituals, games, play, enactments, touchings, and so on. Of course we then find ourselves speaking and writing about these things and by thus subsuming them within these symbolic codes fail, while we so describe them, to discern their own symbolic function or that of our description. Perhaps it is their often more reflexive, unconscious, and embodied nature that allows us, while in the act of signifying them verbally, to forget them as signifiers themselves. But the way in which such things may be verbally denoted indicates precisely where it is in a larger symbolic environment that speech is most necessary and valuable. Speech is supremely economical, requires minimal muscular energy, needs no materials, is multi-directional, can be produced immediately, its own temporal structure can represent that of events occurring in time, it can be inflected and modulated, is a common possession, and can be both highly articulate in its precise references as well as richly ambiguous. Hence it will suffice for legal definitions and passionate outbursts, for erudite discourse and for jokes, for arguments and for songs, for instructions and for poems, for plain speaking and for deceit, for confessing and for lying. And it is perhaps the extraordinary ease with which we appear to accomplish these most complex and subtle of activities, the very transparency of speech, that blinds us to a realization of verbal language as a symbolic means, to the fact that we live all the time with spoken language as an artifact, as a representation only of reality. We are inclined to neglect just how continuous it is with other symbol systems and this obscures the constraints within which such a method representation operates. The failure of speech adequately to apply is difficult to see just because it is difficult to describe. It cannot, for example, picture the place of a part in a whole as a map does, compare finger prints, inform others of what sort of person we are as well as keep us warm as clothes do, picture the play of light on a surface, convey exactly how someone looks or moves, actually indicate the humour, tragedy, or majesty of a human face, and so on.

A way of placing the gamut of expressive possibilities and the symbolic modes upon which they depend within a model of the body and the mind with their dispositions might be made clearer as follows. Given the fluctuating circumstances we pass through in life and the inner states these give rise to – our desires, fears, disappointments, confusions, and perturbations – there are, roughly speaking, three ways in which we may respond to them. We can embody our response in immediate and concrete action; we can withhold any action; or reveal our feelings indirectly by representing them. To put the matter slightly differently, we can either conceal an inner state and with varying degrees of self-awareness suppress its realization in behaviour, or reveal it, and if we reveal it we can do so in two characteristic forms – as direct expression or in the form of a representation or description.

Of course I do not mean to suggest that these alternative outcomes are as rigidly separated as such a schematic description suggests. An event may be described tearfully, involuntary laughter may interrupt the telling of a joke or attempted silence, a slip of the tongue may betray our feelings, we may struggle to control our feelings and express them in an unintended form such as blushing, weeping, or shaking; actual behaviour may also be symbolically representational as in ritual; indeed that which is symbolic holds such a wide-ranging sway over so much of our social life that we can scarcely distinguish it from real action. Thus the laying of a foundation stone is both a ceremonial and an actual founding of an edifice (see Wollheim 1973: 84–100).

The systematic investigation of ways in which we reveal ourselves and the perception of these by others has formed the traditional subject matter of aesthetics and increasingly of disciplines such as semiotics. In modern aesthetics an understanding of art has brought into play the examination of expression, symbolization, and perception. One may find now in aesthetics detailed investigations of metaphor, representation, exemplification, syntax and semantics, signification, emotion and cognition, of the whole range of our symbolic modes as they are created and perceived. We can expect then that these enquiries will have much to say pertinent to our interest. It seems to me that the most thoroughgoing exploration of manners in which we conceal our inner states is that of psychoanalysis in its various major forms. The vastly complicated repertoire of negative actions and their consequences, the mechanisms of ego defence, denial, repression, projection, the structure of the unconscious, and intrapsychic dynamics are all concepts created in the wake of Freud.

A problem arises, however, when in the interests of our survival in reality as we see it we conceal our inner state, and this problem was at the heart of Freud's enterprise. Concealment, through denial or repression, is not the end of the matter, the pressing inner state does not thereby vanish though that indeed may be the wish we secretly harbour. It is likely to resurface elsewhere in unexpected forms of behaviour, thought, mental agitation, or even perception, which may appear inexplicable. In the case of projective identification for example, the banished thought and its connected effect comes home to roost with a vengeance as an apparently perceived aspect of reality; this is the necessary failure of such a pathological mechanism. A delusional belief may be seen by he who possesses it as accounting for such seemingly impossible experience. So a form of behaviour, or a disturbance of experience, comes into being which we might think of as being symptomatic; it was via such a medical metaphor that hysteria appeared to Freud and Breuer at the end of the nineteenth century. Freud extended the logic of this metaphor of the symptom to an account of how a 'latent' meaning, a concealed psychological dynamic, might rhetorically 'manifest' itself in a behavioural expression. Hence we may be unable truly to conceal an inner state or volition, it will eventually gain expression, often involuntarily and in a distorted and troublesome form, as a kind of scrambled message. Indeed it is clear that Freud thought of repression as lying behind a surprisingly large number of complex human symbolic activities. The repressed thought and attendant emotion may be expressed pathologically in the case of symptom formation or creatively in the case of sublimation.

Paradoxically we might now see how ways in which we conceal our feelings serve in fact to reveal them, and ways in which we reveal our feelings serve also to conceal them. The contribution of psychoanalysis is to have demonstrated how this can be accomplished through the 'condensing' of several meanings together into a composite expressive form, by 'displacing' meaning from one form to another, and by using the latent propensity of symbols to pun with each other in such a way as to both reveal and conceal our thoughts and emotions.

These condensations and displacements operate through fractures or leakages in the narrative form of expression which forms the basis of psychoanalysis. Such leakage allows a 'shifting' or 'turning' of meaning, in ordinary usage referred to as a 'turn of phrase', 'figure of speech', or pun. Linguistic processes of this kind depend upon ambiguity and without it a purely discursive language would be poverty stricken and threadbare indeed. Poetry, jokes, and irony would remain forever beyond our reach.

The clarification of ambiguous expression is a cornerstone of psychoanalytic technique. Freud had drawn attention to the importance of this in his analysis of 'Dora' (Freud 1951a). The analysis examined certain of her words which were 'overdetermined' by virtue of their ambiguity, they allowed of both a 'lexical' or manifest and an 'intended' or latent meaning. The word 'jewel-case', '*schmuckkästchen*', figured in her report of a dream; it referred overtly to jewellery while covertly alluding to sexuality through a resonating set of associations and linkages. Freud called such words 'nodes', 'verbal bridges', and 'switch-words'. Through their indirect mode of representation they provide, like dreams, 'one of the detours by which repression can be evaded' (Freud 1951a:15). Of these words Freud says:

'in a line of associations ambiguous words (or as we may call them, 'switch-words') act like points at a junction. If the points are switched across from the position in which they appear to lie in the dream, then we find ourselves on another set of rails; and along this second truck run the thoughts which we are in search of but which still lie concealed behind the dream.'   (Freud 1951a:65, n.1)

How though can we know which words are being used thus? Generally speaking, the meaning of words in a narrative are contextually determined. In language, at its simplest, the meaning of a word is determined by the sentence of which it is a part; that is, the meaning is assigned textually. If we then ask how the meaning of the sentence is determined we must first look to its encompassing paragraphs which form a narrative or dialogue, then to a type of discourse, and finally to a language in which all these elements are embedded. It is through such interconnected levels that words acquire ramifications and resonances, as I. A. Richards put it: 'Our words commonly take meaning through the influence of other words which we may not think of but which in the back of the mind co-operate in controlling them' (Richards 1936:75); words are connected by their 'interinanimation', are 'overdetermined', and always mean more than they appear to. Hence a single word may allude to several contexts in which it is employed, in which its synonyms are employed, or in which synonyms of its synonyms occur. For example, as Freud and Dora were aware, '*schmuckkästchen*' was a German colloquialism meaning a woman's genitals.

In addition, however, our understanding of a word's meaning may be qualified by the *manner* of its employment. Such 'paralinguistic' features in language may be prosodic; that is, poetic or playful uses of the sound and rhythm of words, their sensuous qualities. The ambiguous nature of a word may be signalled by its position in a sentence, by the letters composing it, or by its rhyming with other words. In speech this may be extended further so that the *act* of speaking qualifies the speaker's meaning. Such actions consist of the rhythm, pauses between, intonation, and pitch of the words – their music as it were, and the gestures that accompany them. Our attention is drawn to the multi-modal context of words and it is the nature of this amplification of speech that, together with its contextual context, creates both intended and unintended ambiguity.

To return to Dora once more, Freud refers to certain of her actions as 'symptomatic acts'. During a session after she recounted the dream featuring the jewel-case, she played with a reticule which she wore as an adornment at her waist: 'as she lay on the sofa and talked, she kept playing with it – opening it, putting a finger into it, shutting it again, and so on' (Freud 1951a:76). This act was a 'node' comparable in its function to a switch-word; through its ambiguity it is both an innocent action and points further afield via associated material to sexuality.[1] Hence in psychoanalytic terms an 'inner speech act' or latent thought may reveal itself in a twofold manner, in actual speech and in behaviour. Dora alluded to certain hidden preoccupations by alluding to them in speech and by unwittingly *picturing or miming them in bodily actions*. (see Bär 1975:19–58).

We may then be too ready to characterize psychoanalysis and related psychotherapies as being essentially verbal, ostensibly they may be but in fact their writ runs much wider than we might suspect. This is indeed suggested by the readiness of psychotherapeutic practice to explore widely differing forms of expression; for example, play in the psychoanalysis of children,[2] 'body armour' in Reichian 'character analysis', pictorial work in Jungian psychotherapy and in art therapy, and re-enactment in 'psychodrama'. The question then needs to be asked, how do these expressive modes, in the context of this volume particularly the pictorial, operate in such a way as to illuminate the matters with which a psychotherapy may be concerned? It is here that we most need to look further than the analysis of the speech act to explanations arising from the interactions of other expressive and symbolic modes.

Further explanations of the operations of non-verbal symbols can be found in the rhetorical interplay that exists between the literal and the metaphorical, between actual and figurative possession of certain properties in an expressive symbol. Ambiguity is a necessary but not a sufficient consideration here; to be figurative or metaphorical a symbol must possess ambiguous properties, but mere ambiguity is not metaphor. A metaphor is the illumination of one realm of related facts, associations, history, and orderings in terms of another. This is accomplished by the interaction of at least two conceptions of different things in the one symbol which refers to them both. In speech a metaphor consists of a single word or phrase which supports the interaction through the intersection within it of different frames of reference: 'he laid his cards on the table' denotes both a declaration of what is in one's hand and one's mind. A metaphor may also reside in *actual properties* jointly possessed by the realms that intermingle in the metaphor and by the metaphor itself; gold, that precious metal out of whose properties so many metaphors have been coined, doubly denotes the pure and the profane, virtue and vice, rarity and abundance, and is both a price one pays but is priceless.

Typically, metaphorical allusion is a running together of the familiar with the unfamiliar, which establishes a kinship between them so that the latter is clarified in the light of the former. What is clarified is usually an undetermined set of relationships and this is accomplished by informing the 'foreign' realm, the target of the metaphor, with known and established relationships from the 'native' realm, the source of the metaphor. The customary schema of known territory is superimposed on that which is unexplored to see if equivalent features match the 'grammar' of the allusion. Metaphor, as Goodman puts it, 'is a matter of teaching an old word new tricks – of applying an old label in a new way' (Goodman 1976:69).

It is equally characteristic of metaphor that it runs in the direction of the less important to the more, a structure within something trivial or of no immediate concern matches a structure within a more engrossing preoccupation. This allusion elsewhere than to the immediate establishes the metaphor's direction or 'turn', the way in which it is 'framed'. For we must see not only how the schemata placed against each other in the metaphor fit, but also how they do not. The two sets of schemata both attract and repel each other and this tension contributes to the metaphor's freshness or shock; 'a metaphor is an affair between a predicate with a past and an object that yields while protesting' (Goodman 1976:69). Thus a metaphor, to be effective, is concerned with more than simple truth or analogy, the comparison effected by it must scandalize current perceptions and by so doing jolt them into a new frame of reference.[3]

This sorting of fresh experience in terms of the more customary is no mere whim of figurative embellishment but is imposed by a rigorous economy necessary to symbolic usage. Everyday language is literally strewn with metaphors both new and old; those in frequent use lose their youth and vitality, attain respectability, tire, and join the ranks of the innumerable 'faded' metaphors that parade through our lives as so many turns of phrase, colloquialisms, and received wisdoms. If we could not, through metaphor, have the means to recast our ordering of experiences into new moulds by transposing different sets of schemata we would labour under the dead weight of a necessarily huge array of terminologies and an impossible bureaucracy of established custom and usage. The extraordinary subtlety and value of metaphor is its ability to create new realms of experience by rapidly and economically shifting elements of existing categories across great distances of space, time, and logic, and, through seeming faults and imperfections in our languages, to cause discrepant frames and levels of experience to fuse together into new entities.

I referred a short while back to metaphors functioning through properties actually possessed; pictures rely upon such possession to a marked degree. Metaphors composed of words depend in the main on conventional denotation, that is, the symbol and that which is symbolized are quite distinct; a word is in no way *like* the object it denotes – although actual possession may figure in the paralinguistic elements of speech forms such as onomatopoeia or poetry. Certainly images may convey conventional symbolic meaning as does the printed letter 'A', a digital watch-face, or even a diagrammatic representation, or topographical landscape. But a landscape, say by Constable or Rembrandt, is not expressively or symbolically important by virtue of denoting a particular locality in Essex or Holland. Pictures literally possess certain pictorial properties that are not required for denotation alone. It is through such actual possession that pictures obtain the ability figuratively to possess abstract properties such as exuberance, sadness, wit, or serenity. Through figurative possession a picture may be said to *exemplify* abstract qualities.

The following is a hypothetical example adapted from Goodman (1976: 50–2). Imagine a picture of a man painted in shades of red which we say expresses anger. Since a picture is insentient how could this be so? We can say of the picture that it (a) denotes a man, (b) literally possesses the colour red, and (c) expresses anger. Through (b) it is a sample of red and is, therefore, denoted by the label 'red'. Outside the picture frame we apply a metaphorical transfer of colour schemata to those of the emotions and this correspondence is then imported back into the picture. Such 'shading' of the emotions is a stock in trade of figurative expression. Through such a process we may say that the property exemplified subsumes the picture much as the picture subsumes that which it more literally denotes.

My example is, of course, highly schematic and any instance of exemplification in a real picture will be much more complex. I hope, however, I have made the logic clear. The metaphorical meaning of objects and actions – what they express – may be conveyed by exemplification. What the substance gold symbolically expresses is bound up in the predicates that denote its qualities; 'gold', 'precious', 'rare', 'pure', etc. What a gesture expresses is to be found in predicates that characterize it as 'agitated', 'impatient', 'expansive', and so on. Forms of expression that depend on substantive possession exist in the material world, their meaning peculiarly consists in them being *things*. Exemplification is nearer to spatiality than is denotation and it is through the subtle interplays of schemata exemplification brings into play, carrying with them the expressive and logical qualities of different sense realms, that pictorial images appear swollen with meanings and significances not immediately apparent – as, for example, in non-figurative painting.

The creative use of metaphorical processes are so striking, so demanding of our attention, that we may overlook, indeed be quite intended to overlook, an implicit consequence of their power. That metaphor is as capable of masking a state of affairs, of dissembling, as it is of bringing it to our attention, a metaphor may *turn* our attention to or away from a perception. If this is so we might regard switch-words, nodes, and symptomatic acts as species of metaphor – as in fact did Lacan (1977). Such 'symptomatic metaphors' seek to obscure rather than clarify, the wider conjunctions hazarded by creative metaphor are, in its symptomatic form, artfully hidden from view.

Symptomatic metaphor may come into being to *remove* unbearably stressful psychological conflict. So persistent may be a thought, together with the emotion and accompanying behaviour it insists upon, but so acutely felt the need for their suppression, that the inner agitation such conflicting perceptions give rise to can only be calmed by repressing their apprehension complete with thoughts, perceptions, and emotions associated with them in the mind. Such an act of repression consists in the complex of apprehensions being shifted elsewhere in the mind. The central ideas and perceptions animating the conflict can be seen as being propelled via a series of metaphorical transformations to a position in awareness where they can be unnoticed. A switch of attention is effected, the trajectory along which thought is directed swerves or turns by means of 'tropes'[4] such as metaphor and exemplification. The syntactical structures operating here may be thought of as identical to those governing genuinely exploratory metaphor; schemata are transferred from one realm to another and one mode may be exchanged with or resonate with others. The essential distinction between the two processes is one of ends rather than means, the goals of open exploration and fruitful comparison are exchanged for those of duplicity – a reversal of purpose is involved.

In order to understand how the creative and the symptomatic functions of metaphor are accommodated to each other we might imagine the metaphor as a vehicle of meaning which focuses attention on unexpectedly alarming dimensions in a situation and as a consequence moves perception to a safer position in relation to the hazards it has uncovered by transpositions of less threatening schemata. The more polysemous and ambiguous of our symbolic modes, while also providing the means for creative uses of metaphor, supply the necessary leakage or escape hatches to effect such flight. An apprehension can thus become embodied as a latent, or 'unconscious', aspect embedded in a richly ambiguous metaphor. This movement 'to and fro' between different encodations of our experience has something of the nature of discourse about it. The back and forth 'shuttling' of tropes between different realms of experience, between different symbolic modes, between the literal and the figurative, and between the moralities of engagement and flight, is, in spite of its sometimes being 'pathological', essentially a mediative function.

A further distinction between metaphorical structures that reveal and those that conceal lies in the 'framing' of the metaphor. A framed metaphor is open to inspection, indeed it might be said to invite it; its frame prefaces it with 'as if'. An 'unframed' metaphor is closed; the transfer of certain schemata, the particular way in which an action is expressive, the figurative allusions involved, remain covert and unconscious, or unassimilated to conscious examination and criticism. Symptomatic metaphor is directed intrapsychically towards an 'inner' theatre of protagonists. Such inner actions may consist of the deepest irony and we may think of them as being laconic communications between two parts of the self carried on out of earshot of a third. Hence the expressive actions which issue from such dissembling are inner directed and characterized by hidden agenda.

A distinguishing feature of metaphor and its symptomatic counterpart is that they tend towards embodiment, even metaphors composed of words usually refer through them to physical phenomena. In psychoanalytic terms they move towards the end of the 'psychical apparatus' concerned with perception; that is, they become spatialized. This spatialization may again serve two purposes. On the one hand to make apparent, to literally show forth, to give an instance of or to clarify; on the other hand to bury, hide, or compress a thought in perceptual space – in fantasy, a projection, a somatic symptom, or a hallucination. The meanings of a visual image, for example, exist simultaneously in the one time and place and are composed of a succession of glances made in a variety of orders and directions. In contrast to a unilinear mode of expression pictorial imagery avails itself of 'overdetermination' and may become the repository of many meanings. Movement along a spectrum of spatiality towards sensuous perception can be accomplished by metaphorical transformations. If the metaphor is hidden, or *repressed*, it exists as a latent aspect within an ambiguous perception. The history of a metaphor's travels remain, however, implicit in its structure; its meaning may betray itself by being exemplified in symptomatically expressive behaviour (see Wollheim 1973:31–53). The direction and framing of these defensive metaphors may be thought of as operating in an upside-down fashion; that is, the position of the home and foreign realms forming the source and target of the metaphor's transposition of schemata are exchanged, we see the source of the metaphor in the place usually occupied by its object – turned inside out as it were. A statement of belief in the form 'they are poisoning me' may metaphorically exemplify the contamination of thoughts via the application of the relatively embodied schemata of *cuisine* to the more abstract ones of thoughts and feelings, a metaphor tentatively begun or ironically unfinished, its completion being blocked or even forbidden by others (see Henzell 1983).

An example may illustrate some features of the foregoing. A woman in her forties makes a painting of a childhood experience. She depicts a hill covered in silver flecks and recounts the happy memory of seeing these during a walk with her mother on some hills near London during the war. The silver flecks represent small metal filaments. The background of the painting is muted and dark. When someone else tells a story of huddling with her family in their house during an air raid she becomes upset and explains that she too underwent such experiences. The suggestion is proffered that the metal filaments in her picture were dropped by German bombers in order to throw radar detection devices off their track. With emotion she then says she remembers hiding alone under the stairs when her neighbourhood was being bombed. She was so terrified, particularly by the dreadful fact of being alone, that she became dumb for two years. Her painting, and her account of it, referred implicitly to this distressing event. It literally denoted a happy experience but exemplified the tragedy underscoring it. The exemplification was twofold. Firstly, the dark tone of the background figuratively hinted at a shadowy area of experience. Secondly, the metal filaments were an instance of a method, one of extraordinary topicality for her, by which something threatening might avoid detection. The traumatic memory of her abandonment during the bombing, and presumably much other associated distress, had not occurred to her at the beginning of the session, only a sense of foreboding and a brittle shining memory which took place, when her speech had returned, in the presence of her mother.

The ramifications of the hidden metaphors originally only alluded to are considerable and, although it may sound odd to say so in this context, quite elegant. The most radical of symptomatic metaphors may be found in the psychoses. Here metaphorical transformations traverse vast abysses of experience and when set forth in words and pictures may attain awesome expressive power, a commentary on the dislocations that can exist between our thoughts and our language, our feelings and our actions. It may be understandable why we should wish, but unwise in the event, to anaesthetize such experience by means of clinical explanation. Art and aesthetic attitude in their full enquiring vigour may save us from such a banal miscalculation.[5]

I have tried to show in this chapter how it is through the more metaphorical and non-discursive of our symbolic modes that our thoughts and feelings find their fullest expression. It is both what we say and how we say it that counts and which together constitute a unity. This unity may be most cohesively and singularly evident in art. To the degree that psychopathology is present this wholeness may be fractured, the surface signification of an expression is belied by the manner of its delivery, and it is the latter which betrays its real denotation. Hysterical lameness may exemplify the thought 'I can't stand it' while ostensibly denoting an honourable illness; the delusional 'they have implanted a bomb in my brain' may, with the addition of 'as if', mean 'I have an angry thought in my head'. Psychotherapists and art therapists may pay attention to paralinguistic and bodily expressions and amplify these by asking their patients to draw and paint so as to allow other metaphors to speak. They may then offer interpretations of these amplifications that are themselves essentially metaphorical. This rhetorical dialogue serves to furnish a context that can transform the symptom once again into a framed metaphor in order to bring into proximity the protagonists of an internal conflict. Psychotherapy of this kind might aptly be compared to an art, an art that by imaginatively, perceptively, and tactfully offering the client different schemata and alternative perceptual domains uncovers the trajectory of his unconscious thoughts and feelings so that these may be fully owned.

Both metaphors and symptoms are fabricated, like works of art the works of psychopathology are painstakingly created artifacts. An assimilation of what we know of metaphorical transformation in art to the study and treatment of psychopathology may rescue a darker domain of human invention from misleading medical determinism, disinter the authorship of such paradoxical creation, and place the responsibility on the shoulders of those perverse artists, poets, and jokers in all of us. Psychopathology may indeed be an extreme irony and precisely because of this has remained largely invisible, unheard, and unremarked on by our sane, rational, and utilitarian consciousness.

Notes

1 'Jewel-case' was the starting point of several interconnected associative chains leading to the idea of sexuality and sexual wetness. It pointed to sexuality through colloquial usage and also via the idea of 'jewel drops', jewellery that hung from the ears. 'Drops' introduced the idea of wetness. Dora's mother had wanted her husband to give her some jewel drops but he did not like that kind of thing. Dora also suffered from nasal catarrh with a distressing discharge, this symptom together with the 'flowing' connotation of the word 'catarrh' led to the idea of displaced sexual wetness. And of course in the session referred to Dora played with her reticule which she wore in effect as a piece of jewellery. Whatever we may think of Freud's notions of the aetiology of Dora's illness and of female sexuality, his study of interconnectedness of Dora's words, actions, and symptoms is masterly.

2 The psychoanalysis of children through their play by Melanie Klein and others not only led to fundamental reformulations of classical Freudian theory but, in the writings of authors such as Hannah Segal, Adrian Stokes, Anton Ehrenzweig, and Richard Wollheim, has had a marked effect on English art criticism.

3 Of the resistance involved in a transfer of schemata Goodman says:

> 'The shifts in range that occur in metaphor ... usually amount to no mere distribution of family goods but to an expedition abroad. A whole set of alternative labels, a whole apparatus of organization, takes over new territory. What occurs is a transfer of schema, a migration of concepts, an alienation of categories. Indeed, a metaphor might be regarded as a calculated category-mistake – or rather as a happy and revitalizing, even if bigamous, second marriage.'   (Goodman 1976:73)

4 'Trope' from the Greek *'tropos'* – a turning point – from which 'tropics' is also derived. A figure of speech in which a word or expression is turned from its more literal meaning.

5 For an investigation of the transformation of meaning in psychosis see Schatzman's study of Schreber's madness (Schatzman 1973).

References

Bär, E. (1975) *Semiotic Approaches to Psychotherapy*. Indiana: Indiana University Press.

Freud, S. (1951a) *Fragment of an Analysis of a Case of Hysteria* (first published in 1905), *Complete Psychological Works* (Standard Edition), vol. 7. London: Hogarth Press and the Institute of Psycho-analysis.

— (1951b) *Introductory Lectures on Psychoanalysis* (Part I) (first published in 1916), *Complete Psychological Works* (Standard Edition), vol. 15. London: Hogarth Press and the Institute of Psycho-analysis.

Glymour, C. (1982) Freud, Kepler, and the Clinical Evidence. In R. Wollheim and J. Hopkins (eds) *Philosophical Essays on Freud*. Cambridge: Cambridge University Press.

Goodman, N. (1976) *Languages of Art: An Approach to a Theory of Symbols.* Indianapolis, Indiana: Hackett.

Harré, R. and Secord, P. F. (1975) *The Explanation of Social Behaviour.* Oxford: Basil Blackwell.

Henzell, J. (1983) Metaphor Reversed: Application of Metaphor to Psychopathology. In *Art and Therapy: A Symposium concerning Uses of Art in Therapy in the UK.* Held as part of the International Conference on Psychology and the Arts, Cardiff. Papers jointly published by Birmingham Polytechnic, Goldsmiths' College, and Herts College of Art and Design.

Lacan, J. (1977) *Écrits: A Selection*, trans. A. Sheridan. London: Tavistock.

Richards, I. A. (1936) *The Philosophy of Rhetoric.* London: Oxford University Press.

Schatzman, M. (1973) *Soul Murder: Persecution in the Family.* London: Allen Lane.

Wittgenstein, L. (1961) *Tractatus Logico-Philosophicus*, trans. D. F. Pears and B. F. McGuinness. London: Routledge and Kegan Paul.

Wollheim, R. (1973) The Mind and the Mind's Image of Itself *and* Expression. In *On Art and the Mind: Essays and Lectures.* London: Allen Lane.

Biographical note

John Henzell   Art therapist since 1960 in a variety of psychiatric hospitals and a founder member of BAAT. SSRC Research Fellow at the School of Art Education, Birmingham Polytechnic (1975–78). Currently Senior Lecturer on the Postgraduate Diploma in Art Therapy (CNAA) and MA in Art Therapy (CNAA) at Herts College of Art and Design, St Albans.

3 | Art therapy as a form of psychotherapy

John Birtchnell

'Man has from earliest times built up an elaborate series of defences lest his carefully sublimated emotions and motivations come disturbingly into consciousness.'   (Lord Platt 1967: 442)

Art therapy combines art and psychotherapy and ideally each is enhanced by its coupling with the other. Art involves the creation of aesthetically stimulating representations of reality. Psychotherapy involves the treatment of psychologically disturbed individuals. On the face of it these contrasting disciplines have little in common. In fact both are concerned with emotional issues and the practitioners of each need to be sensitive and intuitive. There are many forms of art therapy, depending on the proportion of art and psychotherapy involved. There are those who argue that the art therapist is essentially a trained artist who does therapy and those who argue that he is essentially a trained psychotherapist who uses art. In this country at least, the art therapist is usually an artist who has gone on to train in therapy. To my mind, the art component of art therapy is very much subsidiary to the therapy one and it concerns me that the degree of training in therapy which artists currently receive is far from adequate to enable them to be competent therapists.

In previous contributions to *Inscape* (Birtchnell 1977, 1979, and 1981), I have tried to develop some theories about art therapy. In this chapter I have drawn freely upon this earlier writing and carried the discussion further.

Theoretical background

Ideas about art

As a student in 1959, I wrote an article entitled 'Art as I see it'. In it I wrote:

> 'When a stone has been carved into the shape of a woman we see it both
> as a stone and as a woman. Although it is only a stone, we respond to it
> emotionally. We imagine life into it: it becomes filled with the spirit of
> woman.... It attracts us because, although it is not alive, we are made to
> treat it as though it were. A skull or a sea shell have the same effect upon
> us because we know that once these things were part of a living
> creature.... A certain amount of life is left behind. The same is true of a
> ruined cottage or a discarded plough-share.... By painting, an artist gives
> form to what was a free floating idea. The idea becomes embodied. Quite
> an innocent object acquires significance because of the idea which has
> been attached to it. It is like the hermit-crab which has come to live in a
> disused whelk-shell. It has turned the shell to advantage. The painting
> fulfils a need for the artist in that it brings the idea to light: it exteriorises
> it.'   (Birtchnell 1959:47)

Each time an artist looks at his creation it permits a release of emotion
because of the connection he makes with the idea which prompted him to
paint the picture. There is then a degree of circularity operating: the idea
causes him to make some external representation of it and in turn the
representation of it evokes the original idea.

Aesthetic effect then, in part, is due to the fact that the aesthetic creation
both is and is not the object it depicts. We see the nude sculpture as both a
block of stone and as a woman at the same time. Our mind grapples with
this strange paradox much like a dog not knowing what to make of a rubber
bone. Because the shape of the statue is usually flesh we respond to it as if it
were, yet when we touch the stone we find it is not. Similarly the dog gnaws
the bone-shaped rubber because that shape normally means bone and yet its
teeth sink into it. There is however a difference between our response to the
statue and the dog's response to the rubber bone. Nudity is not approved of
in pubic places and undressing is a conventional invitation to intimate
behaviour. Thus looking at the nude statue is arousing because it is a kind of
looking at a naked woman. If challenged by one's conscience, one can
reasonably assert that one is merely looking at a block of stone which
happens, incidentally, to resemble a naked woman. Since bones are not
normally forbidden to dogs, the dog is not conscience stricken and the
rubber bone is presumably nothing more than a source of frustration.
Children's sugar cigarettes are something altogether different and resemble
much more the nude statue. In sucking the cigarette the children are at least

enacting something naughty, whilst at the same time protesting that they are merely eating a sweet.

Like the art and psychotherapy components of art therapy, the medium and the message components of the aesthetic creation can exist in varying proportions and the proportions they exist in can affect the viewer's response. In general, it is most satisfactory when the medium is clearly in evidence such that the viewer does not lose sight of the fact that he is not just experiencing that which is depicted. Thus allowing parts of the canvas to remain exposed or the paint to dribble reinforces the conflict. Similarly using a hard material to represent something which is soft, such as a cast iron bird, or a soft material to represent something which is hard, such as a felt typewriter, add to the paradox.

The mess

Berlyne (1960), a psychologist with a special interest in aesthetics, defined art as something like harmony in disorder or unity in diversity. Besides the interplay of message and medium there is in most works of art a correct admixture of chaos and control. A good deal of art is what I would call 'the harnessed mess'. Freud described art activity as a sublime form of playing with one's own excrement and certainly I think we share with most animals a fascination with that which is extruded from our own bowels. Marjorie Wardle, a music therapist, graphically described her own childhood preoccupation with peeing and how the piece of music 'Rustle of Spring' evoked for her the sound of running water – due in part perhaps to the double meaning of the word spring (Wardle 1979). In a recent workshop I did, a young woman represented, in pictorial form, how she felt sexually aroused as a child by the water running into her bath. As we grow up we are taught by our parents that wetting and messing ourselves is wrong, that we should retire to a private place to perform, and wash our hands afterwards. Even just making a mess is disapproved of and strong emphasis is placed on being clean and tidy. However, perhaps in making mud pies and paddling, children are able to get messed up and wet again. These childhood yearnings are played out by getting covered in mud on a rugby field or jumping into the Trafalgar Square fountains fully clad. I remember some psychiatrists at lunch one day becoming anxious and starting to laugh at the loud trickling noise made by someone pouring out water from a slightly raised jug.

Paintings such as those of Jackson Pollock owe a lot to the fact that they started as wet sloshy messes. Willem de Kooning once said that he started with the puddle of paint, then the picture got sort of pushed out from the puddle. Painting and modelling with clay enable us to make a limited mess. One limit is that it is less messy when it dries; another is that it is restricted to the size of the picture; yet another is that it can be framed, covered with glass, and displayed in an unmessy place like a drawing-room or picture gallery. The aesthetic quality of *objets trouvés* and 'ready mades' is due to the fact that they are discarded junk set up in elegant surroundings. Thus one component of art activity is the opportunity it provides for relaxing controls and letting go, but within a limited framework.

The censor

There exists in all of us a conflict between the way we would like to feel or behave and the way we believe that others would like us to. This has its origins in childhood when our personal need for gratification clashed with our parents' requirements. In psychoanalytic parlance, this is the famous rivalry between the id and the super-ego. The ego, the essential us, that by which we are recognized, represents the mid-way, compromise position between the primitive drives of the id and the discipline imposed upon us by the super-ego. Out of the ego springs sweet reasonableness, the discretion that is the better part of valour, and the expediency that ensures our survival in social situations. We develop into respectable, responsible citizens by putting aside feelings of embitterment, envy, lust, greed, and rage and relegating them to an inaccessible region of the mind called conveniently the unconscious. Freud proposed the existence of what he termed the censor, which controls that which we allow ourselves to be aware of. Drugs, such as alcohol, have the effect of weakening the powers of the censor and enable these antisocial feelings to come to the fore. In certain psychological states, such as mania, we seem able to give free expression to these normally suppressed emotions. When we have sobered up or recovered from these states we either are amnesic about our indiscreet utterances or, if we do recall them, we are both embarrassed and ashamed.

In dreaming, which occurs mainly as we are emerging from deep sleep, there is also a slackening off of the censor's control; though, to counteract this, we tend to be amnesic about what we have dreamt. Also, as a result of the interplay between the pressing forward of suppressed emotions and the pushing back by the censor, we are, in dreaming, capable of the most imaginative aesthetic creativity. Murderous, incestuous, adulterous inclinations are played out in fantasy as are feelings of insecurity, jealousy, and envy. What makes dreams so fascinating are our efforts to camouflage these inclinations and feelings by ambiguous images or by changing the identities of the dream characters. The censor's ultimate defence is to wake us up just before our most cherished wish or dreaded fear comes to pass. So similar are the phenomena of dreams and the pictures created in therapy that it is essential for all potential art therapists to be conversant with the existing literature on dreams.

Wanting to do it though fearing to do it

In everyday life what these various conflicts amount to is a state of mind in which the wish to be openly ourselves is opposed by an equally strong fear of causing offence. As Hamlet said, 'Conscience doth make cowards of us all' (*Hamlet* III. i. 83). In order to cope with this we have developed a wide range of strategies which it would take a whole new chapter fully to do justice to. A striking example of one such strategy was the occasion when the Muppets featured on the Michael Parkinson Show. The usually inhibited Michael Parkinson was able to be much more freely romantic and flirtatious with the glamorous puppet Miss Piggy than he normally was with attractive young women on his show. It was particularly intriguing that the man who was creating the voice of Miss Piggy was sitting right beside him and was thinking up seductive remarks for Miss Piggy to say to Michael Parkinson to which Michael Parkinson was responding. He was therefore responding to this man's voice, spoken through the mouth of a puppet, as though it really was a glamorous woman chatting him up. He was able to respond in this way because the effect was sufficiently like the real thing to evoke the appropriate response, whilst at the same time he knew it was really only a puppet and the voice really belonged to a man. This reminded me at the time of those men who dress up as women and offer themselves as prostitutes to sailors in places like Singapore. The sailors, knowing them really to be men, allow themselves to be picked up by them. Are they making a homosexual response to the young men or a heterosexual response to the women they are pretending to be? They are in fact doing both. They are permitting themselves to be homosexual because the man is masquerading as a woman, and they feel easier about going off with a prostitute because 'she' is really only a man dressed up as one. It is reminiscent of the kind of ambiguous image we create in dreams.

Related to this is acting the part in a play of a character who is doing what one might like to be able to do oneself. One is able to do it because the part demands it and, although one is actually doing the feared or disapproved of thing, one can reasonably argue that one is merely being true to the part and that the author, in writing the part, dictated that one should do it. A slight variation is a young man who asks another young man to go into a chemist's shop and buy a packet of condoms. The second young man is able to do it by explaining to the shop keeper that he is really doing it for someone else. Similarly it is easier to dictate an offensive letter for a secretary to type than to write the offensive letter oneself. This reminds me of a story I once heard of a medical student who was asked by a little boy in hospital if he would write down on paper anything the boy said. It began as a sort of joke. The boy thought up all manner of obscene words and he thought it very funny that the student was prepared obediently to write it all down. Gradually the boy asked him to write about various sexual fantasies he had about his parents and later about the student and a female student who also sometimes visited him. By this strange device of dictating to the student the boy was able to distance himself from what he was actually saying and perhaps, because it was the student who was doing the writing, he could blame the student instead of himself. At the same time of course, the student, by agreeing to write it, was conveying that it was alright to say these things and have these fantasies.

Telling a story or writing a story, play, or poem about someone who feels the way you do or who does that which you are not sure you are capable of doing is another way of being one step removed from fully committing yourself. By changing the character in some non-fundamental way or changing slightly what he is doing you are making it possible to deny that it is really you that you are writing about. On the other hand you are dropping fairly big hints for some sympathetic reader to take up with you. Whether you confess to the true identity of the character depends upon how safe he makes you feel. This is getting very close to the kind of situation that commonly occurs in art therapy, and in painting there is more scope for ambiguity, since you can represent yourself as an animal or even an object. You can also make it not very clear whether the character in the picture is actually doing what is depicted.

Exposure and self-revelation

Much of what I am saying boils down to the simple question, 'Dare I reveal my true self to the world?' Fritz Perls, the originator of Gestalt therapy, wrote, 'Take responsibility for your every thought, your every feeling, your every action' (Perls 1978). This is not easy, but it is one of the principal objectives of the form of art therapy I shall describe here. Part of my preoccupation with nudity is that it is a concrete form of self-revelation. I would contend that the ambivalent feelings many people have about nudity are to do with a kind of conviction that the various imperfections of their bodies represent the imperfections of themselves. Exercises in aspects of physical self-exposure may therefore facilitate the more subtle revelation of motives and preoccupations. In line with what I have been saying, it is clear that a nude painting or photograph is not the same as an actual nude person. I find it intriguing that the artist's or photographer's model enters into a, usually financial, contract to expose herself in the privacy of the studio. Thereafter, thousands of reproductions of the painting or photo-graph are distributed throughout the world, but though these reproductions reveal to the viewer, with considerable accuracy, what the artist or photographer saw, he and he alone was the person who actually experi-enced the model exposing herself. The reproductions, though stimulating in themselves, are merely coloured canvas or photographic paper. Slightly more intimate was the experience I had of a patient showing me some nude photographs of herself which her man friend had taken with his new instamatic. In a workshop situation participants are usually prepared to make authentic drawings of themselves nude and show them to each other, though they find it much more difficult to undress. In fact such drawings prove to be useful in that they do to some extent feel like exposure and also enable the person to make quite personal statements about his or her body.

An alternative to total self-exposure is exposure of parts of the body and if done seriously can evoke strong emotions. The exercise of pairs of people exploring each other's hands or of a group of people sitting in a circle comparing feet can acquire the quality of self-exposure because the hand or foot becomes a substitute for the body itself. Because we mostly keep much of the body covered, the face normally does come to represent the entire body and our emotional responses to parts of the face are responses which would be more appropriate to those parts which remain hidden. The adornment by women of their eyes is to some extent a displaced adornment of their breasts, which their eyes physically closely resemble.

Practical application

Art versus art therapy

From what I have said in the previous section, it can be concluded that the work of art represents a compromise position between various conflicting needs: the message versus the medium, chaos versus harmony and, perhaps most important, outspokenness versus propriety. There are ideas pressing to be expressed and inhibiting constraints limiting the extent to which they can be made explicit. Freud (1951) used the term 'secondary elaboration' to describe (predominantly in the dream, but it applies equally to the work of art) the moulding together of the components of the composition, to create a semblance of logic and coherence. This is related to what the psycho-analyst Herman Nunberg called the synthetic function of the ego, namely the need we have to arrange ideas into orderly and meaningful patterns (Nunberg 1931). This is the end point towards which the artist is working and where he wants to stop. This is his creation, all neatly parcelled up, the extent to which, at the moment of completion, he is prepared to commit himself. Many artists express the conviction that a work of art speaks for itself and that it is a heresy to suggest that there is a hidden psychological content, of which the artist may be unaware, that can be extricated and highlighted. Other artists, whilst acknowledging that there may be a hidden psychological content, strongly resist any attempt to seek it out, fearing that if the source of their inspiration were unearthed, they would lose their touch and the spell would be broken. There are still others who believe that it is sufficient to make the aesthetic statement in order to resolve the conflict which led to it. They speak of the therapeutic value of art, and consider that patients can paint their way back to health without the assistance of a therapist. It is my belief that various forms of aesthetic pursuit, whilst being satisfying in themselves, do not bring emotions and conflicts near enough to the surface; or if they do, we do not hold on to them long enough to work with them.

Part of the job of the art therapist is to move in and disentangle the neat and elegant statement of the aesthetic creation, break down the veneer of orderliness, and get back to the underlying turmoil before it was tidied up and made acceptable. I do not deny that one needs to execute this disentangling process with the greatest care and sympathy, for the art work was put together in the first place in order to accommodate a number of conflicting themes and, in the finished product, these are ingeniously interlocked. What cannot be too strongly emphasized is that therapists are not normally let loose upon the work of professional artists and they would, quite reasonably, not be too popular for putting forward their considered analyses. The pictures created in art therapy are done so, in the full understanding by their creator, that they may be psychologically dismantled in this way and, to a large extent, this affects the way they are put together. That is they are usually fairly crude, not particularly beautiful, and have pretty obvious clues left for the therapist to pick up. Also quite often they have writing over them which perhaps indicates that their creator is quite willing for the content to be dealt with on a verbal level.

The scope of art therapy

It would be appropriate at this stage to enumerate, with examples, the special features of art therapy and the ways in which art can contribute to the psychotherapeutic process.

1   Unlike dreams, art therapy creations can be presented in concrete form for all to see. The choice of colours and materials used are sometimes significant. It is not just what is depicted, but how it is depicted and how what is depicted is talked about. The picture, once it is created, forms, like a photograph, a permanent record of the state of mind of the subject and of the way he construed his life situation and the people important to him at the time. It can be referred back to minutes, weeks, months, or years later and viewed in conjunction with subsequent pictures. A sequence of pictures can often graphically reveal changes in attitudes or relationships over time.

2   It must always be recognized that pictures are produced for a specific person or group of persons. In this respect they are a manifestation of

the relationship between the subject and the person or persons they were painted for. This should be respected and pictures should not be shown around to other people without the subject's knowledge or permission. Although, technically speaking, pictures painted in hospital are the property of the hospital, from a psychotherapeutic point of view they are strictly the very personal property of the person who painted them. He has the right to decide whether they should be preserved or destroyed. In fact it may have been the knowledge that they could subsequently be destroyed which gave him the courage to paint them in the first place. The destructibility and therefore evanescence of art therapy creations is an important quality; for sometimes the actual destroying of a picture and the way it is destroyed can be a positive component of therapy. Also when a picture is destroyed, in a sense, it is as though it never was. On the other hand, if a picture ever existed, even if no-one other than its creator ever saw it, the statement it incorporated will have left its mark somewhere in the subject's memory and nothing can ever quite be the same again.

3 Art therapy can permit, in fantasy at least, the recreation of something that is lost or past. It enables the subject to return to a relationship which has broken up and communicate with someone with whom he is no longer in touch. He can reconstruct a disturbing scene such as a serious accident or moment of embarrassment. He can draw a picture of someone who has died and tell that person what he never got around to saying, or retract things he regrets having said. He can depict himself at an earlier age or recreate an early family scene. A particularly effective strategy is to propose that he speaks as he draws, speaking in the present tense and the first person singular, using words and a tone of voice appropriate to the age he is supposed to be. He can be encouraged to represent moments of early sexual experimentation, particularly cherished moments, or experiences of sexual harassment. With the representation of these past scenes comes the emotion associated with them and with the expression of that emotion may come the release of some current inhibition.

4 It can enable the subject safely to represent in pictorial form that which he finds frightening, such as being in a confined space, handling snakes, or addressing an audience. He can reproduce frightening dreams like falling through space or running naked through the streets. He can speak as if he is in these situations and allow his emotions to be expressed. He can be encouraged to make new versions of the scenes which are even more disturbing. In this way he can learn more about what the fears are about and, by rehearsing them in this pictorial way, become less frightened of them. Similarly it is possible to write in letters of increasing size, and in progressively brighter colours, words or

phrases he would like to speak aloud or shout, as a stage towards actually doing so.

5 It can permit the subject, in fantasy at least, to indulge in disapproved of or forbidden acts such as embracing or making love to someone who is unavailable, having sexual relations with a parent or sibling, having a homosexual relationship, or a heterosexual relationship if he is homosexual, practising perverse sex, being excessively cruel or sadistic, setting fire to buildings, destroying precious objects, or behaving outrageously. These may represent latent or suppressed motives the partial expression of which allow their more complete assimilation into the personality. Accepting and owning the less acceptable aspects of oneself means that less energy is spent denying their existence.

6 Related to this is the possibility of being safely irrational or frankly psychotic on paper. It is quite acceptable to draw wildly crazy things, be totally ridiculous, regress to being infantile, allow incomprehensible nonsense to spill out, make an utterly chaotic mess, and give free range to one's imagination. It could possibly be argued that such outpourings in the medium of art may keep the individual sane. There are unfortunately still those who use the pictures painted in art therapy sessions as aids to diagnosis and such people may not appreciate that mad pictures are not necessarily painted by mad patients.

7 Much of what is expressed in art therapy would come under the heading of metaphor. A subject may represent his situation by imagery such as heavy weights hanging from his neck, being covered by a glass dome, tossing like a cork in the sea, being an insignificant speck in an empty landscape, surrounded by locked doors, or fluttering above everything like a butterfly. He may depict himself as transparent, meaning that people can see right through him or as literally fused to someone he feels close to.

8 Finally the pictures may not allude to what was or what is but to what might be, such as impending disaster; what could be, like a successful outcome; or what the subject would like to be such as married with children, of the opposite sex, taller, thinner, more powerful, or famous.

Art therapy and the cathartic therapies

Because of the resemblance of aesthetic creations to dreams, art therapy has traditionally fitted in well with either the analytic psychology of Jung or Freudian psychoanalysis, for both Jung and Freud have written a great deal about the nature and interpretation of dreams. Whilst in no way wishing to deprecate these approaches, I would like to propose that with the advent of the 'new' or 'action' therapies art therapy has taken on a new lease of life. These have their origins in the writings of Wilhelm Reich, a contemporary of Freud, who laid great stress upon the value of catharsis, that is the dramatic release of powerful emotions (Reich 1960). Interestingly Breuer and Freud in *Studies on Hysteria,* first published in 1895, demonstrated the effectiveness of catharsis in the treatment of women with various hysterical disabilities (Breuer and Freud 1951). Subsequently however Freud made few references to this approach, preferring instead the more long-term and less dramatic piecing together of significant events in the patient's life story. The most extensively developed of the new therapies is that which has been called Gestalt therapy. Fritz Perls, whose name is that most associated with it, has proposed a new way of looking at and talking about dreams and this can be fairly readily applied to the pictures created in art therapy (Perls 1973). He says that each character and each object featuring in a dream is essentially part of the dreamer. He should therefore be able to own these various facets of himself and speak out of them. If for example he dreams about a fast, powerful motor car it should be possible for him to be the car and say what the car feels. This principle applies equally to the characters and objects depicted in art therapy.

The primary object of the cathartic therapies which, besides Gestalt therapy, include the primal therapy of Arthur Janov (1973), the new identity therapy of Daniel Casriel (1971), and Alexander Lowen's bioenergetics (1967), is to enable the subject to establish contact with suppressed emotion and give vent to it. The means by which this is done is by holding on to small stirrings of emotion and trying to join up with them more completely. In bioenergetics, it may be a physical gesture which represents such a stirring, in which case the subject may be encouraged to exaggerate the gesture and keep repeating it. In primal therapy the patient, using baby talk, calls, and screams, is urged to express his deepest feelings towards his parents. In new identity therapy, the therapist thinks up a particular phrase which seems to encapsulate the feeling and suggests that the subject tries speaking it and repeating it. If using the phrase seems to come close to, but does not quite lead to an emotive discharge, a slightly different phrase or different emphasis may be suggested. In Gestalt therapy, when a particular word or phrase seems to be accompanied by a tremor of the voice or evidence of unrest, the subject is encouraged to 'stay with that feeling' and asked to repeat the phrase a number of times saying it louder and with more emphasis. This often causes progressively more emotion to enter into the expression or for new and more forceful remarks spontaneously to spring to mind. Sometimes, because of the pressure of emerging emotion, the words degenerate into mere noises and the subject begins to weep bitterly.

These methods can readily be adapted to art therapy with great effect. In line with Perls's principles of dream analysis, the subject can be asked to take the part of a character or object represented in the picture and say what the character or object may be feeling. Alternatively, and more commonly, it may be suggested that he addresses one of the characters or objects. This is in accordance with the point made earlier in the chapter, that a picture of a person or thing is not the same as that person or thing, and yet carries some of their characteristics. Thus it represents a safe, half-way stage. The subject can shout at and accuse a drawing of his mother though find it difficult to do it to her face. As with physical gestures or words, some feature of the picture which appears to be the most relevant can be drawn again only larger and more prominently. The subject can once more try being it or speaking to it.

The pictorial versus the verbal in art therapy

One issue on which the more art-orientated art therapists and the psychotherapists who merely use art may sometimes differ is the extent to which the therapy should be kept at the pictorial level. Since it is my conviction that the aesthetic statement is as far as the creator is prepared to go in making explicit his inner conflicts, I see my role as a therapist in assisting the subject to bring these conflicts nearer to the surface. One of the concepts of Gestalt therapy is that the subject should be encouraged to take risks, like for instance daring to whisper something personal and embarrassing into his neighbour's ear. Similarly the subject in art therapy should be encouraged to take pictorial risks. A slight suggestion of murderous intent could be transformed in a subsequent picture into a blatantly murderous act. If the subject draws his father with a large frightening penis, he could perhaps in the next picture draw an enormous penis, perhaps with words coming out of it.

It is my practice to use the picture as a focal point for therapy which, in the main, involves talking about and talking to the pictorial content. During the course of this process new pictures may be suggested as a means of sharpening the focus, but these are essentially only quick sketches, so as not to interrupt the flow of talk or the building-up of emotional tension. The therapy is primarily achieved by the emotion released and the insight gained through talking. In fact progress is made by being able to say in words that which is only pictorially represented. It is possible to go a stage further by translating words into action. Thus a person who has progressed from depicting a murderous scene in a picture to expressing and experiencing murderous feelings in words can be persuaded violently to enact these feelings by pounding cushions. Similarly a woman who has drawn her obese abdomen and progressed to saying how she feels about it can be invited to uncover her own abdomen, touch it, and talk to it.

In various ways such as this art therapy can merge imperceptibly into psychodrama. For example a man can draw the faces of his family members, attach elastic to them, and string them on to the heads of selected members of a therapy group. He can then literally address his remarks to them and they, if they know enough about his life situation, can respond appropriately to him. In turn, he or another group member, can draw his own face, turn it into a mask, and then change masks with another family member. In this way he can feel what it is like to be that person and be addressed by the person wearing his mask. The final step of course is to return to his real family and put into action what he has rehearsed in the drama group.

Transference considerations

So far I have said little of the role of the therapist in art therapy or of the transference and countertransference phenomena which inevitably develop. Because art therapy is to do with bringing unconscious or partially conscious emotions nearer to the surface and daring to be more openly oneself, the super-ego, which derives from parental control, is forever in evidence and needing to be taken notice of. As with the medical student and the little boy, a central function of the therapist is that of a more permissive parent, assuring the patient that it is alright to make references to forbidden issues and give expression to forbidden emotions. He has therefore to convince the patient that he knows what he is doing and that it is safe to trust in him. At the same time, the therapist must be aware that he carries a heavy responsibility and, for this reason alone, must make it his business to learn as much about his craft as possible. As well as this, he must be a reasonably stable person, aware of his own emotional problems and as sure as he reasonably can be that his motives are honourable.

Since, by encouraging the patient to be more open, the therapist is setting himself up in opposition to the patient's parents, he is laying himself open to a good deal of hostility and reproof which he needs to be able to tolerate. Perhaps paradoxically, he often also comes to be cast by the patient into the parent role and he must appreciate that many of the strong positive and negative feelings which become directed towards him do not really belong to him at all. At the same time he must be aware that some of the themes brought out during therapy trigger off emotions in him which are to do with his own family relations.

Concluding remarks

This chapter, unlike a number of others presented in this book, contains a lot of theory, but no case material and no precise guidelines for practice. The best way to learn about method is to attend an actual workshop and Brown (1980) gives an account of her experience in one of my workshops. My primary intention in writing this chapter was to justify my particular approach in terms of my own views about art. I hope I have conveyed the impression that I see no rivalry between psychoanalysis and the cathartic therapies: the latter have evolved out of the former and art therapy can profitably draw upon both.

References

Berlyne, D. E. (1960) *Conflict, Arousal and Curiosity*. New York: McGraw-Hill.
Birchnell, J. (1959) Art as I see it. *Jabberwock* (Journal of Edinburgh University Renaissance Society): 45–8.
— (1977) Alternative Concepts in Art Therapy (1). *Inscape* 1(15): 11–14.
— (1979) Catharsis. *Inscape* 3(1): 3–6.
— (1981) Is Art Therapeutic? *Inscape* 5(1): 15–17.
Breuer, J. and Freud, S. (1951) *Studies on Hysteria* (first published in 1895), *Complete Psychological Works of Sigmund Freud* (Standard Edition) vol. 2. London: Hogarth Press and the Institute of Psychoanalysis.
Brown, S. (1980) Dr. John Birchnell: Art Therapy as Essentially a Form of Psychotherapy. *Inscape* 4(2): 21–2.
Casriel, D. H. (1971) The Daytop Story and the Casriel Method. In L. Blank, G. B. Gottsgen, and M. G. Gottsgen (eds) *Confrontation: Encounters in Self and Interpersonal Awareness*. London: Collier Macmillan.
Freud, S. (1951) *The Interpretation of Dreams I & II* and *On Dreams* (first published in 1900), *Complete Psychological Works* (Standard Edition) vols 4 and 5. London: Hogarth Press and the Institute of Psychoanalysis.
Janov, A. (1973) *The Primal Scream*. London: Sphere.
Lowen, A. (1967) *The Betrayal of the Body*. London: Collier Macmillan.
Nunberg, H. (1931) The Synthetic Function of the Ego. *International Journal of Psycho-analysis* 12: 123–40. Also in *Practice and Theory of Psychoanalysis*. Nervous and Mental Disease Monographs No. 74. New York: International Universities Press, 1961.
Perls, F. (1973) *The Gestalt Approach and Eye Witness to Therapy*. New York: Bantam Books.
— (1978) Esalen Catalogue (July–October). Big Sur, California: Esalen Institute.
Platt, Lord Robert (1967) Medical Science: Master or Servant? *British Medical Journal* 4: 439–44.
Reich, W. (1960) *Selected Writings*. New York: Farrar, Straus & Giroux.
Wardle, M. (1979) Music Therapy and the Therapist. *Inscape* 3(1): 26–31.

Biographical note

John Birchnell At school I had a keen interest in art. I was also interested in science, particularly biological science. Whilst still at school I read Freud's 'Three Essays on Sexuality' and was an immediate convert. I went to Edinburgh University to study Medicine with the intention eventually of becoming a psychoanalyst. During my time at Edinburgh I attended evening classes in art and read through about half the complete works of Freud. On graduation I went straight into psychiatry though, strangely, never got round to having a psychoanalytic training.

By way of a compromise I got the Aberdeen University Diploma in Psychotherapy. In Aberdeen I was introduced to art therapy by Joyce Laing and together we made a film on the paintings of a psychiatric patient. The film, which is called 'A Young Man Preoccupied with his Nose' is available from Concord Films. The same patient was subsequently described in a paper entitled 'An Analysis of the art productions of a psychiatric patient who was preoccupied with his nose' which was reproduced in E. Ulman and P. Dachinger (eds) *Art Therapy in Theory and Practice* (Schocken, NY, 1975). Joyce also introduced me to BAAT which I joined in 1967. My interest in science has led me, since 1967, to remain in full-time psychiatric research. From the early 1970s I have been progressively more influenced by the cathartic therapies and from 1978 have realized the potential of combining these with art therapy.

Currently: Scientific Officer, Honorary Senior Lecturer and Honorary Consultant Psychiatrist, MRC Social Psychiatry Unit, Institute of Psychiatry, De Crespigny Park, London SE5 8AF.

Qualifications: M.D., F.R.C.Psych., D.P.M., Dip. Psychother.

4 | Alternative models for describing the development of children's graphic work: some implications for art therapy

J. K. Dubowski

At approximately eighteen months of age the human child starts to draw. Mark-making activity at about this time is spontaneous. If paper and crayons or other suitable materials are made available the child will produce drawings. If not, no matter, the child will move his or her finger over a steamed up pane of glass, some dust on the floor, or the earth outside. This ability and eagerness to produce marks seems to be innate.

There has been an interest in the study of early child art since the close of the last century. Since that time authorities have studied and published accounts of the development of drawing skills in early childhood. One of the earliest accounts was by Herman Lukens who described the development in terms of chronological age (Lukens 1896). Other authors followed him. A full review of the literature to the present day is well out of the scope of this study. *Table 4.1* shows in historical perspective how these theories of the development of art in childhood relate to each other.

This paper will be concentrating on the first part of the table. Most of the authors listed in *Table 4.1* refer to this stage of development as the 'scribbling' stage. I will refer to it as the 'pre-representational' stage, as it is the stage of artistic development prior to the child having the ability to represent an object in his or her drawing that is clearly recognizable to an audience.

At about eighteen months of age the child starts to show an interest in mark-making activity. At this early stage the child's mark-making is described as locomotor scribble as the individual has not yet established a co-ordination of the hand and eye that allows control of the type of mark

Table 4.1 *Artistic development of the normal child (from 18 months–12 years)*

Authors	Age of child											
	1	2	3	4	5	6	7	8	9	10	11	12
Lukens, H. (1896)		scribbling			the golden age (child blends story and picture)				the critical period (the child's judgement of his art stagnates his efforts)			
Verworn, M. (1907)		unconscious physioplastic stage (scribbling)				unconscious ideoplastic stage (symbolism used to express ideas)				conscious ideoplastic vs physioplastic		
Burt, C. (1921)		scribbling		line	descriptive symbolism		realism		visual realism — repression			
Lowenfeld, V. (1947)		scribbling — disordered substage, lack of motor control; longitudinal substage, lack of visual motor control; circular substage			pre-schematic		schematic		dawning realism		pseudo-realism	
Piaget, J. (1950)		sensorimotor period / pre-operational period			intuitive thought stage		concrete operations period				formal operations period (age 11–15 years)	
		pre-representational drawing period (18 months–4 years)										

that he or she is capable of achieving. As the child develops the marks become increasingly more complex until by the age of four most children can draw a simple representation of the human form. The most primitive type of figure drawing is that which is commonly called a 'tadpole man', a simple representation made up of a circle for the head, sometimes containing marks that represent features, and two vertical lines drawn below the circle representing the legs. Many of the accounts of the development of art in children are attempts to describe the process by which the child arrives at the ability to produce representative drawing.

I have described mark-making in early childhood as a spontaneous activity. This is certainly true of the eager eighteen-month old who has just embarked on that developmental journey towards becoming an artist. Prior to the time that the activity arises spontaneously a child can be coaxed into producing a drawing. The activity at this time is usually unattended and marked with unco-ordinated limb movements. There is a lack of motor control and the child shows very little interest in the activity. The child needs to have developed some degree of hand–eye co-ordination before mark-making becomes a spontaneous activity.

In my work as an art therapist in the field of mental handicap, I am frequently called to assess the mark-making development of patients. On one occasion I was seeing a group of children on an (severe) ESN ward. A Down's Syndrome infant of fifteen months was in temporary care on the ward at the time. The child was sat up in a cot with high sides. I lowered a drawing board with a sheet of paper next to him and offered him a marker. He took this from me, but as his grasp was poor he dropped the marker onto the sheet of paper. It left a dot. The child immediately picked up the marker, investigated both ends, decided on the working end, and started to dot all over the sheet of paper. No other type of mark was produced. The child had good hand–eye co-ordination coupled with attention and curiosity. He had observed how a specific movement had resulted in a mark being produced, and through experimentation was able to reproduce the mark.

It is not very long before a child realizes that different limb movements will produce different types of marks. The child experiments with this notion and in so doing expands his or her repertoire of different marks. The activity changes from one that is simply a locomotor activity to one that is under the visual control of the child. As can be seen in *Table 4.1* the child then goes through other more complex stages, concentration and attention increase, and more than one type of mark is combined on the same drawing. Complex forms emerge, the child starts to notice that some of his drawings resemble real objects – Luquet's 'fortuitous realism' stage: 'a scribble whose meaning is discovered in the act of making it' (Luquet 1929: 29). Eventually the child combines marks in order to produce representations; the first is usually the 'tadpole man' already referred to and from then on drawings become increasingly complex as the individual's skill develops.

Piaget describes this development as a 'semiotic function' (Piaget and Inhelder 1966). Piaget describes his sensorimotor period as follows:

'The sensory-motor mechanisms are pre-representational, and behaviour based on the evocation of an absent object is not observed until the second year.... At the end of the sensory-motor period, at about one and a half to two years, there appears a function that is fundamental to the development of later behaviour patterns. It consists of the ability to represent something (a signified something: object, event, conceptual schema, etc.) by means of a "signifier" which is differentiated and which serves only a representative purpose: language, mental image, symbolic gesture and so on....'   (Piaget and Inhelder 1966: 52)

Piaget places drawing within a scheme of stages leading to the appearance of the semiotic function. He places drawing specifically between a stage of 'symbolic play' and 'mental image'. Piaget describes symbolic play as a game of pretending. This is the capacity to make something stand for something else outside reality. During the stage of symbolic play which occurs about the time that the child starts to draw at the end of the first year and before the end of the second, the child learns to represent events in imitative gesture, and these are sometimes accompanied by objects which at this stage are becoming symbolic. Luquet's first stage in children's drawing development in which he includes his fortuitous realism is in many ways a form of 'playing' with the act of drawing, as the child has not set him- or herself a task of attempting to represent anything.

Play becomes an important factor; Piaget categorizes three distinct stages of play:

1 Exercise play, this occurs during the early sensorimotor stage of development, does not involve a symbolic function, but consists of repeating an action in order to retain and adapt it, and then to use this adapted pattern for simple 'functional pleasure'. The pleasure comes out of causing an event and by so doing confirming the newly acquired skill. Again this description agrees with the locomotor-type scribble often repeated.

2 Symbolic play; the game of pretending as already described.

3 Games with rules; these are, according to Piaget, transmitted socially, such as hopscotch, and so on.

Out of these three basic forms of symbolic play comes a fourth, games of construction. During this final stage the individual makes the transition from play to work. Piaget includes under this heading of play 'intelligent creations'. This notion is in accord with Burt's period of 'artistic revival', which comes after the stage of 'repression' as shown on *Table 4.1* (Burt 1921). Piaget's stages of play seem to agree very well with the development of drawing skills. The stages describe the transition from primitive scribble on the one hand to complex relationships between marks on the other. The development between the two can be said to relate to the development from pre-representational to representational drawing or to the semiotic or symbolic function.

All of the studies so far mentioned have emphasized those stages that follow the earliest representational stage. Indeed this is true for most of the studies about child art. The pre-representational stages are described only in terms of how they contribute to the process of representation. Where the pre-representational stages have been examined, the studies have been based on completed drawings, rather than on the mark-making behaviour that leads to the drawing. One of the most notable examples of this are Kellogg's excellent studies of children's scribbles (Kellogg 1955 and 1970). Kellogg collected more than 100,000 drawings and catalogued the collection. Her account of the development in children's drawings seems to be based on a study of the collected drawings, rather than an analysis of the drawing behaviour leading to their completion – an impossible task with so many drawings.

The art therapist, as a clinician, is first and foremost concerned with treating the patient. The nature of the therapy often has within it the notion that some drawing, painting, or other form of 'art' is produced. The work of art, in my opinion, is secondary to the act of production. The therapist's first concern should be with this, the creative process. With young children the initial problem might well be helping the individual to grasp the skills necessary to produce meaningful marks – meaningful first and foremost to the child and only secondly to the therapist. An understanding of the developmental processes leading to that skill is invaluable. So far I have described this development by highlighting some of the existing literature on child development. Now I will discuss some of the implications of that developmental process.

We have seen that developmentally play occurs before art. Like early stages in the development of drawing, locomotor activity is an early stage in play. A simple example of this is the infant who repeatedly moves his arm to touch a suspended toy above the cot. The infant notices that touching the toy makes it move and repeats the activity to re-affirm that the touch is responsible for the movement. Eventually, through this re-affirming experience, the activity is assimilated and can be used for other things. But this is a very primitive form of play that occurs in early infancy. What is the nature of play? Crook offers the following definition: 'Play is more or less goal-less, is carried out for the fun of it, is relatively unrestricted by fatigue, and is usually conducted with subjective self-awareness' (Crook 1980: 317). The statement is meant to be applicable to both child and adult play. Play as an activity is in itself fulfilling. Crook calls it 'autotelic': 'Autotelic activities then are modes of human action in which total involvement to the exclusion of introspective self-examination is the prime characteristic' (Crook 1980:319).

Kramer compares human and animal play: 'Characteristically, animals at play spontaneously produce a broad range of behaviour germane to their species – not just behaviour belonging to the realm of hunting and food gathering, but ... the whole repertoire of social signalling' (Kramer 1981:49–51). The importance of this final point is stressed:

> 'It seems that the importance of play should be attributed more to the opportunity it affords the immature animal to become acquainted with its species' entire repertoire of behaviour, including actions that would otherwise occur only under extreme stress ... social signalling can be rehearsed without serious consequence. For instance, a weak animal may make threatening gestures before its elders without being summarily punished for this impudence.'
> (Kramer 1981:49–51)

This, of course, is no less true for the human child. Unfortunately, many individuals cared for in large institutions suffer from environments that do not encourage this type of behaviour. Through play an individual has the opportunity to learn new skills relating both to manual dexterity and social skills. The development towards representation in drawing, through playing with mark-making behaviour, is also the development towards an important communicative skill.

Kirkland makes the following statement pertinent to our enquiry: 'Curiosity is triggered by attention to environmental anomaly. Sustained and persistent effort applied to resolve curiosity, leads to skill development and finally, application of this skill to solve other problems' (Kirkland 1979:31). This statement describes a process similar to that taking place in the example (above) of the child touching the suspended toy: the resulting movement is the environmental anomaly which triggers curiosity, the re-affirming activity of repeatedly touching the object is the effort applied to resolve the curiosity, and assimilation is the resulting skill. Kramer has shown that social skills are also mastered in this way. Can the 'process' of play as described be applied to development in drawing? When a child is drawing, particularly at the pre-representational stages, a single type of mark is often repeated on the same drawing. Later the child plays with combinations of marks – at first only two types of mark share the same drawing, later three or more patterns emerge and are again played with. Eventually specific patterns that are conscious representations develop.

I have described the development from play to art ontogenetically, that is in terms of an individual's development from birth. Dissanayake (1974) has attempted to describe the relationship between play and art phylogenetically, that is in terms of its evolutionary development. She argues that art is a social activity: 'Like play, artistic behaviour, even though it might be private, takes the artist outside himself, puts him into a relationship with an "other"' (Dissanayake 1974:7). This process can be described in terms of the relationship between the work of art and the perceiver: 'Moreover, a perceiver may not be aware only of the object as an other, but also of its maker and thereby reaching a feeling of identification with them both' (Dissanayake 1974:211). Dissanayake argues that as man evolved as a social animal, any social activity is to be seen as possessing selective value: 'Social institutions progressively freed individuals from dependence on instincts, which preclude innovative behaviour, and allowed knowledge to be accumulated and transmitted' (Dissanayake 1974:214–15). Arguably, there is a relationship between the degree of evolutionary development and play behaviour. Moreover any form of play that is communicative in nature must be of the utmost importance to such a socially cohesive species as man. Representational mark-making or art as an innate activity must also be of prime value and importance.

I have stressed the importance of the pre-representational stages of drawing development in the context of play. The art therapist working with young children who, for some reason or other, have not yet reached the representational stage, gives the child the opportunity to play and experiment with mark-making behaviour so that the child may be able to develop further. Reasons for individuals working at the pre-representational stages other than simply chronological age and normal developmental growth might be mental handicap, physical handicap, emotional problems, or social deprivation. Some individuals regress because of trauma or other reasons and will exhibit these early stages in their drawing. Are the drawings produced at these pre-representational stages open to any form of interpretation other than the developmental model as described?

Piaget has stressed that play has a symbolic content in it. Dissanayake stresses that play has a strong metaphorical content. Child psychoanalysts, notably Melanie Klein (1959), use the play activity of children as the starting point of the analysis. If during the pre-representational stages of drawing the child is engaged in playing with marks, is this as readily interpretable?

In play, objects, both animate and inanimate (playmates and toys), can represent an infinite number of situations. A ball of paper thrown across the floor in front of a kitten will elicit hunting behaviour. The ball of paper represents prey to the kitten. This manifestation of play using an object metaphorically is applicable also to human play, when a child uses a toy to represent another. Arguably the same kind of process also occurs when the child is engaged in drawing at the pre-representational stages. He might not have the skill necessary to give an object or situation a definite outline; he might not at this stage grasp the concept that lines can be arranged to give objects and situations outlines. All the same, as Luquet has pointed out, the marks might, to the child, represent some kind of event; in his play the child might stumble upon a shape in his drawing that suggests an outline to him – Luquet's 'fortuitous realism'.

Freud wrote of children's play: 'The child at play creates a world of his own by re-arranging the things of his world in a new way that pleases him' (Freud 1951a: 143–44). The metaphorical content in play, invested in an action or object, can have an infinite number of meanings to the child. In the example of the kitten and the ball of paper, the elicited response is stereotyped, the metaphorical content is prey. The kitten playing with the ball of paper is experiencing a pleasure-orientated activity (this is one of Dissanayake's points concerning the nature of play (Dissanayake 1974)). The complexity of play in the child allows for this process to work at a complex unconscious level. Freud states:

> 'The child in play endeavours to master unpleasant experiences. He does this by reproducing a situation that has (in reality) been too much for him originally, by repeating the situation in this way the child goes over what has been done to him.'   (Freud 1951b: 15)

Through play the child can experience feelings of mastery and omnipotence. In this way play serves the child's ego.

In children's play, actions and objects take on symbolic meanings. Play at this level operates on a similar principle to art. In evolutionary terms the complexity of play and its relationship with art has arguably contributed to our ascent. Dissanayake takes up this point in comparing the self-rewarding aspect of play, one of her major principles of play, with art. Desmond Morris points out that even chimpanzees, when encouraged to draw or paint, will do so without external reward (Morris 1964). The ability to produce without external reward allows the creator to produce novelty. This might, in the phylogenetic past, have led to the production of tools. There is a difference between tool use, exhibited in chimpanzees, and tool making, only exhibited in man. 'The non-serious, functionally useless activity of play might then in fact be responsible for two of mankind's most important characteristic activities; the 'practical' fabrication of tools and the 'spiritual' creation of works of art' (Dissanayake 1974: 214).

In what way are we to use the complexity of this development in therapy? I have suggested that even without intention on the part of the child to endow his drawings with symbolic content, to give an outline, form, or shape to an external 'other', the very activity is endowed with some metaphorical or symbolic meaning. I have emphasized the nature of re-affirmation in this type of mark-making behaviour. 'Locomotor activity' as a descriptive term is physiological in nature. That is, it describes the types of limb movements used to carry out the activity. The description of developmental stages following locomotor scribble also rely heavily on physiological terms. The increasing complexity of the drawings produced by the child are described in terms of increased complexity of mark as a result of increased motor control and hand—eye co-ordination. In the literature there does not seem to be any analytical interpretive basis for accounting for children's drawings until after the representational stages have been reached.

In describing play the term 'autotelic' was introduced. This term suggests that play is an activity that is done for its own sake. There are no ulterior motives involved. Through play the child learns to experience, in a safe situation, potent types of behaviour that will be useful in later adult life. That is to say, play allows the individual to be self-assertive without threat of consequence. Any self-assertive activity is an 'ego' activity. In psychodynamic terms, the human child's struggle away from the mother towards independence is the development of the individual's ego. Play is used during this struggle, through play and the use of transitional objects the child builds up an ever increasing distance from the mother figure (Winnicott 1971). One of the activities used during this period of the child's psychodynamic development is mark-making through drawing and painting.

In psychodynamic terms, the ego is the mechanism by which an organism achieves the needs of the id or instincts. The super-ego is an extension of the ego and is to do with social conformity; that is, to ensure that the actions used by the ego to satisfy the id are socially favourable. The dynamics of this system constitute a psychic economy.

Can this model of psychic economy be used to describe the drawing skills in early childhood? Drawings produced by a child during this period are a record of the child's ever increasing ego strength. The period leading up to a time when the individual is able to assert selfhood – that is, a degree of independence – is a period of ego growth as well as physiological growth.

In a normal child psychological and physiological growth occurs side-by-side. That is what we mean when we say that an individual is well-adjusted. Mentally ill and handicapped children suffer imbalance between the two types of development. It is acknowledged that intellectual impairment limits the capacity for abstraction, this interferes with language development and also the capacity for symbol formation (Piaget's semiotic function) and problem solving.

Clearly, care must be taken in any interpretation of the drawing activity of mentally retarded individuals. Even a comparison between early stages in the drawing activity of the normal child and the pre-representational marks produced by the retarded individual must be made with caution. Although the drawings produced by these two sets of individuals have common elements, the processes leading to the production of the drawings differ. Any study based on a simple analysis of a collection or collections of drawings by the normal and subnormal population will clearly be limited because of this factor.

Any valid interpretation must be based on observable facts. Some form of discipline is needed to collect the data required for interpretation. The finished drawing is never enough. Many of the studies of the development from scribble to representation have been shown to be based on the interpretation of drawings rather than an investigation into the activities responsible for the production of the drawings. It is in this area that I feel that art therapists can be making a vital contribution to our knowledge concerning the development of a certain type of behaviour. This type of study that art therapists might involve themselves with may contribute to our knowledge concerning the evolution and nature of art.

Art therapy with mentally retarded and autistic children: some notes

Some mentally retarded individuals and some children that are classed as autistic, because of the severity of their handicaps, may never reach the representational stages and be able to use drawing symbolically. However, if the potential for development is there this needs to be nurtured by the therapist or teacher. Development will not take place without the individual having the opportunity to experiment and play with mark-making behaviour. My experience as a therapist working with the mentally handicapped has led me to make the following observations. First, there is a marked increase in investment during periods of mark-making activity at and following the start of the representational stages, the activity seems to become increasingly important to the child, the child's attitude to the activity changes in terms of the amount of time he will spend at it. Attention while engaged in mark-making behaviour also increases. The child's attitude to the finished drawing is a measure of this investment. The child exerts ownership over the drawing, asks for his or her name to be put on the drawing, for the drawing to be hung on the wall, or to take the drawing home or back to the ward. A child, in my experience, will only infrequently make these demands at the earlier pre-representational stages of development. Second, while engaged in human figure drawing the child frequently relates parts of the drawing to his or her own body. For example looking at a hand while drawing with the other one, lifting clothes to local a navel prior to drawing one. These observations lead to a notion that the first human figure drawings produced by the child relate to that child, they are statements of 'self' or ego. The development leading to the ability to assert selfhood in this way is a period of ego growth as well as physiological growth (see Dubowski 1982).

Within the framework proposed by Piaget is the assumption that the child's perceptual motor development runs parallel to the development of drawing. The ability to produce a circle comes at precisely the same time as the child is capable of perceiving the Gestalt experience. (The Gestalt experience, simply, is the ability to recognize a configuration by separating a figure from a field. This is achieved by being able to recognize a figure's edges which separate it from its background or field.) Linguistic skills are also developing at this time, enabling the child to appreciate the symbolic potential of his graphic productions. Within the child's psychodynamic development, the ego is emerging, enabling the child to invest the drawings with meaning that is concerned with a sense of identification. The first representational figure drawings produced by the child are pictures of the 'self'. The ability to produce human figure drawing is complex. A number of developmental processes work together; a deficit in any of these areas will hinder the process, sometimes making the step from pre-representation to representation impossible. Many mentally handicapped individuals develop some verbal skills but have perceptual problems that may prevent their ability to perceive their own bodies. Institutionalization often hinders the development of ego strength making it difficult to develop linguistic skills. Infantile autism is an example of this type.

However, even at the most primitive level of the developmental sequence the individual is able to follow strategies that enable drawings to be produced; even the most basic locomotor scribble is produced, by definition, through postural consequence – the types of marks will be determined by the way the child holds an implement in the hand, the size of a line will be to some extent determined by the child's reach, the length of the child's arm. The posture of the child in relation to the sheet of paper will to some extent influence the type of mark that will be produced.

Even at these early stages the child seems to be capable of setting up goals, in the form of following a defined set of rules in order to achieve certain aims. That these aims are achieved in the form of drawing strategies that most children seem to follow is evident in the similarities of drawings at the various stages of drawing development as described in this chapter. It is the nature of these goals, rule structures, and strategies that are difficult to define. The materials used, such as medium and type of implement, have an obvious effect. Factors such as posture, grip, and handedness, can be seen to influence both type of mark and, more significantly, placement of that mark on a given picture surface. The fluidity of paint lends itself to types of mark-making that differ from the quality of line produced by an implement such as a pencil or crayon. Different sizes of picture surface lend themselves to different types of motor activity, from gross to fine movements, all influencing the resulting drawing. The goal to fill in a large sheet of paper effectively lends itself to gross motor movements, the same goal on a small sheet of paper to finer movements. Once a goal has been set by the child and the task of achieving it begun, the circumstances change. A picture surface, once initially marked, offers a secondary problem, that of relating future marks to what already exists. The difference in strategy to cope with this problem will depend on the type of marks that the subject is using at the time. The more discrete and separate the type of marks, the more flexible the possible response to the secondary problem from the already marked surface. Diversity of marks and movements used in the production of drawings, along with a capacity to respond to novelty, seem to be the factors that most influence the flexibility or rigidity of responses during drawing. Learning and further development in a given area arises out of a situation where attention to novelty triggers responses in behaviour that are adaptable in such a way as to solve the problem arising from the novel situation, and finally assimilating that response for future use.

The construction of a drawing by placing several single marks in some sequence offers a far more potentially novel arrangement on a picture surface than a drawing produced by a prolonged single movement. The problem of attention is one that has implications concerning the opportunity to achieve the maximum developmental potential of an individual. Many handicapped and institutionalized patients, including children, adopt behaviour patterns that are now clinically termed 'stereotypic'. Studies into stereotyped movements and subnormality in children have been undertaken by many authors. Forehand and Baumeister describe stereotyped behaviour in the following terms: 'Highly consistent and repetitious motor or posturing behaviours, the adaptive consequences of which, if any, are not immediately apparent' (Forehand and Baumeister 1971:79–87). It has been suggested that the function of stereotyped acts is to reduce arousal. Studies into the behaviour of autistic children by Hutt and Hutt (1970) support this hypothesis. In observing the behaviour of 'autists' in social situations they found that the intensity of stereotypes increased following encounters of mildly agonistic types which, 'in all probability indicates an increase in level of arousal or excitation' (Hutt and Hutt 1970:175–205).

Although researchers have submitted differing assumptions and the studies have been concerned with different client groups, there seems to be agreement that stereopathy serves as some form of self-regulatory or homeostatic function. That is, that stereotyped behaviours occur at times when the level of stimulation available to the individual is either too low or too high. People who adopt these types of behaviour obviously have difficulties with their attention structures making concentration during any task difficult.

The repetitive nature of the mark-making behaviour of many mentally handicapped children and adults, and to a lesser degree, institutionalized psychiatric patients, suggests that while engaged in drawing they are adopting a stereotyped act. However, if the individual is able to concentrate and attend the activity of drawing – and this is often the case when, although drawings are made up of single units or marks, these are placed in an orderly way and more than one drawing of the same type is produced – then the term 'stereotyped' as applied clinically does not seem applicable to drawing. Further confusion concerning this term exists in its use to describe the type of repetition noted in the behaviour and drawings of emotionally disturbed individuals, particularly children. Emotionally maladjusted children frequently develop rigid inflexible patterns of acting. This pattern type behaviour can be a form of escape to avoid having to adjust to a new situation. Avoidance of new and, therefore, threatening situations as a complex psychological defence might result in a maladjusted child drawing patterned pictures of a simple type, and these drawings might resemble those of severely mentally handicapped individuals whose 'stereotyped' response to mark-making behaviour is a result of abnormal attention structure; the art therapist needs to know the distinction between these differing causal factors.

What I have attempted to show is that the development from the basic scribble to the first representational drawing is a part of that development towards a semiotic or symbolic function, a development towards unique human consciousness.

Normal children manage the developmental sequence quite easily, there appears to be an innate drive forward. The individual child, in his or her drawing, through experimentation, through play, and through learning skills by solving problems arrives at the unique human ability to 'represent' in drawing, in painting, and through other plastic expression. Further, the first representations produced by that child appear to relate to that individual's concept of 'self' before the concept of 'other'. This phenomenon – that the first representation by a human is that of a 'figure drawing' – suggests that this development, together with language, contributes to the semiotic function which allows us to perceive ourselves as different and individual beings: in psychodynamic terms, this is the ego. The complexity of our social lives depends on this capacity to separate ourselves from the other, both environmental and individual. Many forms of mental handicap and autism, as well as trauma and other psychiatric problems with children, often prohibit or slow down normal development resulting in individuals who have not achieved the separation and live in a world of confusing objects in which they have no place. Drawing towards the representational stage and beyond offers those individuals the opportunity to develop towards a sense of 'self'. Art therapy is, therefore, an appropriate and valid treatment in these areas.

Illustrations

The following are two examples, out of a total of thirty-eight drawings produced in one session, of 'tadpole' type of early representational drawings by a mentally handicapped adolescent.

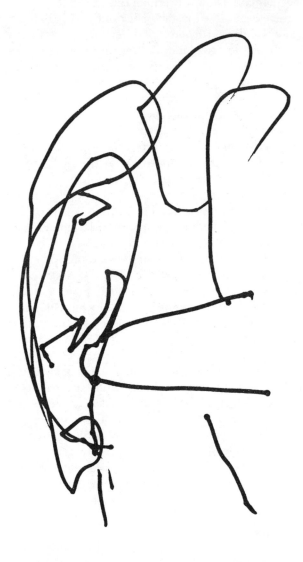

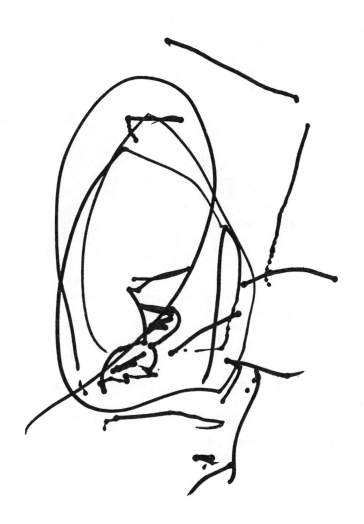

References

Burt, C. (1921) *Mental and Scholastic Tests*. London: P. S. King.

Crook, J. (1980) *The Evolution of Human Consciousness*. Oxford: Oxford University Press.

Dissanayake, E. (1974) *An Hypothesis of the Evolution of Art from Play*. Oxford: Pergamon.

Dubowski, J. K. (1982) Alternative Models for Describing the Development from Scribble to Representation in Children's Graphic Work. Proceedings of the two-day conference: 'Art and Dramatherapy', Hertfordshire College of Art and Design, St Albans, 22 and 23 April.

Forehand, R. and Baumeister, A. A. (1971) Rate of Stereo-typed Body Rocking of Severe Retardates as a Function of Frustration of Goal-directed Behaviour. *Journal of Abnormal Psychology* 78: 35–42.

Freud, S. (1951a) *The Poet and Daydreaming* (first published in 1908), *Complete Psychological Works* (Standard Edition) vol. 9. London: The Hogarth Press and the Institute of Psycho-analysis.

— (1951b) *Beyond the Pleasure Principle* (first published in 1920), *Complete Psychological Works* (Standard Edition) vol. 18. London: The Hogarth Press and the Institute of Psycho-analysis.

Hutt, C. and Hutt, S. J. (1970) *Behaviour Studies in Psychiatry*. Oxford: Pergamon.

Kellogg, R. (1955) *What Children Scribble and Why*. Palo Alto, Calif.: National Press.

— (1970) *Analysing Children's Art*. Palo Alto, Calif.: National Press.

Kirkland, J. (1979) Interest: Phoenix in Psychology. *Bulletin of the British Psychological Society* 29: 31–41.

Klein, M. (1959) *The Psychoanalysis of Children*. London: The Hogarth Press.

Kramer, E. (1981) *Childhood and Art Therapy*. New York: Schocken Books.

Lowenfeld, V. (1947) *Creative and Mental Growth* (3rd edn). New York: Macmillan.

Lukens, H. (1896) *A Study of Children's Drawings in the Early Years*. Pedagogical Seminary no. 4.

Luquet, G. H. (1929) L'evolution du dessin enfantin (The development of children's drawings). *The Bulletin of the Binet Society* 29: 145–63.

Morris, D. (1964) *The Biology of Art*. London: Methuen.

Piaget, J. (1953) *The Origin of Intelligence in the Child*. London: Routledge & Kegan Paul.

Piaget, J. and Inhelder, B. (1966) *The Psychology of the Child*. London: Routledge & Kegan Paul.

Verworn, M. (1907) Kinderkunst und Urgeschichte (Child Art and Early History). *Korrespondenz der deutschen anthropologischen Gesellschaft* 27: 42–6.

Winnicott, D. W. (1971). *Playing and Reality*. London: Tavistock.

Biographical note

J. K. Dubowski Postgraduate Diploma in Art Therapy (CNAA), Herts College of Art and Design, St Albans, 1976; since then has worked extensively with mentally handicapped people; until recently was Head Art Therapist at Cell Barnes Hospital, St Albans. Currently, Rank Xerox Research Fellow, awarded through Herts College of Art and Design and this chapter is based on unpublished doctoral dissertation entitled, 'An Investigation of the Pre-representational Drawing Activity of Certain Severely Retarded Subjects within an Institution, Using Ethological Techniques'.

5 | # The child and art therapy: a psychodynamic viewpoint

Margarita Wood

I hope to explore a network of ideas which have a child playing and painting at its centre, so I would ask you to leave the culture of the adult world for a moment and follow this child, who merely for ease of writing, is a boy. And for the sake of simplicity also, the word 'painting' will have to cover the use of any plastic medium, any tactile substance, that the child might use to create an image.

A world without words: the beginning of relationship and the search for meaning

We have all been children yet even when helped through our forgetfulness, there is a qualitative difference between childhood memory recalled and the live child who, demanding help in therapy, leads us back on a return journey to his own, more recent beginnings.

At the very beginning, we find ourselves in a world of great clarity, even if rather short in focus, filled with sensation. There is a rate of learning never again to be equalled, as the sensory world is explored, and loss of stimulus is cause for distress. Acutely perceptive of body/world yet with little ability to communicate, the baby learns to recognize the mother's face and voice within the first few days after birth (Carpenter 1975).

Later, when the child makes wordless images of this time, it seems that there are moments when things are clear and others when all is confused; there is no inside nor out, no up nor down, no defined 'me', no 'not-me', but a fluid clustering of sensation and emotion. It is a world where parts may represent the whole, and a single attribute or sensation may provide the hook for a cluster of contiguous events and the responses to them; where a multitude of meanings may co-exist. This rich ground for future development becomes impoverished for the child left unstimulated or made anxious, and where there is trauma or disruption, the clusters of effect-plus-meaning are blocked off to avoid further distress; they can remain unmodified by any search for reality and coherence, as knots of unfinished business and anxiety which can cause disturbance later on in the child's life.

One of the reasons for the return journey in therapy is to find the meaning that is lost.

As language becomes an important means of communication, the small child attempts to match the meanings he has found with those that appear to be attached to words. Usually the 'fit' is reasonable, but where discrepancies persist, a gap between inner and outer worlds may broaden to produce confusion and isolation. This becomes tragedy when the meaning of words is contradicted by the feeling of relationships surrounding them, by the actions which accompany them, or by the inflection in the voice which utters them. At best, language inevitably brings out some loss in richness of association, words tending to express a linear sequence of thought in time, although poetry may make a bridge to that multiplicity of meaning and relationship more readily held by an image. Too often acquisition of language means a closure on entire areas of experience which can be but poorly expressed in words, and access to earlier, more fluid modes of thought and feeling is lost.

Painters such as Chagall (Haftmann 1973) and Hieronymous Bosch (de Tolnay 1965) can take us back, charm, or unsettle us. Magritte (Torczyner 1977) evokes disturbing echoes from a world of unpredictable objects and people, having no permanent nature, size nor substance, location nor relationship with other objects; and where space is a mystery. He attacks the conventional link between word and object and we are forced to relinquish hard-won ideas, relieved that these things are rendered harmless in the wit of the painting. It is less easy to dispose of the death and separation which are also present.

Magritte exposes us to the austerity and fear of loss in relating, and such loss is the second reason for the return journey.

A world without words: 'unless we are artists'

The interweaving structures of meaning and relationship develop and change throughout life and at any point may become knotted or broken. However, early damage makes for the more profound effect on the personality and occurs at a time when communication is wordless.

The question of very early experience and development has received increasing attention over the last decade from psychologists such as Bower (1977) and many others. Yet fifty years ago, pioneers in the study of the child, such as the psychoanalysts, Anna Freud and Melanie Klein, and the paediatrician, Margaret Lowenfeld, sought to understand how the infant stores up memories of meaning and relationship in the body and its functions, and in the archaic images which form the mental counterpart of sensory experience; and how later on, children may demonstrate their original encounters with an unpredictable world, through play and picture-making. They were followed by others such as Erik Erikson and Erich Neumann, Freudian and Jungian respectively, and by D. W. Winnicott, a paediatrician and analyst, who extended his own special insights from a Freudian base.

All these sources influence my description of the live child whose growth into play and painting we are attempting to follow. But first, a brief look at the common ground shared by these varied psychodynamic approaches to the non-verbal experience, and some thoughts as to how art therapy can relate to them and make its own contribution.

The Freudian definition of fantasy provides a broad base of agreement:

'By the term "unconscious phantasies" we mean the most primitive psychic formations, inherent in the operation of the instinctual urges.... Unconscious phantasies occur not only in the infant, they are part of the unconscious mind at any time, and form the matrix from which pre-conscious and conscious processes develop ... they are pre-verbal, or rather non-verbal. The words which we use when we wish to convey their content and meaning are a foreign element, but we cannot do without it – unless we are artists.'   (Heimann 1955:24)

In the Kleinian view 'reality experiences immediately influence and are influenced by unconscious phantasy ... unconscious phantasies can determine what kind of causal sequence is attributed to events' (Segal 1964–73:14, 15). Even if a perfect maternal environment were possible, aggressive and persecutory fantasies and anxieties would still arise. Lowenfeld pointed to sources of such anxieties:

'Small children are in a peculiar position in regard to their own bodies. Sensations from them arise almost continually, powerful urges to movement, violent phenomena like vomitting or diarrhoea, noises of their own crying, the feel of substances and the mystery of sleep.... Time also in the sense of process of time, has no meaning for them; each experience, as it arises, dominates the field of consciousness.'   (Lowenfeld 1964)

Physical and emotional pain have a unity for the young child, there is no description, no localization, and he cannot stand apart from the discomforts of an unstable metabolism (Lowenfeld 1931:195–96). The incomprehensible experience and strong feelings together produce fear, and often there is insufficient understanding from parents and other adults, to mediate the experience or offer adequate outlets for expression. This experience becomes the ground of pre-verbal thinking (Lowenfeld 1937) in which sensation and effect are fused together in a unique and idiosyncratic way.

The same questions concerning infant experience are framed in Jungian terms (Neumann 1973), together with a study of the wealth of images we carry with us out of infancy (Neumann 1955). Heimann's 'unconscious phantasy' (Jackson 1960) is considered as equivalent to these 'archetypal images' which convey the life experiences common to us all (Jung 1959). Such images that arise in infancy become elaborated with maturity, give form to culture, and are of changing significance in each phase of life, or they may remain unmodified, binding energy and delaying maturation (Neumann 1961).

There would seem to be general agreement that images are the primary containers of experience. It follows that a representation could convey that content and make a bridge into language. We need to emphasize that picture-making in all its forms is a universal mode of communication, no more confined to the gifted than is the use of language.

Theories can usefully help us organize our ideas but they can also set limits on expectation and perception. Freud considered that visual expression could be given only to concrete subject matter and not to the interrelation of elements: 'Thinking in pictures is, therefore, only a very incomplete form of becoming conscious' (Freud 1951b: 21). Picture-making as a means of communication remains underestimated in much psychoanalytical thought.

I hope to show that 'thinking in pictures' lies at the root of awareness. The verbal form may have to be rephrased many times before the right nuance of meaning is found, and further transcriptions may have to be made at subsequent times. This is made possible, and possibly made tolerable, because a painting holds the essential communication, for as the eighteenth-century painter, William Hogarth, said in his *Apology for Painters*: 'Drawing and painting are only a more complicated kind of writing' (Hogarth, ed. Kitson 1968).

A world without words: 'the pictures in my head'

'How do I know what I think until I've said it!' said the child, for thoughts just seem to happen, like falling over or having a surprise. But often it is a case of 'how do I *know* until I've played the pictures in my head!'

Play brings the world within the child's grasp and takes him out into society, providing the means to externalize his thoughts and feelings, to experiment with links and relationships, to find new outcomes, or to absorb past experience by making a form in which it can safely be repeated; he can explore ideas about body functions, about birth, and sex, and death. He can encounter the great archaic images common to all and find ways of representing the more unique aspects of himself and others.

This wide spectrum of activity is an essential part of the child's healthy growth, and has attracted the attention of therapists over many years (Lowenfeld 1969 (1st edn 1935), Erikson 1950, Winnicott 1971). More recently, play has become the focus of research in child development (Trevarthen and Grant 1978), and it is seen as arising out of the mother's playful imitation of the baby's own actions. This 'social play' is the 'necessary precursor of solitary fantasy play.... When he plays on his own a child communicates with himself inside his own head.... He is, in effect, trying out his ideas on himself and to do this he must surely know that there exist ideas and intentions other than his own' (Trevarthen and Grant 1978: 566–69).

The mother's mirroring, imitative playing endows the child's actions and responses with meaning and enables his own playing to follow (Winnicott 1971: ch. 9). A sense of objectivity and separateness, however, is not a prerequisite but a gradual achievement within the play. We need not know the source of an idea in order to play with it as an *objet trouvé* or something we feel we have created for ourselves; 'me' and 'not-me' have permeable boundaries and intentions may be located anywhere. The important thing is the child's discovery of some sort of space, or place, in which he can explore those ideas and pictures in his head.

The 'potential space' (Winnicott 1971) is where inner and outer realities can interact and objects found seem to be created to meet the moment. The child can realize this potential in actual play-space and time, only if he feels the world is safe enough. The necessity for trust is recognized everywhere to be of prime importance; without trust anxiety fragments all attention. Solitary playing cannot be discovered if the child is his own caretaker, for continuity must be held by another in whose presence he can play alone (Winnicott 1965a).

The making of a mark is a form of playing which contains the flow of activity and mirrors it back to the child. The child is caught in an exchange with his own meaning and so acquires a knowledge of it; he is within a reflective process. Reflection 're-enacts the process of excitation and carries the stimulus over into a series of images which, if the impetus is strong enough, are reproduced in some form of expression' (Jung 1960: 117).

'Those pictures in my head' are discovered on the outside, and the child may become as active in his response to the image he had made as he was in the original dyadic relationship with his mother. The self-encounter may be self-confirming and lead to further exploration or the child may repudiate the image to the point of denying authorship, experiencing again the negative aspects in the original mirroring. Yet again, he may attempt to gain mastery over the frightening or intolerable by destroying the image. All the responses and strategies of the mirror reaction (Pines 1982) can be found.

Painting can be an appropriate medium for this playing and the most adequate mirror in which the child can encounter himself. Giftedness adds its own problems but when it fades, as in Nadia (Selfe 1977), many questions remain unanswered.

Nadia, as a young child, had an incredible ability to draw yet suffered severe disability in language and social skills, and it was not possible to test her intelligence. Her drawing skills are inexplicable in terms of the ordinary child's development. While we may be amazed by the aesthetic impact of her horsemen, we must turn to the nature and function of the mirroring which may override the value and cultural status of giftedness. Faced with such impetus towards expression, perhaps we should consider hallucinatory elements combined with eidetic recall, comparable to those exploited by artists such as William Blake in his works on the 'Ghost of a Flea' (Bindmann 1977; Tate Gallery Catalogue 1978). Television, even seen peripherally, is a rich source of horses and other images.

Nadia began to draw horses and horsemen with great fluency when she was just over three years old. Locomotion and aggression are certainly conveyed, and with such fierce emphasis on the eyes that we cannot avoid the encounter. Perhaps something was being said about the beginning which equates the eye and the breast as the mother mirrors the feeding baby? It is possible that Nadia was attempting a new beginning, drawing in the presence of her mother, now restored to her after a period of three months in hospital with breast cancer. The absence had been total and very distressing; it followed a series of events in the previous two years, patterning repeated loss of her mother and the facilitating environment (Winnicott 1962). In spite of real damage in both mother and child, and apart from damage that might have been fantasied, safe holding and potentiality was restored.

Intense graphic activity erupted out of passive withdrawal and Nadia was observed in animated and reflective interaction with what she had drawn. Her drawings conveyed a quality of aliveness usually buried or split off from her everyday self.

In later drawings, made when Nadia was just over six-and-a-half years old, the dominating eyes had gone, vanished into a vacant pinhead, while the focus became attached to the crossed legs and feet of seated female figures. Was this a retreat from direct contact, or did it reflect the receding presence of her sick mother? Yet the graphic pressure remained, line upon line as the flow of the ballpoint pen carried the seeking gesture forward, repeatedly, to explore the points of physical contact, leg crossing knee.

Then, from the age of seven, the extraordinary giftedness faded. Within a special school, Nadia sought ritualistic forms of continuity and dependability, achieved some social skills, some integration, while highly sensitive to separations. The horsemen only appeared as occasional, transitory forms on steamed-up windows.

Was the loss of spontaneous drawing really the price paid for some sort of normality? Her language can surely never approach the eloquence of her drawing. Perhaps we should look for the answer in the death of her mother when she was seven years old. I suggest that the loss carried with it the search for meaning and relationship which lay behind the drawing; the mirroring space was shattered; the spontaneous graphic playing could not bring resolution for the task was too great.

Art therapy: triple reflections in a triangular space

A child may be caught in a struggle to state a problem in order to know it, yet continually fail because of the problem's archaic, split-off, or inadmissible nature. Or he may be caught up in a statement which does not change with repetition because change is prohibited or too dangerous. Or he may be held fast, reflecting problems which largely belong to others, in the same way as some artists reflect their society. Whatever the overburdening factors, the explorative dialogue with the painting fails; it becomes a closed repetitive system, even within a supportive environment.

Painting in the presence of the therapist alters the intention and the dynamic balance; dyad becomes triad. This may be described as a triangulation around the potential space.

Painting ceases to be part of the general flow of playing and becomes the focus of therapy. As the precipitate of the interaction between inner and outer worlds, the painting becomes a third world, unchanged by attitudes, time, or distortions of memory, yet different aspects of meaning and relating can be discovered on different occasions. As the centre of a triplex structure, the painting can survive a degree of impact from denials and distortions, and hold together fragmented elements from the other worlds, while continuing to make a statement about the contents as a whole. This statement may be central to an accumulation of interpretations and exchanges between child and therapist, before its content is exhausted.

The presence of the therapist produces a complementary triangulation in the mirroring process. The child is caught in response to self or to experience as reflected in the painting, and in response to the therapist's receptivity, whether or not interpretation is made.

The counterpart of the child's sense of having created what he has found, or finding what he has created, is the therapist's acceptance of the painting, in form, content, and emotional tone. The therapist mirrors, and reflects upon, the dynamic process from first mark to finished state, so gaining a knowledge of the child's receptivity to insight, capacity to assimilate past images, or to explore them further, and a sensitivity to those necessary periods of just waiting.

The third aspect is the interpersonal exchange between child and therapist encompassing the therapeutic alliance, and the transference and counter-transference within the alliance. The roots of this alliance in art therapy, whether this is implicitly or explicitly acknowledged, lie in the child's creative imagination – that is, to 'the capacity to form images and recombine these into new patterns' (Plaut 1966:131) – and the child may find himself mirrored in this way for the first time in his life. The alliance, as a contract, may also be new in the child's experience of adults, in its non-directive support of self-discovery and acceptance of need, and the child's acceptance of help; in spite of cultural damage and preconceptions, the child usually responds to the therapist's expectations.

The elements of the classical, dyadic transference, the projections of the child's inner world onto the therapist, are present, but their expression and resolution take place within the picture-making, unless they are clearly impeding that process, or are set in direct defence against it, or yet again, if the child is unable to enter that state in which painting is possible. Although an art therapist may work directly with the transference, it is here that we find the boundary between two specific techniques.

Freud originally defined transference as an intra-psychic process where there is a penetration of unconscious content and forces into preconscious feelings and wishes (Freud 1951a:562–63). These intrusions of 'transfer-ences' may be found in many forms, in dream, fantasy, and play, but in therapeutic and analytic technique, the focus is narrowed onto the person of the therapist in an exploration of original relationships. My plea here is for a wider recognition of the original concept, for only then can we respect the integrity of the therapeutic process which we observe in art therapy.

Some aspects of experience, such as body processes in infancy, find uneasy containment when projected onto another person. The non-human environment can offer a more simple transference medium, and, 'by acting as a kind of shock absorber' (Searles 1960), allows a new exploration of an overwhelming event through a symbolic enactment. Blocks in the thera-peutic process can occur when the child centres all his fears and aggressions on the person of the therapist, and so finds the situation and the relationship intolerable.

The symbolic enactment and its product are subject to the mirroring process which carries its own subtle interpretive action. In contrast to 'acting-out' which may be seen as a non-reflective event, aimed primarily at reducing anxiety, this 'in-actment' is modified as it proceeds, possibly through a series of images which mark the shifts in the child's understanding of a traumatic event, or of aspects in a relationship.

This is well illustrated in a brief study of 'Mark' (Cohen 1971), a five-year-old boy who became increasingly disturbed, attempting to act-out a magical solution and invite punishment, after he survived a fire in which his little brother died. His parents held their grief in silence and Mark was left to draw conclusions out of his own feelings of sibling rivalry.

Two years later he found help and, after several months of art therapy, he produced a cartoon strip drawing which encapsulated the tragedy. While making the drawing Mark found his own missing words and buried grief, supported and encouraged by his therapist, and a new understanding of the accident emerged. The drawing 'was a perfect mirror in which he could view what actually happened. He expressed surprise that he could recall the tragedy so vividly, and he verbalized that he could see that he had not killed his brother' (Cohen 1971:18).

The child makes tangible his transferences and confusions, and is active in their elucidation until he is able to integrate them. Insight is often achieved through the child's own interpretive efforts, and both analyst and artist have to surrender claims to 'creativity' out of respect for the 'potential space'.

In art therapy, we are concerned with an image-making process within a specific area of dynamic interactions, and our particular focus here is on the child at a time before he can create culture (Winnicott 1971:ch. 7), although he has some degree of creative capacity. Here, he is involved in a particular mode of reflective playing for a particular purpose.

The hidden mirror: some thoughts on interpretation and counter-transference in art therapy

The therapist's support is an informed one and is based not only upon the reflective attitude but also upon a counter-transference response which is essentially adaptive to the child.

Originally, the psychoanalytical term 'counter-transference' applied only to unconscious, maladaptive responses, and was cause for vigilance and further work towards insight and self-knowledge by the therapist. Currently, there has been a wider, more positive approach from analysts such as Racker (1968), Fordham (1974b), and Lambert (1981). They put forward ideas of therapeutic empathy and identification across unconscious levels with accommodating shifts or 'de-integration' (Fordham 1974a). It is as though the therapist becomes a pliable vessel with a good-enough fit around most of the yet unknown contents put into it, until the time comes for recognition through reflection. But the vessel also has to tolerate unknown contents which distort it, and the therapist realizes a burden of feelings and ideas, not personal belongings, and not necessarily evoked by the overt situation but existing concurrently with it.

In his painting, the child makes his own vessel, but the art therapist is still subject to the overspill of unconscious content, at unconscious levels of interaction. It is often that which is formless and unbearable, as well as being unspeakable, and it is liable to arise when the child is pressed inwardly, or by outer events, beyond his capacity to imagine or to tolerate.

The therapist may feel battered and useless for no apparent reason. The therapist is also in a counter-transference relationship with the painting and can feel inexplicably exercised in response to it.

There is another aspect in art therapy which parallels the psychoanalytic experience but which carries its own distinctive knowledge and insight. It emerges from the therapist's experience as an artist in a reflective attitude towards his own work, and the apprehending of the hidden, inner process which accompanies it. Projection, introjection, identification, and empathy are inherent in any participation with the arts, but as in psychoanalysis, a vicarious understanding is not enough, and personal experience of the process is needed to inform the therapist's empathy with the painting child. It is essential that the high anxiety surrounding symbolic processes (Kris 1952; Ehrenzweig 1967) can be held by the therapist who also apprehends the shifts in the child's condition as he paints.

Premature moves by the therapist can be felt as very intrusive and persecutory. The chance mark or the clever remark can rob the child of his creative moment, causing the image to be rejected as 'not mine'. Impingement by the therapist's ideas may produce compliance or inflation in the child, with similar losses of integrity and of being real in his own right; this false dependency hampers that process of healthy 'forgetting' which permits there to be a future. Interpretation easily becomes a form of robbery, or an infilling of the child's potential space, so the therapist needs to communicate with great care.

Art therapy makes a distinctive contribution in allowing for the privacy of self-discovery, and in holding the paradox of being found and yet not found (Winnicott 1965c), particularly important in adolescence. Comments on active imagination echo here, for 'we get to know aspects of our nature which we would not allow anybody else to show us and which we ourselves would never have admitted' (Jung 1954: 496).

Art therapy: the matrix as sanctuary

Given a good-enough therapeutic alliance which accepts products without censorship, the child finds himself contained by the therapist within an actual place, although the person and place may be merged in his experience as the matrix within which he creates his own containing forms. It is here that anxiety can take on a lower pitch, allowing the action of imagination on old patterns of thought and feeling. This becomes possible when the child feels that someone is present who has either been that way before, or who can understand what is needed; someone who can give support to the more mature part of the child's personality, enabling him to work towards integration, and who shares and survives his experience with him.

The matrix holds the reality of inner experience in contrast to the actuality of the outside world, without collusion or judgement. The child may then find his way through illusion or delusion to the proper ground for his hurt, the original cause for rage, persecution, loss, or despair, without being labelled mad or bad, as the case of Mark has already shown. Art therapy does not offer an easy solution, however, as the matrix, like other forms of help, may be rejected, doubted, attacked, and at times, felt to be destroyed, before the child can start work within it.

Painting can only take place where separation has begun, when the child can be alone, if only briefly, in the presence of the therapist. If this state has not been achieved, we have to help the child to find it. The severely fragmented child whose primary experience of being mothered has been inadequate, disrupted, or damaged, needs to find that essential relationship, perhaps in a residential setting (Dockar-Drysdale 1968), before he is capable of any of the symbolic processes on which art therapy is based. Traumatic experience which leads to secondary damage or deprivation is more appropriately met by art therapy. The mute or inarticulate child may find a way out of isolation, and the child whose perceptions have been denied or confused by family pathology may establish his own truth. The symptoms on referral may be a means of obtaining help, concealing the real needs that emerge later in therapy.

The matrix: mediation and containment

Mediation and containment over time form a therapeutic continuum at both concrete and psychological levels. Content which is too raw or overwhelming can be mediated or held; images that are especially valuable or particularly frightening may be given into safe keeping, until the child has sufficient strength to acknowledge them as part of himself. Blindness to the image on the part of the therapist can amount to an abandonment for the child, echoing the original trauma, but sometimes the child obstructs mediation so the therapist has to 'get it wrong' in order that the past experience is communicated.

Mediation lies not only in help to regulate the flow of content and give location in time, place, and person, but it also lies in the plastic media, the stuff of picture-making. The right 'media' can have a profound effect on the child's system of defence and initiate a very active symbolic process. Obsessional blocks may give way in a wash of colour, ego strengths can be enhanced by gains in skill, and aggressive energies may be safely expressed in materials such as wood or clay, where destruction is integral with construction. The underlying fluidity can be allowed, the incoherent fragments, incongruities, and confusions can emerge out of a chaos and find some kind of resolution. The possibility of such a chaos in which there is a hidden order (Ehrenzweig 1967) touches upon the essential nature of the non-verbal world. Where the chaotic is held by some minimal form, a few scrappy marks, anxiety may also be held.

However, mess, poverty, or fragmentation in form and content may also be part of an attack on meaning which is unbearable, a continual breaking of links which leads to an inner, self-imposed deprivation (Henry 1974).

There are also times when it would be inaccurate to describe content as having been repressed in the sense of having been lost to consciousness; it may be emerging out of body tensions and sensations which have never before reached consciousness, or possibly it is new content arising out of the maturational process.

Thus Max, aged seven, unmediated in his infancy by his depressed mother and unsure about his body boundaries, managed eventually to piece together odd bits of paper to form a bizarre body image, and then filled it with sensation so intense it seemed inhabited by creatures living independent lives inside him. Itchy snails crept around inside his scalp, hunger rumbled like lions and tigers, while in the pit of his stomach, crocodiles devoured their own bones, and a kangeroo leapt about in his bowels and caused erections with its tail.

Within the matrix, the child creates his own mode, literally and metaphorically, giving characteristic form and colour to the task in hand. Ideas and effects press upon skills, and the lability of the child is seen within a single painting. Where emergent fragments of buried experience gather together in a series of paintings, feeling, tone and idea may be carried in the colour, while movement and the structure of relationships are embodied in the form, but often there is a fusion of these elements; the more archaic the image, the more abstract its expression, as in the archetypal images of early infancy, and in the cyclic return of those images in the maturational process (Neumann 1955 and 1961).

Such a series was painted by Anna, aged seventeen, giving form to infant witness of the primal scene, as pre-verbal ideas of body function fused with excitement, and feelings of envy and jealousy were mixed with the fear of violence. The paintings made comprehensible the traumatic and contradictory elements of sexual experience in infancy, and showed how they informed and darkened the new sexuality of adolescence, also endangered by violence.

On the other hand, adolescents may find their experience given a form in adult culture. Gina, aged sixteen, gifted and yet unable to use her potential, found a large print of Hieronymous Bosch's triptych 'The Garden of Delights' (de Tolney 1965). The suggestive imagery appeared as an eloquent description of her infancy, and she moved through the oral delights and frustrations in the first two panels, to areas of increasing persecution and the final warlike destruction in the third, which echoed with family violence and the loss of her mother in a clinical depression.

Poetry and music can also lead in and out of painting, the underlying tonal qualities conveying the meaning, and like the therapist's murmured comment, can be heard when the child is ready to hear. The non-verbal, unmediated experience becomes accessible to words.

The waking dream: in conclusion

For some children, painting embodies an immediacy of experience and response, as in a waking dream, which would be unbearable apart from the presence of the therapist. As infants these children were particularly vulnerable to common traumatic events such as hospitalization, severe marital conflict, and maternal depression; all felt a loss of mediation and failure of the facilitating environment. However, the capacity to play and to paint remain sufficiently intact for them to make use of the therapeutic matrix.

The pictures reproduced here were all key statements about those original experiences, produced in an active dialogue with the material and within the transference as broadly defined. These statements shaped the therapy that followed and, most important, they were subject to the triadic mirroring which facilitated understanding and change.

Roger was the second of three children and born into an ordinary caring family, although both parents tended to be reserved. A year before Roger's birth, an encephalic child had been stillborn, and, fearing another, his mother cut herself off from the subsequent pregnancy and childbirth, and the initial contact with Roger. Within a few days Roger developed enteritis and was isolated for two weeks in an incubator, naked and tube-fed. When returned to his mother, he refused the breast, refused to be held, and would feed only when tightly wrapped, his bottle propped beside him.

In those two weeks he had suffered from loss of relatedness with his mother, from loss of holding, and from sensory deprivation and hunger. His mother was unable to penetrate the barrier he created to protect himself from such fearful experience.

Roger grew up as a detached child, who did not like to be touched, never showed much affection or feeling, and found it difficult to play with other children. He was referred by his school when he was nine years old as a friendless child, disruptive, and underfunctioning. His initial experience had become elaborated to produce a persecuting world.

Therapy was accepted but he remained blinkered behind long eyelashes, guarded from contact, hypersensitive to touch, sound, and body temperature, filling his sessions with obsessional drawings of silent battles. Gradually he thawed, became less persecuted, and found his own words to describe his complex drawings in pencil and ballpoint pen. He began drawing pictures of sea battles, depth-charges, and rising sea levels, all

Illustration 5.1

images of a failing maternal world, but became more animated. Then, on finding a safe therapeutic relationship, he drew and spoke about his terrible, ancient hunger.

A man on board an enemy ship woke to find a 'caterpillar' (like a feeding tube) over his bed, imagined a monster, and called out 'Help!' for a doctor, all simultaneously. Then the man fell overboard and became a giant who declared 'I was hungry' while a stream of shells from the battle ship poured into his mouth. The giant was transformed, in rapid succession, from a little monster without teeth, caught between shark fins, into a large monster with many teeth and a caterpillar on his hat, and then into a fourth monster with canine fangs and flippered hands, assaulted by shells from the ship. The monster was so hungry that he did not know whether he was biting or being bitten; and yet at the same time, it was all in the imagination of the man still on board the ship. A large helicopter, like an observing adult, hovered overhead. Roger had to take flight like 'the angry swallowing fly who looks as though he doesn't know what to do with himself'.

In therapy, Roger later found restoration of his infant world, becoming a lively, warmer child. A fisherman-ego gained control over the biting creatures in the water and fishing became a hobby. Finally, he could describe therapy as taking in 'nice things like soup and ice cream and horrible things like dinosaur's blood'. He remarked: 'I came to work here and became a milkman [baby] and then – I became me!'

Charlotte, a bright seven-year-old, had a delicacy belied by outbursts of energy discharged at random, and she accompanied painting and play with dramatic dialogue and song. Her needs, unmet by her mother's limited capacity to imagine, had found expression in therapy so the stealing and wet beds had eased, but her anxious, butterfly mind continued to frustrate her efforts at school.

When drawing 'The Rainbow Hut', she gripped the wax crayon in her fist, infant fashion, and used it with great freedom, in contrast to her earlier, obsessionally neat, felt-tip renderings. Inside 'The Rainbow Hut' was a microcosm, with a little red sun, a baby in a pram, a 'little robot', and a butterfly. Two worlds seemed co-existent, an inner mother/baby world and the paternal sun in the world beyond.

'Then the rain poured down and the black clouds came.... All the clouds went over the sun and the sun didn't come out again after that!'
The scribble storm filled the outer sky, like quarrelling parents and the sun-father left, rarely to return, but the little robot was able to protect the baby.

'It's a mother, not a robot!'
The idealized world was maintained until hunger struck.

'It's not a robot! It's a snake! ... with a red tongue and fire all over the baby!'

Illustration 5.2

The hungry attack and the parents' sexual conflict fused, and identities became confused.

'The hut broke!' And the scribble-weather erupted inside.

Although she maintained that the baby was still safe, the butterfly was painted a little later in damaged flight, sharing red paint-blood with Charlotte.

The destruction of the idealized 'Rainbow Hut' brought Charlotte face-to-face with the angry discharge between mother and baby which had previously been projected into the marital conflict.

Lorraine's mother had been deeply depressed at her birth, although she had been more available to the sister born two years later. By the time Lorraine was twelve years old, her mother, still fragile, was anxiously aware of her early failure. But Lorraine was underfunctioning, difficult at home and school, jealous of her sister, graceless in movement and manner, and alternating between dependence and sullen hostility.

Lorraine's painting was produced half-way through two years of therapy, and it marked the point where she could begin to separate from the

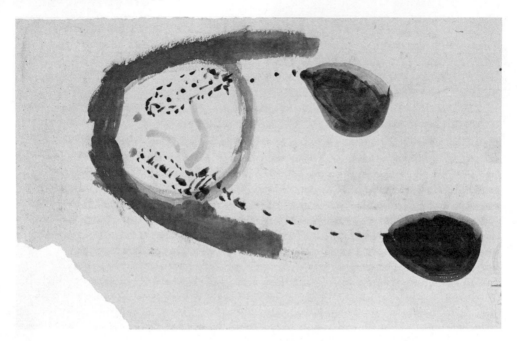

Illustration   5.3

depressed mother whom she still had inside her. This was difficult to achieve as she had to be sure of her mother's continuing aliveness as well as her own, just as she had to do as an infant (Winnicott 1965c: 191–92).

In the painting, the pale face smiles gently through black tears that flow into large, black, tear-drop breasts. The tears appear to flow horizontally along the figure and at right angles to the observer: it is from such an angle that the young baby would see the mother, while feeding – milk and tears are equated.

Separation also meant the recognition of the old anger, felt to be very dangerous and destructive, remaining from the time when her mother was not sufficiently present nor aware of her baby's needs. This anger had been turned inwards, new depression had fused with the old sadness, and Lorraine had been trapped in her infant world.

Much support was needed from home and school in order for Lorraine to bear to come to therapy. How tempting it was to take flight and leave all the hate and mess behind. Gradually, she came to understand the paradox that the right time to leave was when it felt all right to come. Lorraine gradually became alive in her own right, and grew from sullen child to attractive young adolescent, ready to leave therapy. When I asked her if I might include her picture in this book, she generously agreed, and looking at it, remarked, 'Oh yes! I did that when I was young!'

References

Bindman, D. (1977) *Blake as an Artist*. Oxford: Phaidon.

Bower, T. G. R. (1977) *A Primer of Infant Development*. San Francisco, Calif.: W. H. Freeman.

Carpenter, G. (1975) *The Mother's Face and The Newborn*. In R. Lewin (ed.) *Child Alive*. London: Temple Smith.

Cohen, F. W. (1971) *Mark and the Paint Brush*. Austin, Texas: The Hogg Foundation for Mental Health, University of Texas.

Dockar-Drysdale, B. (1968) *Therapy in Child Care*. Harlow, Essex: Longmans.

Ehrenzweig, A. (1967) *The Hidden Order of Art*. London: Paladin.

Erikson, E. (1950) *Childhood and Society*. Harmondsworth: Penguin.

Fordham, M. (1974a) Notes on the Transference (first published in 1957). In M. Fordham, R. Gordon, J. Hubback, and K. Lambert (eds) *Technique in Jungian Analysis*. London: Academic Press.

— (1974b) Technique in Counter-transference (first published in 1969). In M. Fordham, R. Gordon, J. Hubback, and K. Lambert (eds) *Technique in Jungian Analysis*. London: Academic Press.

Freud, S. (1951a) *The Interpretation of Dreams I & II* and *On Dreams* (first published 1900–01), *Complete Psychological Works* (Standard Edition) vols 4–5. London: Hogarth Press and the Institute of Psycho-analysis.

— (1951b) *The Ego and the Id* (first published 1923–25), *Complete Psychological Works* (Standard Edition) vol. 19. London: Hogarth Press and the Institute of Psycho-analysis.

Haftman, W. (1973) *Marc Chagall*. New York: Harry Abrams.

Heimann, P. (1955) *A Contribution to the Re-valuation of the Oedipus Complex*. In M. Klein, P. Heimann and R. Money-Kyle (eds) *New Directions in Psycho-analysis*. London: Tavistock.

Henry, G. (1974) Doubly Deprived. *Journal of Child Psychotherapy* 3(4): 15–28.

Hogarth, W. (1968) *Apology for Painters*, ed. M. Kitson. Oxford: Oxford University Press.

Jackson, M. (1960) Jung's Archetype: Clarity or Confusion. *British Journal of Medical Psychology* 33(2): 83–94.

Jung, C. G. (1959) *The Archetypes and the Collective Unconscious, Collected Works*, vol. 9, part I. London: Routledge & Kegan Paul.

— (1960) Psychological Factors Determining Human Behaviour (first published in 1936). In *Structure and Dynamics of the Psyche, Collected Works*, vol. 8. London: Routledge & Kegan Paul.

Klein, M. (1950) *The Psycho-analysis of the Child*. London: Hogarth Press.

Kris, E. (1952) *Psycho-analytical Explorations in Art*. New York: International Universities Press.

Lambert, K. (1981) *Analysis, Repair and Individuation*, Library of Analytical Psychology 5. London: Academic Press.

Lowenfeld, M. (1931) A New Approach to the Problem of Psycho-neurosis in Childhood. *British Journal of Medical Psychology* 11(3): 194–227.

— (1937) A Thesis Concerning the Fundamental Structure of the Mento-Emotional Process in Children. Paper delivered to the British Psychological Society.

— (1964) The Study of Preverbal Thinking and its Relation to Psychotherapy. Paper delivered to the Sixth International Congress of Psychotherapy.

— (1969) *Play in Childhood* (first published in 1935). Bath: Chivers.

Neumann, E. (1955) *The Great Mother*. London: Routledge & Kegan Paul.

— (1961) The Significance of the Genetic Aspect for Analytical Psychology. In G. Adler (ed.) *Current Trends in Analytical Psychology*. London: Tavistock.

— (1973) *The Child: the Structure and Dynamics of the Nascent Personality*. New York: Putnam.

Pines, M. (1982) Reflections on Mirroring. *The Journal of Group Analysis* 15(2): suppl. 1–25.

Plaut, F. (1966) Reflections on Not Being Able to Imagine. In M. Fordham, R. Gordon, J. Hubback, and K. Lambert (eds) *Analytical Psychology, a Modern Science*. London: Academic Press.

Racker, H. (1968) *Transference and Counter-Transference*. London: Hogarth Press.

Searles, H. (1960). *The Non-Human Environment*, Monograph Series on Schizophrenia 5. New York: International University Press.

Segal, H (1964–73) *Introduction to the Work of Melanie Klein*. London: Hogarth Press.

Selfe, L. (1977) *Nadia, a Case of Extraordinary Drawing Ability in an Autistic Child*. London: Academic Press.

Tate Gallery (1978) *William Blake* Exhibition Catalogue. London: Tate Gallery Publications.

Trevarthen, C. and Grant, F. (1978) Infant Play and the Creation of Culture. *New Scientist* 81(1): 566–69.

Torczyner, H. (1977) *Magritte: Ideas and Images*. New York: Harry Abrams.

Tolnay, C. de (1965) *Hieronymous Bosch*. London: Methuen.

Winnicott, D. W. (1965a) The Capacity to be Alone (first published in 1958). In *The Maturational Processes and the Facilitating Environment*. London: Hogarth Press.

— (1965b) Providing for the Child in Health and in Crisis (first published in 1962). In *The Maturational Processes and the Facilitating Environment*. London: Hogarth Press.

— (1965c) Communicating and Not Communicating Leading to a Study of Certain Opposites (first published in 1963). In *The Maturational Processes and the Facilitating Environment*. London: Hogarth Press.

— (1971) *Playing and Reality*. Harmondsworth: Penguin.

Biographical note

Margarita Wood studied Fine Art at Hornsey College of Art and the Royal College of Art, where she became interested in art therapy. Having worked in a wide variety of settings with psychotic and neurotic adults, children, and adolescents, increasing concern with children led her to a Diploma in the Psychology of Childhood at the University of Birmingham and later to train as a child psychotherapist at the Institute of Child Psychology (Lowenfeld).

She currently works as a child psychotherapist in a Family and Child Guidance Clinic, and is also engaged in research under the aegis of the Child

Research and Development Unit, University of Nottingham, into image-making by children with severe learning disabilities.

Margarita Wood finds the two disciplines of art and psychology inform and complement each other in her work as both artist and therapist. Commissioned works include 'The Fall of Icarus', RAF Memorial, Wickenby, Lincs.

6 | A Jungian approach to art therapy based in a residential setting

Martin Robinson

Those not entirely foreign to C. G. Jung's work may anticipate a certain friction from the introduction of some of his ideas into a residential setting for young people. In many ways it involves the meeting of two fundamentally different approaches to therapy – the one being in essence an individual's introversion or turning inwards to explore depth within himself and uncover creativity with which to share with the group, while the other – the all-embracing world in miniature of a therapeutic community – demands a strong adherence to group processes and boundaries and, in order to preserve loyalty to pre-established principles, tends to frown on what it may negatively term as 'hole in the corner' activities. A community concerned with this form of identity often fosters an almost excessive extroversion. However much an aspiring art therapist in such a situation may experience a sense of trying to fit round pegs into square holes, it often proves a valuable experience because it raises many important issues in an age when group processes are gaining more and more impetus and many new insights arise from seeing these two worlds in proximity.

This chapter is not concerned with giving precise identity to any particular therapeutic situation although many experiences and examples are drawn from work in a residential setting. Rather it is an exploration of the many problems raised by the introduction of a certain form of art therapy into a pre-existing therapeutic framework and attempts to throw light on deeper more universal issues which lie behind them. It is only through a community facing some of those issues that the very considerable potential for creative art therapy can be realized and much work may have to be done before circumstances permit art therapy the freedom to reach the level of success that it can in a private setting. The decision to introduce art therapy is often in principle recognized as worth while by everyone concerned but few see what it may entail in re-adjustment. A therapeutic community makes for very fertile ground given its strongly familial, even tribal, character and the energy generated by a large group of adolescents and young adults each with their own intense personal problems of identity, of relationship, and of authority with which to contend is very considerable indeed.

Most immediate is an explanation of just what in this case is meant by a 'Jungian' approach to art therapy. Such a loose word as Jungian, which incidentally Jung himself is reputed to have deplored, suggests a multiplicity of vague meanings. When one further considers that there are many different approaches to the image even among Jung's followers – who are notorious for their encouragement of art as an aid to therapy – it is safer simply to state one's own viewpoint within the wider context of one's training.

Far from having a ready-made set of formulae with which to lend Jungian or Freudian significance to particular motifs – a common enough practice but one which seems to say more about the therapist than client – I try to preserve an attitude of mind that remains as open as possible to the uniqueness and specific feeling content of an image and a belief in the self-regulating nature of the psyche which is communicating a particular message through the image for anyone who is prepared to see. Over and above the predisposition to value the psyche in this way is an attitude to art therapy that is less concerned with straightening out disturbed behaviour and modifying symptoms than with centring on the overall importance of the emergence of evidence of the Self of the individual as distinct from evidence of ego in the art work produced. While I shall return to this theme later it is just worth mentioning that this is not an arbitrary distinction. Most people do not bother to separate the source of one sense of 'I am' from another and so would regard an attempt to do so as unjustifiably abstract. But if, as I firmly believe, art therapy is to make its contribution to a serious study of human nature, it is worth making a few stabs in the dark about the ways in which art work can convey the fundamental questions of identity. To give the discussion a Jungian flavour we could take the ego to mean the centre of the field of consciousness and as such the subject of all personal conscious acts (Jung 1978: 3). The Self is much more than this, since it also includes unconscious and impersonal or collective parts of the individual's psyche and as such can be considered as the personality as a whole. Art work which expresses a sense of wholeness or totality has an impersonal and universal flavour and quite a different energy level to art work which is the product of the ego. The hallmarks of the latter are felt in work which conveys an air of clever inventiveness, aims at impressing an audience, and aggressively demands recognition. I have no intention of underrating or discounting this art work, but merely want to suggest that its particular intention imposes its own limitations.

In order to approach the idea of unconscious content in art it is worth pointing at the parallels to be found between dream content and spontaneous or unintentional art work. Jung like Freud and many since attached great importance to the interpretation of dreams. While both men considered the dream to be an expression of the unconscious mind, Jung's personal approach was based on the principle that the dream was indicating something profound and meaningful in itself (Jung 1964:28). Instead of following Freud's method of using the patient's free associations to lead away from the dream content towards the complexes that cause neurotic behaviour, Jung insisted on returning constantly to the exact nature of the dream in the belief that it was not merely making disguised comments about generalized complexes – for example the Oedipal complex and its various ramifications – but, much more important, using metaphorical images to be very specific and precise about the individual's own condition in regard to these complexes and offering hints on how the dilemma might best be resolved. In other words Jung's approach includes an attitude towards the unconscious mind which involves considerably more respect than one which simply regards it as a repository of repressed fears and desires. It seemed to Jung that a patient would derive more energy and encouragement to resolve his difficulties from grasping the specific meaningfulness of his particular dream than by being furnished by the analyst with generalized interpretations concerning for instance his anger with Father or his ambivalence towards Mother.

Holding in mind this attitude to the dream, why should one not regard a painting by someone undergoing therapy in the same way? That is, not just as interesting evidence from the therapist's point of view from which to make a quick diagnosis, but as intensely individual and intimately connected with the changing and developing feeling life and values of the painter which is the area in which he experiences a sense of himself in relation to the world in however fragmented or defended a condition that might be. As such, a painting discussed in isolation is as limited in application as an isolated dream, since it is only through the dream series or picture series, forming an organic process that reflects the kaleidoscope of the psyche, that one begins to build a whole picture of the person and the direction in which the psyche is meaning him to go.

If the therapeutic process is to remain in contact with the person then it cannot content itself with picking out significant motifs for intellectual interpretation but must try to preserve contact with the real dynamic which is the gradual process of transformation.

This can be illustrated by a brief example from Greek mythology. There is much literature explaining how the myths can be regarded as presenting in analogous form the archetypal framework of the various psychological complexes (Campbell 1975). If we take the well-known myth of Theseus and the Minotaur and concentrate only upon the separate motifs we might make a list as follows: King Minos – super ego; Minotaur – uninhibited sexual desire of which the owner is ashamed; labyrinth – complex in which the monster is buried or lost from consciousness and which consumes all new energy; Theseus – ego which overcomes the neurosis. If we do this we could easily miss the underlying theme in the myth of the process of change from one fundamental psychic attitude to another. The myth begins from a position of fixed and static ego centricity symbolized by King Minos who in order to further his personal interests refused the god's demand to sacrifice the divine bull and in consequence got lumbered with a monster. Much positive energy had to be sacrificed to this tyrannical ego condition before the appearance or birth of the hero, the new element in the psyche who could liberate the individual from its devouring monster because he had made his journey into the labyrinth and out again and there made contact with the aspect of the god who had previously been denied. In other words by penetrating deep into the unconscious he has gone beyond the personal and can then benefit the world at large with the riches he has gained.

The slow rather laborious process of inner change in the story is also symbolized by the fragile and tenuous thread with which Ariadne (the hero's feminine counterpart or Anima) furnishes Theseus and without which he would have been lost in the labyrinth and the hero's task defeated. The tenuous thread often half hidden, scarcely recognizable, that connects a person's dreams or pictures together over a period of time and leads through so many often unaccountable twists and turns is in itself the process of healing. All too easily the individual's ego interferes with the direction which the unconscious psyche wishes to pursue or the therapist alters the course through encouragement along preconceived therapeutic channels. Very often a therapist's disapproval of images or colours which he considers negative or unhealthy or too daemonic is conveyed to the patient who then paints what the therapist wants to see. Then the patient loses the thread and finds himself in a blind passage or cul-de-sac that produces disillusionment or loss of libido.

Of course a picture is rarely such an unconscious product as a dream, being constantly subject to modification by the conscious sense of what the person wants to depict. In a sense the picture or sculpture belongs equally to both conscious and unconscious worlds and presents a kind of dialogue between the two. It is probably impossible to paint a picture that does not betray any unconscious attitudes or predispositions. Even when setting out deliberately to illustrate a story from a given source the unconscious tends to impose its own stamp and then details which depart from the given text contain particular significance pointing to important blindspots. How easy it is to impart to a portrait the same emotional expression that one is in fact feeling on that particular day.

One broadly built, almost muscle-bound youth I once worked with, whose hysterical rages were carefully concealed from everyone by a polite and an apparently considerate demeanour, drew the portrait of a friend of his with almost obsessional attention to surface detail and texture. While the face of the sitter was in profile and almost entirely lacked interest, the folds on the hunched shoulder which occupied most of the centre of the picture surface were rendered with excessive care. The symmetrically placed lights and darks of the folds of the jersey instantly conjured up the full face of an agonized and imprisoned old man who seemed doomed – like Michelangelo's slaves – to be for ever incarcerated in the underworld. The portrait, ostensibly of the friend, had become in reality a portrait of the artist's own unconscious problem. That he was suffering from an overwhelming problem at an instinctual level which constantly poisoned his sense of self-worth and prevented the normal expression of pain seems to be borne out in a dream he once related and a picture he painted to illustrate it of a deep pit in the desert in which he watches from high up on the craggy lip a young man being stung to death by huge scorpions.

Perhaps even more telling is a second of his pictures, also obsessionally detailed, of a brick wall, each brick carefully outlined and shaded, but pierced with small round holes through which poked the trapped hands and feet of elongated, spidery men. That he chose to exhibit this picture in a room reserved for group therapy seems to indicate the rack-like discomfort at an instinctual level which he felt in being pinned down, so to speak, and exposed in public to intellectual interpretation. Outwardly he never expressed these feelings in words and remained a model of community respectability, but was felt by others to be isolated and untouchable as if surrounded by an impenetrable wall. That his problems were I believe essentially concerned with a negative aspect of the Mother while the group discussions turned incessantly on the oedipal struggles with the male group leader did little to ease his particular inner conflict. While the interiorized rejecting Mother constantly inhibited an expression of his infantile rages, he was in no position to contact his own enormous potential energy with which he could have assumed the Father qualities and so resolved the oedipal conflict. Something which went wrong at a very early stage in his inner life had to be resolved before he could actually enter into the communal life, the intellectual values of which he so stalwartly upheld and at such great cost to his own maturity.

Before moving on to a fuller exploration of these group values one last and central theme concerning Jungian psychotherapy requires examining further. Jung attributed special importance to art work in which he found evidence not of psychopathology and neurosis, but of what he called the Self. The Self to Jung was of far greater significance in the psyche than the ego which he defined as forming the centre of consciousness. If the ego preserves consciousness by standing against the inroads of the unconscious, the Self resolves this inherent conflict by its situation mid-way between the two, relating equally to both, and thus forming the centre of man's totality (Jung 1981).

Large collections of spontaneous art work by small children have been formed in which motifs of 'wholeness' occur (Kellogg 1970). These are often of a geometrical or numerical nature such as the circle or square and reflect adult symbols of wholeness from every culture from the earliest times of man. These universally employed symbols suggest first and foremost an inner desire for order and inner security which has a fundamental influence on the sound development of the personality. Kalff, trained as a Jungian therapist, has developed the Lowenfeld world technique of sand play (Kalff 1980) and regards the manifestation of the Self in the work of her patients, many of them children, as a necessary precondition for the development of a sound ego; she points to many cases of a weak or neurotic ego development where this manifestation of the Self has failed to appear through some environmental deficiency in early life.

Both Kalff and Winnicott, working from a Freudian basis, lay great emphasis in their writing on the importance of the right kind of therapeutic space in which the patient's Self can be given the opportunity it never had previously to constellate itself. When Kalff describes the 'free and sheltered space' (Kalff 1980: 29) in which the child gradually comes to feel fully accepted and gains the sense of security which is a precondition for developing potential, not just of the ego but of the total personality, she is, I believe, almost exactly echoing Winnicott in his well-known formulation of the 'potential' space. The achievement of the 'I am' should, says Winnicott (Winnicott 1971), take place in the 'holding' environment provided by the 'good enough' mother. The individual is later able to forgo the actual mother's support because of the establishment of an internal environment. If this is lacking it is essential that the therapeutic space should recreate that opportunity for the constellation of the Self. Winnicott describes it as a space in which inner reality and external life both contribute, an area created between therapist and patient where fantasy and reality meet. It naturally develops into an area of play and creativity in which the art therapist for one is ideally placed to cultivate.

The establishment of this kind of 'holding environment' or 'free but sheltered space' within a community set up specifically to provide therapy for young people should not, one might imagine, in theory at least, meet with much opposition.

In order to realize how threatening and potentially disruptive the creation of individual therapeutic bonds which so easily constellate the mother/child relationships are within a therapeutic community, one has to examine carefully the structure and central dynamic of the community. To define a therapeutic community is problematic. There is no one model. One has to define the group and the therapeutic aims. Therapeutic communities (Hinshelwood and Manning 1979) have grown since the war in a variety of settings. Some are annexed to prisons and mental hospitals, others have evolved out of the old approved schools, others were pioneer establishments in their own right. Some aim to provide psychotherapy, others rehabilitation, others education, many a combination of these.

Most subscribe to a policy of democracy which involves participation by inmates in much of the decision making, encouragement of the verbal expression of feelings, and close social proximity of staff and inmates. While the democratic measures give the inmates a sense of self-worth and resonsibility for themselves and each other, there is of necessity a hidden authority structure behind the apparent freedom. No form of therapy appears to work without definite boundaries.

Since the central theme of this chapter is the exploration of the conflict between individual therapeutic needs and group therapeutic needs, particularly of an organized nature – a problem which is sufficiently widespread to be recognized by all institutions mentioned – it is possible to make several general observations. Since my experience has been with the treatment of young people, mostly male with severe personality disorders, I will limit the observations to that area.

There are more therapeutic communities for boys than girls. The reason for this is probably because boys are easier to control in groups than girls, will more naturally embrace systems of justice, hierarchy, and tradition, and are more inclined to accept the value of group morale. Many workers in the field would rather deal with the more overt acting-out of disturbed boys which calls forth qualities of will and personality in them than the often more submerged, undermining, and hysterical acting-out of disturbed girls which so often puts them in contact with their own unresolved problems.

The institutional umbrella I am describing then has strong masculine overtones, has the democratic elements previously mentioned, but also a strongly maintained authority pyramid. It is largely and purposely cut off from the outside world, an environment which is often experienced by inmates as an island refuge in the midst of a hostile world 'out there'. The life of the community revolves around its community meetings where matters at every level are discussed, from solving behaviour problems and administering sanctions to exploring personal and group dynamics all of which often become confused. The community meeting is experienced in many ways – as a bull-ring where aspiring young matadors test out the power and strength of the bull authority; as a place of initiation where an individual may, according to the mythology of the institution, attain manhood and a new identity through making a public declaration of his support for the community values. The raising of one's voice in a large group, often passively hostile to the values upheld, attains an almost phallic significance. Lastly the community meeting can, on occasion, act as a large therapy group session.

The institution makes enormous demands on the individual – he must participate, communicate, and analyse his own and others' motives. He is told repeatedly that the community will collapse without each one pulling their weight. Having arrived full of his own particular problems he finds that instead of dealing first and foremost with them that his biggest problem is one of resisting what the community demands. Whether he can overcome the resistance depends largely on his willpower and ability to suppress anxiety and hysteria. If the psychic wounds are deep and he is by nature introverted then the community demands can form an agonizing experience. No private life is acceptable, no careful guarding of some area. Everything is coerced or dragged into the open.

So the problems to be overcome in a therapeutic community are not so much a collection of the individual's personal problems but the stereotyped resistances to institutional life that requires of the individual no less than everything. The institution becomes the mother, its director the father. The transferences both good and bad are intense because they are set up to be so. The resistance comes in a multitude of forms: hysteria, rage, resentment, envy, rivalry, passive rebellion, boredom, torpidity. They have behind them all one central dynamic – the child-like seeking or stealing of personal attention which the individual craves more than anything else. Wanting parent figures all to himself he is forced to accept only his share as part of the larger family group.

The extent to which the same issues of authority, boundaries, and transference so often repeat themselves is not coincidental. It is because the community life and therapeutic structure predetermine the issues. It is as if the community as a whole has agreed at some subliminal level upon a certain fantasy or myth that must endlessly be replayed. Each individual psyche becomes penetrated and dyed by the same shared internal contents. In this situation it is very difficult for one member to say with any certainty whether he is actually feeling angry for instance or even murderous towards father or whether he has been required to intraject the feeling and is merely acting as spokesman for a collective dynamic.

It is highly debatable whether being required to experience the transference willy-nilly is a healthy and therapeutic procedure or whether it has a dampening effect on the psyche and prevents creativity. It most certainly inhibits spontaneity.

I have spent some time outlining the system of therapy often current in a therapeutic community. This is necessary to show with any conviction where the main brakes on successful art therapy may occur. The chief difficulty to be overcome is in creating a 'safe' space in which the individual allows his defences to drop and, through feeling unconditionally accepted by the therapist, can in turn accept the support offered. In community life of this kind it is common for everyone to scrutinize each other's behaviour to make sure it conforms to community morality. Each member has a duty to report infringements of boundaries. This is not regarded as 'grassing' but as 'responsible friendship'. It is probably true that the survival of the community depends on this peer group surveillance which makes discovery inevitable. Without it the subversive elements would quickly produce a state of anxiety and chaos. It does however militate against the individual feeling free to express himself spontaneously. In a community which uses much psychoanalytic terminology everyone watches for the Freudian slip. When one person is brave enough to paint a snake he will be inundated with derogatory jokes about the Freudian significance. Apart from the fact that snake symbolism extends over a far wider area than the obvious phallic symbol inevitably seized on by adolescent boys in groups, it goes without saying that the essence of successful art therapy is spontaneity and a non-judgemental or condescending attitude to such a valuable and sensitive activity as giving expression to the unconscious.

Another important problem is the more insidious one of a negative attitude to the unconscious which is in turn connected to a negative attitude to the feminine. A milieu which is predominantly masculine and adolescent attracts its own mythology. Emphasis is on the pecking order, rivalry, display of aggression. Where the valued image is macho, the myth Herculean, there is bound to be a corresponding devaluation of feminine values of creativity, intuition, caring, compassion, relating. The boys come almost invariably with serious maternal problems and deep feelings of rejection. Their internalized mother image is often the terrible, devouring mother, the witch. While inwardly bound to her, outwardly they are predisposed to devalue her. This attitude is easily transposed to a profound distrust of the unconscious. When an institution as a whole allows the feminine to be devalued then however natural and nourishing the environment, the facilities, the food, the activities, somehow one senses a lack overall, a top heaviness, an artificiality which never quite meets the bedrock needs of the individual. The boys' fragmented instincts are looking for a level of reality in which to root themselves and which only mother can provide.

An atmosphere of rivalry and competition where potential libido is caught and dissipated in the tension between authority and delinquency betrays an inner loneliness and loss of Self. When the focus is on what an individual does positively or destructively towards the group and there is little room for simple acceptance of the person as he is apart from his behaviour, then the sense of security and confidence that should accompany ego achievement is missing. The ritual airing of negative feelings, so prized by the therapeutic community though usually involving painful exposure and much group pressure, seems rarely to go beyond a certain relief at having attained respectability. But the individual is left without the deeper experience of personal meaning that can transform the disclosure of deep secrets.

The real value of the group experience seems to lie in those rare moments of sunshine when the individual is able to make his disclosure without coercion from a deeper layer of feelings, and then all the envy and blocking mechanisms of the peer group dissolve in the recognition of feeling expressed, and the group generates for a time a remarkable cohesion and unity.

Groups relying on verbal exchange are often in danger of separating themselves from the core of feeling which they are attempting to uncover. Participants soon learn the rules of a subtle game of hide-and-seek. Psychologizing becomes a sophisticated art of not saying, let alone experiencing. Those in command of the language find themselves in a position of power which their egos are only too willing to exploit. The power 'to therap' is experienced by the victim as infinitely more threatening than physical or mental superiority and evokes a corresponding powerful resentment.

If in the treatment of deeply concealed psychological hurt we take the analogy of the physical wound, no-one would find it surprising, or irritating, or subversive if the sufferer flinched at the very approach of the nurse's scissors, let alone the panic induced by the exposure and probing of the unhealed wound itself. It is not to be wondered at that subtle defence mechanisms are in operation under the threat of the often uncompassionate analytical interpretation.

One of the most frequent motifs in the paintings produced is that of walls or fences that shut out, separate, and compartmentalize. One painting of suburban semis and their gardens viewed in tunnel perspective, giving an impression of unending claustrophobia, included rows of garden fences placed horizontally up the picture plane like hurdles. The few occupants of the gardens conversed with each other across their fences. They were all therefore cut off from each other below the waist. Whilst the picture was well constructed and tidily executed the stereotype nature of the figures and their gardens and the sameness of the house façades conveyed the almost desert-like poverty at an individual and instinctual level with extraordinary accuracy. Another powerfully telling image in this connection was one of a cow seen through strands of barbed wire.

One of the negative emotions most frowned upon in a therapeutic community meeting is the expression of boredom. It is usually interpreted as repressed aggression particularly towards authority. Seen in addition as posing a threat to group morale and participation, it is often summarily confronted and dealt with. The confrontation approach usually increases the feelings of frustration felt by the bored person who then reacts aggressively thereby proving the original interpretation. It is however possible to see boredom as a quite ordinary reaction to a situation in which nothing new is being offered, nothing stimulating or creative. A situation in which there is no element of play.

When theoretical interpretation is respected more than the person then a situation arises where the person's behaviour is adapted to suit the theory. Soon after art therapy was introduced to the community a dream was related to which I attach considerable importance. The dreamer found himself walking upstairs from a dark basement where in the dream the art studios were situated and where in the company of the art therapist he had just painted a snake encircling an egg. He took the painting up from the empty studio and similarly deserted ground floor to the top storey of the house where he met all his peers who ignored him and his work and continued to move from one group therapy room to another, talking incessantly to each other as they did so. The meaning of the dream is clear not only on a personal level for the dreamer but also in what it mirrors of the institution of which he was part. The top of the house – the intellectual and ego level – was full to bursting. The almost empty art studios, the area of creation, were situated in the basement representing in its darkness the as yet unexplored unconscious. The basement despite its low and neglected appearance nevertheless possessed a wealth of unrealized potential symbolized by the cosmic egg protected by the snake, but which the collective, upstairs, was not yet prepared to assimilate. When an institution grows in this subtly lopsided way then it usually involves being cut off from most genuine emotional experiences.

In an institution where a certain degree of acting-out and expression of feeling is tolerated in order to provide material for group therapy, it is common for the art department to be expected to absorb a large share of the frustrated and pent-up feelings. A non-verbal activity like art can be a safety valve for the newer members of the community who are not yet able to describe their feelings in words. Sometimes individuals too hysterical to be objectively dealt with elsewhere are directed towards the open art sessions where it is hoped they will find some release through play with the large number of simple art techniques and nursery activities provided. While this 'potty training' aspect of art therapy plays an important part in the community life, the space provided for a more profound kind of art therapy is often put at risk. If the space should, as I believe, aspire to be 'free but sheltered' then it cannot afford to contain too large a burden of violence. It is of course important that aggression should be safely allowed out, but it is also important that art therapy, in this kind of institution, should not become identified only with this task. It is possible for aggression, once set free, to run unchecked in the belief that this is therapeutic, and then it is discovered too late that a certain person's behaviour has become crystallized in a destructive form. The space is no longer a shelter but an atmosphere buzzing with angry vibrations. The right kind of space is only possible if the community as a whole regards it as valuable.

The adolescents, when they arrive and for a long time subsequently, are suffering above all from a lack of inner security and a feeling of not belonging. One telling picture portrayed this feeling of isolation exactly. A tiny boat is sailing along the horizon – a fragment of self caught between a deep red sky with three menacing clouds above and the vast inhospitable blue green sea of the unconscious below. An imaginative landscape painted jointly by two of the older inhabitants nearing the end of their stay seemed also to suggest a great deal about their inner state. The picture was impressively painted in the style of a seventeenth-century Dutch winter landscape. Each artist had taken one side of the picture. The painter of the left-hand side placed a uniform row of leafless trees and a fence on the frozen ground and left an empty area of snow in the centre. The right-hand side included amongst the frozen trees a small cabin reached by a bridge across a depression in the ground and through the window the ruddy glow of a fire could just be made out. It is not too far-fetched to read into this picture some indication of how each had dealt with his frozen feelings. As it turned out only the one who had painted some warmth into his part of the landscape was able to sustain his identity when confronting the problems he had to face in the world outside.

Of the many who came to paint or sculpt on a regular basis and whose work formed a coherent series, one in particular showed in his pictures – again mostly landscapes – how unconsciously and quite spontaneously he gradually discovered or uncovered much of his potential creative energy through painting. Introverted and morose but intelligent and destined for further education in literature, he came only in his last year to art therapy but in a spirit of play. Because he had no ego invested in attaining renown as a painter he did not worry unduly about technique but took to painting immediately in colour with enviable ease and naturalness. Since he was only playing (though with deadly seriousness) he could paint without intention and so in giving himself up to it the play developed into a kind of magic action which conjured up life. One of the first pictures was of a menacing landscape with a row of mountain peaks on the far horizon separated from the foreground by a cold green sea. The centre of the picture was dominated by the black outspread branches of a leafless tree but right at the centre between the shoulders so to speak he painted a vortex in an aggressive spiral of yellow and orange – a face? a flower? the sun? mother? Whatever it was to the painter it represented a burst of new life in an otherwise utterly unfulfilled and bleak personality.

A large number of paintings followed this arrival of volcanic energy on the surface; a vivid portrait of a female member of staff – the only one he felt relaxed with – then another landscape, now with warm green fields but surrounding a mine shaft and buildings in browns and yellows at the centre of the picture. A mine shaft is a clear entrance into the deep underworld and for the painter it coincided with a newly discovered extroversion and creativity in which he found the energy to assert himself in a positive way and relate to others, and his academic work flourished. A later painting of a river flowing between fields was altogether more peaceful and abundant. A small, roofed structure on a pole like a shrine was placed on the right bank and then like ghostly afterthoughts in pale white water colour he painted a small fence in the foreground and a tiny gallows with figures in the sky like the paling remnants of a tortured past.

In conclusion it is important to add that my apparent criticism of the structure of therapy in the community is not intended to be dismissive but simply to indicate its possible limitations. In this respect it is worth returning briefly to the dream of the snake mentioned earlier. If we are prepared to accept that the dreamer's snake need not only signify personal sexuality in the usual Freudian sense then we find a way to approach the source of much else besides; primitive emotion, the realm of the imagination, and in a sense the unconscious as a whole. To suppress it or bottle the snake up through too rigid or formularized an approach to therapy leaves a vital area of the psyche unexplored. To paint the snake and then bring it up to consciousness was not just an attempt at self-healing by the dreamer. To bring the conscious and unconscious life of the community into relationship and mutual respect requires a bridge. The snake was taken in the right direction – upwards; it was also wrapped around the egg – the symbol of the as yet unrealized Self and the new life of which the community needed to take care. There is no doubt that art therapy can perform – if allowed – a vital function as the bridge in this kind of institutional drama.

References

Campbell, J. (1975) *The Hero with a Thousand Faces*. London: Sphere.
Jung, C. G. (ed.) (1964) *Man and His Symbols*. London: Aldus.
— (1978) *Aion. Researches into the Phenomenology of the Self*. New York: Bollingen.
— (1981) *Symbols of Transformation, Collected Works*, vol. 5. London: Routledge & Kegan Paul.

Hinshelwood, R. O. and Manning, N. (1979) *Therapeutic Communities: Reflections and Progress.* London: Routledge & Kegan Paul.
Kalff, D. M. (1980) *Sandplay. A Psychotherapeutic Approach to the Psyche.* Santa Monica: Sigo Press.
Kellogg, R. (1970) *Analysing Children's Art.* Palo Alto, Calif.: National Press.
Winnicott, D. W. (1971) *Playing: Creative Activity and the Search for Self.* London: Tavistock.

Biographical note

Martin Robinson After obtaining a degree at the Courtauld Institute, Martin worked in Adult Education and Art Colleges teaching Art and History of Art. In 1974, he studied for a PGCE, with the intention of working in schools and linked this with the Art Therapy Diploma at Herts College of Art and Design, St Albans in 1976. Since then, he has worked in special education, mainly in residential communities. At present, he is involved in a training in Jungian analytical psychology.

7 | The use of art therapy in the treatment of anorexia nervosa

June Murphy

Introduction

The large amount of recent publications on anorexia nervosa has created considerable interest in the disease which has become alarmingly common – one in every two hundred adolescent girls is at present starving herself, possibly, in some cases, to death.

This chapter examines the role of art therapy as a treatment for this highly complicated disorder. The following notes and observations are the results of my own experience working with inpatients in an adolescent unit over a period of four years. Art therapy techniques were introduced as another dimension in the therapeutic programme for those suffering from anorexia nervosa.

Historical background

Historical medical evidence suggests that the disease, known today as anorexia nervosa, appeared in the Middle Ages, particularly among pseudo-mystics and women 'possessed by devils'. Richard Morton is credited with the first detailed description, in his *Phithisiologia, seu Exercitations de Phithisis*, (1689), where he referred to the condition as a 'nervous consumption', distinguishing it from tuberculosis by its chief characteristics of amenorrhoea, lack of appetite, constipation, extreme emaciation, and overactivity. Gull (1868) defined a clear symptomatology introducing the term anorexia nervosa as a modern clinical entity. Progress in definition was made subsequently in terms of a 'pure' psychiatric disorder, but this was reversed after the turn of the century as physicians attached more importance to the presenting physical emaciation. Thus, the term 'anorexia nervosa' fell into disuse. In the late 1930s, anorexia nervosa was re-established as a disease of psychological origin. Since then, however, approach to treatment remains divided according to emphasis on the physiological or psychological problems. Russell (1979) and Crisp (1983) have made important contributions to the psychobiology of the disease, while, in the United States, treatment has tended to be conducted along psychoanalytic lines (Bruch 1974).

Anorexia nervosa: towards a clearer concept

Since the 1930s, publications have appeared consistently without establishing a clear aetiology of the disease. Bruch (1974) suggests that further confusion has arisen from the fact that anorexia nervosa is not a 'static' condition and its very existence constantly provokes new problems, with patients coming to attention at various stages of their illness. She argues that to 'explain' the complex picture with one psychodynamic formulation has resulted in exposing stereotyped explanations of a condition which defies such a simplistic approach.

None the less, anorexia is quite common; 95 per cent of cases being female. Recent surveys show that it is present in severe form in one in a hundred girls with middle-class backgrounds and one in every three hundred girls with working-class backgrounds. True anorexia nervosa is based on three diagnostic criteria defined by Russell (1979): self-induced loss of weight with severe inanition, persistent amenorrhoea (or an equivalent endocrine disturbance in the male), and a psychopathology characterized by a dread of losing control of eating and becoming fat.

In the majority of cases, there is evidence of an abnormal relationship between the anorexic and her mother. The mother is excessively anxious about the well-being of her daughter. At the same time, the pubescent daughter feels her changing body is frustrating her unconscious desire to remain a child. Jeammet (1981) stresses the importance of the adolescent, transitory period between childhood and adulthood, as it demands the necessity to establish a separate identity, away from the family, and must include coming to terms with sexual maturity.

Macleod, having suffered the disease herself, described how she rejected womanhood by reversing her own natural biological process, not because she preferred manhood, but because she preferred girlhood (Macleod 1981:77). Having disposed of unwanted flesh and menstruation, she had become 'pure' and 'clean' and therefore superior to those around her: so superior that she considered herself beyond criticism. Dunseith (1978), also a former sufferer, expressed a similar view that anorexia nervosa could be viewed as the physical indication of a silent protest, and one against a permissive society or the inevitability of womanhood:

> 'Willy-nilly, nature is impressing upon the girl the sexual function in society. By refusing food either she is subconsciously rejecting the function and finding escape in starvation so what she loses are the two assets peculiar to women, breasts and fertility; or she does not yet feel mentally equipped for it. Nature is getting out of hand: it has to be slowed down.'   (Dunsieth 1978:169)

This recourse to anorexia nervosa indicates a failure in the patient's ability to symbolize and verbalize her inner conflicts, resulting in her becoming 'a prisoner of her own identification object' (Jeammet 1981). The patient attempts through an eating disorder to be in control of her own life and to acquire an identity. The drive to succeed in the anorexic is realized in the potential destruction of an intolerably precarious 'sense of self'. Macleod clearly describes this:

> 'driven as I was towards success by anxiety and the fear of failure. In reality, I was back where I had started – in a position of helplessness and hopelessness – but with one important exception. I had something I could call my own; my disease, my unique neurosis, which I perceived as my thinness.'   (Macleod 1981:83)

Body image and perceptual disturbance

One of the outstanding problems concerning the anorexic's personal body image is the fact that anorexics constantly see themselves as overweight when, in reality, they are emaciated. Schilder defines body image as 'the picture of our own body which we form in our mind; that is to say the way in which our body appears to ourselves' (Schilder 1935:4). He suggests that the body image is moulded by one's interactions with others, and to the extent that these interactions are faulty, the body image will be inadequately developed. In earlier studies in body interest and hypochondriasis in children, Levy (1932) recognized that derogatory attitudes had a very strong effect. The mother's attitudes and reactions to bodily functions other than eating can be highly significant and can greatly influence her daughter.

Connected with this is the anorexic's desire to be thin. Such is the anxiety about weight gain that hunger signals become blurred by emotional blocking. Bruch (1974) suggests that this disturbance may stem from being incorrectly 'programmed' from childhood – the true anorexic has had few opportunities to correlate hunger with the need for food. From infancy, the mother has responded to every sign of anxiety from the child by pushing food into her mouth, thereby preventing the natural learning process of adopting appropriate behaviour to satisfy bodily needs. The over-protective mother can never conceive of the child as a person in her own right, with original needs of her own. The anorexic's preoccupation with being thin is also endorsed by the western 'obsession' with the concept of beauty achieved through the pursuit of thinness. Bruch (1974) describes this as a distortion of social body concept, from which the potential anorexic may derive many of her values.

Problems arising within a therapeutic approach

Central to any treatment approach in anorexia nervosa is the understanding of the difficulties surrounding the anorexic's 'stance' or position. When less concern is focused on the more spectacular symptoms of the illness, such as weight loss and disturbance in eating, it quickly becomes clear that the long-term prognosis is dominated by psychological obstacles such as poor social, emotional, and sexual adjustment, constant anxiety, phobic and inhibited behaviour. These difficulties are most apparent in emotional relationships and personal communication. Jeammet (1981) recognizes the nature of the anorexic's defiance, continually hurled at her parents, the therapist, and at herself. Behind the defiant attitude lies a certain ambivalence, with her need for relationships on the one hand, but also with the accompanying fear of being deceived and of becoming too dependent. It is important that the patient is allowed to abandon her defence system for the establishment of a psychotherapeutic relationship. Her defiance must be understood in order to avoid entering a power struggle in which the therapist tries to defeat these defensive manipulations by, for example, isolating her.

A strict behavioural approach to treatment lays emphasis on the presenting physical symptoms and so concentrates on weight gain. This usually involves the introduction of a therapeutic 'contract' which has three main aims:

1 To remove the patient from the family situation and from possible physical danger.
2 To move her from an anorexic regime to overcome her familiar defences and to give up the status quo.
3 To make demands on her as a way of demonstrating an interest and showing her that she will not be allowed to regress or be totally involved in herself.

Implementation of the contract is best achieved by a consistent approach. The therapist must be seen to be firm and predictable, as flexibility is construed as a sign of weakness, or worse, seen as indifference. Within the framework of a therapeutic relationship and the protection of the contract, the patient is encouraged to achieve a previously decided on target weight.

A contrasting approach to the behavioural 'contract' is treatment through psychoanalysis. Bruch (1974) points out that certain patients do not appear to respond to the traditional model and disappointing results have led her to re-evaluate the patients' needs. She found that, in spite of gaining some insight, a basic disturbance in the anorexic's approach to life remained untouched. Any attempts at interpreting unconscious meanings only represented a repetition of the interaction between patient and parent which reinforced the patient's concept of 'mother always knowing how she felt', with the subsequent implication that the anorexic did not know how she felt herself. It became apparent that any 'interpretation' only confirmed the patient's own sense of inadequacy and interfered with the development of self-awareness in her own psychological faculties.

Art therapy: a new dimension in the treatment of anorexia nervosa

The anorexic patient therefore presents as a person, physically emaciated, with deeply entrenched social and psychological problems. Therapeutic approaches already described tackle the different extremities of these problems. But their interconnectedness necessitates a more eclectic approach. The anorexic cannot benefit by being 'forced' to eat and therefore gain weight, nor can she remain alive solely by being helped to understand the emotional paralysis of her condition. Changing her abnormal eating patterns can become possible, however, when at least some of her underlying problems have been resolved, particularly those with her relationships and personal communication. She needs to be involved in a therapeutic relationship and introduced to a more direct method of communication.

Art therapy is a psychotherapeutic method where the creative process is utilized and the central medium of communication is pictorial rather than verbal. Some aspects of art therapy make it more appropriate as a treatment process than the more traditional methods previously outlined. Concentrating on a painting in an intensive psychotherapeutic relationship removes the focus from the patient and provides a safer, less threatening arena for therapeutic work. Pictures can therefore facilitate personal exploration, for example, fantasies, self-image, and can also provide a safe vent for feelings such as anger, depression, and fear. In the same way, pictures can be used to express and thus clarify love–hate relationships and other ambivalent feelings which predominate in most adolescent experience. In the case of the anorexic, more specific issues can be confronted, such as her difficulties in personal relationships, particularly with her mother; preoccupations with self-image, thinness, bodily functions; and obsessions and fads in eating and other maladjustments in behaviour.

One of the most important aspects of art therapy is that the patient must participate in her own treatment, and thereby her own recovery. The patient is responsible for active participation in sessions rather than maintaining long periods of silence, which may leave her with a sense of despair and helplessness thus maintaining the status quo. The actual process of painting helps to break down the defensive/defiant mechanism that operates, particularly in the early stages of treatment. The initial commitment to paper is a statement of a commitment to therapy. By expressing herself in this way, the confusion and ambivalence which the anorexic tries to conceal will be externalized on paper. The images produced provide a starting-point within the therapeutic relationship, and help to clarify problems central to the anorexic's position, particularly that of her identity.

An identity crisis is a problem which many adolescents experience, but in the case of the anorexic, this is exacerbated in its concealment by the more obvious physical and psychological symptoms of the disorder. Bruch (1974) suggests that the anorexic has always been told how she feels, therefore a traditional interpretive approach has found to be lacking. A painting is unique to the individual; its contents 'belong' to the creator. In this sense, using art in therapy involves actually working with tangible products, expressions of the anorexic, which help to show that she has feelings of her own, albeit hidden and confused ones. Jung describes this clearly:

'The patient can make himself creatively independent through this method, if I may call it such. He is no longer dependent on his dreams or on his doctor's knowledge; instead, by painting himself he gives shape to himself. For what he paints are active phantasies of that which is active within him. And that which is active within is himself, but no longer in the guise of his previous error, when he mistook the personal ego for the self.'
(Jung 1954:49)

Working together in discussing the paintings or art forms by interacting with the therapist helps the patient become aware of her confusion and possibly work towards a more clarified sense of self.

The activity of painting can be cathartic, and therefore therapeutic, if some emotions are released and worked through in the therapeutic relationship. In the case of the anorexic, the issue of control is central; she wants to remain in control of herself and attempts to control other people by preventing them controlling her – that is by keeping them away. In some cases, the fear of losing control is tantamount to the fear of losing her whole existence. This fear is uppermost when the anorexic begins to paint, which involves a marked step into the unknown. This may be the main reason why she would resist participation in art therapy altogether. The activity of painting erodes defensive barriers and thus has the cathartic effect of allowing feelings to be expressed. The anorexic struggles with this in the fear of losing control of these emotions. However, one important point is that the patient can also learn to master and control images on paper, which in turn leads to a sense of security, and can also lead to an exploration of the issue of needing to be in control. Only by losing control can the learning experience of regaining it be achieved. The anxiety of losing control for the true anorexic is so strong that she has built rigid defence mechanisms to prevent this happening. As painting provides a means of expression which is unfamiliar, it can perhaps loosen some of these established barriers and bring the patient to the position of awareness that these defences are operating. It is possible, however, that the patient will quickly learn to adapt her defences to prevent herself from becoming 'exposed' through her art work. Although this seldom happens, the art therapist must be sufficiently skilled to understand her need for this adjustment and work with it in a constructive way.

Participation in art therapy is often hampered by the anorexic's general defensiveness. The approach to the patient and the style of the therapist is therefore of paramount importance. Most anorexics are threatened by novelty and change but yearn to communicate and have a need to be understood. Thus, in the early stages of therapy, a non-directive approach would seem most appropriate. Allowing the patient to work at her own pace, in the safety of a confined environment, and also within the confines of a flexible relationship, establishes initial trust and allows the patient the tenuous process of getting in touch with her feelings and responses. As emphasis is placed on spontaneous drawings and paintings, the decision is left to the patient to choose to what extent she wishes to project images of her dreams, fantasies, conflicts, and wishes during the course of therapy.

Patients are initially referred for individual sessions by a consultant psychiatrist. Sessions usually last for one hour in the early stages of therapy, but these can be lengthened to one hour and a half. Certain anorexics are involved in sessions while on complete bed rest, as prescribed in the 'contract' approach. When sufficient progress had been made in terms of target weight, opportunities are made available for group work, employing projective techniques, art therapy games, face painting, and the construction of imaginary worlds through paper and clay. The advantages gained in being given the means to become involved in new relationships is a great step forward, as hitherto the anorexic's relationships had probably been confined to family life or to a friend acting as her 'narcissistic' twin.

Assessing the effects of art therapy

The perceptual disturbance of body image is often acute in the anorexic condition. Anorexics see themselves as fat, when they are, in reality, extremely thin. Human figure drawings can act as indicators of this distortion. Those done by anorexics are usually disproportionate and child-like; the arms and legs are drawn as appendages with feet corresponding to the 'quarter-to-three' position. Whether the use of figure drawing might help in correcting this distortion in perception is of great interest to art therapy and its application in treatment. There is very little documented evidence of this as yet, as well-controlled experiments in the area of body image are relatively new.

In 1981, a study was set up at Goldsmiths' College to investigate the effectiveness of art/psychotherapy as a treatment for sufferers of eating disorders such as anorexia nervosa and obesity. As most of the subjects were experiencing body image distortion, certain techniques to facilitate an awareness of actual body size and a more realistic self-image were central to the investigation. Using a group of such patients, a series of exercises concentrating on certain parts of the body were introduced. These included using video, masks and make-up, paintings of ideal self, and a group activity of making life-size models which acted as their 'other' selves. These activities were all recorded on video by the patients themselves. The results of using this direct approach of confronting the body shape are still to be published and will be received with interest.

While working with anorexic patients, certain important aspects came to light concerning the spontaneous art work produced in therapy. Some of this material was used as part of the Goldsmiths' College study to assess changes in self-perception in certain individuals, based on the identification of certain recurrent 'themes' or 'motifs', which might reveal attitudes towards body (or self) boundaries.

First, anorexics rarely drew the human figure in any of their art work and seemed to experience some difficulty if asked to do so. As has been suggested, this may be connected with their distorted body image (Waller 1981). When a figure did appear, it tended to be either long, thin, and boy-like or a caricatured, doll-like girl with long hair and nipped in the waist, usually standing in a bed of flowers. This could be seen as a portrayal of an idealized self, which may stem from the failure of the anorexic to accept a real sexual identity: 'The sexual body is blotted out in order to allow exhibition of a fetish body; phallic in nature, erect and immutable of which the anorexic wishes to be the sole creator' (Jeammet 1981:118).

Many of the paintings reflected the anorexic's stark social environment within the confinement of the family and generally her lack of social interaction. Invariably, the paintings depicted images of isolation and often the fact that the patient had been bullied or ridiculed at some stage in her life. The general isolation from fellow members of her peer group became more evident within an art group where a genuine fear of participation is coupled with a very real inability to express her inner feelings.

One of the most striking features to emerge was the consistency of recurrent imagery which was spontaneously produced in the individual sessions. Certain themes and motifs seemed to fall into the following categories:

1 Concise extrinsic patterns, for example, whirlpools and bottomless pits.
2 Animals, usually dogs and horses.
3 Flowers and plants, cacti and thorns (see *Illustration 7.1*).
4 Landscapes and gardens.

It seems that the above categories corresponded to the different stages of therapy. As therapy developed, the images were generally produced in this particular sequence, indicating a progression towards more expressive imagery. However, paintings were not always produced in this order. It was noticed that after weeks of developing more open imagery, a return to drawing concise patterns occurred. This coincided with the patient expressing feelings of despair and of being locked in an insoluble situation. These patterns usually heralded a return to former defensiveness and some acting-out behaviour, refusal of food, and other 'obsessional' behaviour such as ritual washing.

It is difficult to explain the significance of these images. Whether they reflect the various stages of the anorexic condition in terms of resolving some inner conflicts, or whether the expression of these images actually brings about or promotes therapeutic change, is impossible to say at this stage. The reticence of the anorexic to talk directly about her feelings, and her general defensive attitude to her paintings and also towards the therapist, leave interpretation more a matter of speculation. Some links can be made, however, between the content of the paintings and anorexic behaviour patterns. These become more certain as therapy progresses and the anorexic begins to feel more able to ascribe some personal meaning to the images produced.

For example, the intricate patterns and vortex that appear, most noticeably at the beginning of therapy, could be an indication of the anorexic's barriers of personal expression and human involvement. A return to these patterns in the later stages of therapy has already been noted as a 'regressive' step and provides further evidence that these images reflect defensive behaviour generally. The dogs and horses seem to throw light on the anorexic's urge for exercise. The majority take pleasure in very long walks with their dogs or riding for hours on horseback; this corresponds with their lack of fatigue and overactivity, which are notable features in the anorexic's behaviour. The variety of plant forms which appear spontaneously are drawn with general competence and great attention to detail. It is possible that these are indicators of how the anorexic perceives herself,

Illustration 7.1

as it is not unusual to hear a remark such as: 'I feel like a cactus today.' This does seem to suggest some progress towards self-reflection.

The landscapes and trees were images that usually appeared in the later stages of therapy. A general pattern emerged as the composition 'progressed' from one tree to a set of two trees in a landscape, and were usually painted in symmetrical balance. Jung referred to the tree as the 'wonder-working plant'; it is possible that these trees are archetypal configurations. Jung suggested that when these fantasy products are drawn or painted, they very often fall into symmetrical patterns that take the form of the mandala: 'If a mandala may be described as a symbol of the self seen in cross section, then the tree would represent a profile view of it: the self depicted as a process of growth' (Jung 1968: 272). The striking features of the trees, set in the landscape, is that one is usually blossoming and healthy, the other contrastingly dead and stick-like. One suggestion is that the trees represent an expression of the two opposing aspects of the 'self'.

An example of this is given in the following description of a painting done by a sixteen-year-old girl (see *Illustration* 7.2). The picture is a well-organized composition with two trees: a conifer to the left and a sparse leaf-less species to the right, which are joined by a path leading to a bridge. A

Illustration   7.2

fence is in the foreground with a yellow moon emerging from behind clouds. A small forest is placed to the left of the picture and the landscape is covered by a heavy layer of snow.

The patient complained of some frustration, in that the images she had wanted to paint had not corresponded with what she had actually produced. Apparently, she had hoped to achieve a sense of stillness as appreciated on a winter afternoon – the snow all white and untouched, the path and bridge between the two trees leading up to a small village with 'friendly', lit-up windows. The village had not been realized in the painting as the rather leafless tree on the right restricted this. She described how this picture reminded her of 'happier' times; of Christmas cards, in particular, and she felt that this represented an attempt to kindle more 'romantic' thoughts and aimed at a sense of togetherness. The two trees seemed to have given her difficulty as she expressed disappointment in not actually painting the sparse tree on the right as leaning towards the healthy looking spruce on the left. She felt that she had longed to do this but some inner dissonance had prevented her.

Another patient, aged twenty-six, gave a history of seven years of amenorrhoea, of frequent overeating, followed by self-induced vomiting

Illustration 7.3

with accompanying feelings of self-disgust and guilt which she experienced after such episodes. As she appeared to have an overwhelming fear of losing control, a non-interpretative approach was applied in the sessions, which was perceived as less threatening and gave her a sense, at least, of being in control of the images she produced. Her pictorial products over a five-week period were prolific, and the imagery that developed became increasingly metamorphic. She seemed particularly adept at expressing her dreams and tended to stay with this topic throughout her treatment programme.

One dream depicted a pair of brown gloved hands (drawn distinctly like wings, see *Illustration 7.3*). In the dream, her brother had presented her with these gloves and on wearing them she promptly flew through the air. Between the gloves is an aerial view of a farm with yellow and green 'patchwork' fields. Three figures, barely discernible and drawn in faint pencil, suggest one adult and two small children. She expressed surprise that these images should have disturbed her and stressed her inadequacy at drawing the human figure.

Generally the themes of 'flight' and plant symbols dominated this patient's work. In her last painting, she did draw a human figure, in the shape of a pregnant woman with a small female child, but only the backs of the heads are shown. These two figures were standing in water. The subject matter in her drawings revealed this young woman's preoccupation and efforts at dealing with certain conflicts which arose from her distorted concept of self. Just as in the former patient's landscape, the plant symbols like the two trees, may suggest a polarity of opposites and a symbolic dissociation in her psyche.

Conclusion

What can be deduced from the spontaneous production in art therapy of these images by anorexic patients? Some might argue that these pictures merely reflect the maintenance of a defensive stance. However, the fact is that the pictures do indicate a progression, or change, in content over the course of therapy. From this, it seems that the paintings reflect the particular stage and state of the inner world of the anorexic at one particular time. This is seen to correspond with behaviour and the manifestation of symptoms. For example, the reversion to making patterns was seen to coincide with a general regression in behaviour. Further work on this subject will reveal whether the expression of archetypal images, recurrent in the anorexic's paintings, has any long-term effect over time in terms of the therapeutic value of externalizing some aspects of the self, which might otherwise remain concealed.

While it is relatively easy to effect a short-term weight gain, this does not take into consideration the underlying factors of the disorder. Art therapy provides another dimension in the treatment of anorexics, and allows opportunities for lines of communication to be opened. Communication through art therapy enables some channelling of feelings, stemming from psychic conflict, which the patient had previously found no other way of expressing. The use of art can be seen to help in conceptualizing the underlying problems, while the therapist must be able to tolerate the anorexic's indifference and to 'listen' to the patient. Art therapy aims to help the anorexic to achieve self-awareness and a sense of autonomy without misusing eating functions in bizarre and irrational ways.

Finally, success with anorexic patients is not forthcoming by using art therapy techniques alone – the art therapist cannot work in isolation but needs to liaise with an experienced multi-disciplinary team. Team efforts with the involvement of the family facilitates the progress in the treatment of this complicated condition. Such efforts might include the participation of the whole family in art therapy as a group. Certain endeavours can be ambitious and sometimes bear fruit, but as Crisp reminds us, despite the various treatment approaches 'most anorexics recover, a few die, but some can never be reached' (Crisp 1983:16).

References

Bruch, H. (1974) *Eating Disorders, Obesity, Anorexia Nervosa and the Person Within*. London: Routledge & Kegan Paul.

Crisp, A. H. (1983) Anorexia Nervosa: Diagnosis and Prognosis. *Psychiatry in Practice* 2(13): 13–16.

Dunseith, B. L. (1978) Personal View. *British Medical Journal* (24 June): 169.

Fisher, S. (1972) Body Image. In T. Polhemus (ed.) *Social Aspects of the Human Body*. Harmondsworth: Penguin.

Gull, W. W. (1868) The Address in Medicine Delivered before the Annual Meeting of the British Medical Association at Oxford. *The Lancet* 2: 171.

Jeammet, P. (1981) The Anorexic Stance. *Journal of Adolescence* 4(2): 113–29.

Jung, C. G. (1954) The Aims of Psychotherapy. In *The Practice of Psychotherapy, Collected Works*, vol. 16. London: Routledge & Kegan Paul.

— (1968) *Alchemical Studies, Collected Works*, vol. 13. London: Routledge & Kegan Paul.

Levy, D. M. (1932) Body Interest in Children and Hypochondriasis. *American Journal of Psychiatry* 12: 295–311.

Macleod, S. (1981) *The Art of Starvation*. London: Virago.

Russell, G. (1979) Bulima Nervosa: an Ominous Variant of Anorexia Nervosa. *Psychological Medicine* 9: 429–48.

Schilder, P. (1935) *The Image and Appearance of the Human Body*. Psyche Monographs no. 4. London: International Universities Press.

Waller, D. (1981) 'Anorexia Nervosa and Art Therapy'. Unpublished paper, Goldsmiths' College, University of London.

Biographical note

June Murphy Presently employed as a Senior Art Therapist at Darlington Memorial Hospital, Co. Durham. Studied Art and Design at Newcastle upon Tyne College of Art and Industrial Design and Social Studies at the University of Hull. Has been a teacher of Art in a secondary school, and has been employed as an art therapist in a variety of places including The Retreat, York; Naburn Hospital, York; York Social Services Department, Ashbank Assessment Centre; Clifton Hospital, York. Is a full member of BAAT and currently a supervisor for Art Therapy students at Goldsmiths' College, University of London.

8 | Art therapy for people who are mentally handicapped

Janie Stott and Bruce Males

Mental handicap

In this chapter we shall take a practical approach to the role of art therapy and place it in the broader context of the modern philosophy of care for mentally handicapped people.

As we begin to examine some of the issues related to the use of art therapy with mentally handicapped people, it is essential to consider the nature of mental handicap and the general direction of care for this section of society.

In the past, terms like mental retardation and mental subnormality have been used to refer collectively to three quite distinct phenomena; subnormal intelligence, reduced social and physical skills, and deviant behavioural patterns.

Use of such imprecise terminology has often made it conceptually, as well as practically difficult to distinguish between individuals' inherent mental limitations and the social handicaps they experience because of the effects of their impairments and functional disabilities on their way of life. This lack of clarity of understanding has been significant in the creation of undue public and, in many cases, professional pessimism regarding the problems of mentally handicapped people.

There has been a widely held assumption that because severe mental limitations are normally due to incurable defects acquired from before or around the time of birth, behavioural disabilities and abnormalities observed in mentally handicapped people were similarly incurable and not amenable to 'treatment'.

Why do these misconceptions exist and where do they come from? In 1971 the White Paper 'Better Services for the Mentally Handicapped' (DHSS 1971) was published. This document outlined the desired direction of service for this client group for the next twenty years. Basically, it describes a move from institutional to community care. It can be viewed as a response to the public attention brought to bear on conditions in hospitals in 1967 and 1968 and its very positive recommendations have resulted in substantial improvements in conditions and services, most significantly, a reduction was made in the number of hospital places from 49,000+ in 1971 to 44,000 in 1977. The White Paper target is 27,300 by 1991.

How did these hospitals develop in the first place? The White Paper itself states that the foundations of the service that existed in 1971 were laid in the 1920s and 1930s. What this publication does not explain is that there was a sociological reason for the segregation. The White Paper omits this and we would contend that this omission in itself can be seen as indicative of the deep-rooted nature of the problem of coming to terms with the existence of mentally handicapped people in our society (Males 1981).

It is not as if the process which led up to the first major legislation to affect the mentally handicapped, the 1913 Mental Deficiency Act, was not well documented.

In 1896 the National Association for the Care and Control of the Feeble Minded (NACCFM) was set up and acted as a pressure group for lifetime segregation of defectives. Their emphasis on the prevention of the expression of sexuality was motivated by middle-class fears about working-class fertility and was fuelled by the Eugenics Movement's scaremongering about the likely decline in the talents of the British people.

In 1908 the Radnor Commission was set up to make legislative recommendations. It reported that feeble mindedness was largely inherited and that prevention of mentally defective persons from becoming parents would tend to diminish the number of such persons in the population.

During the 1910 General Election the NACCFM campaigned on the issue of discouraging parenthood in the feeble minded and other degenerate types and the building of separate institutions. The 1913 Act established the basis of that separate service which would exclude mentally handicapped people from other welfare and social agencies as well as from the educational system (Heaton Ward 1977).

As late as 1929 the Wood Committee saw mental defectives as a continuing threat and perhaps even hunted out more wide-reaching answers not unheard of elsewhere in Europe at that time. 'If we are to prevent the racial disaster of mental deficiency, we must deal not merely with the mentally defective persons but with the whole subnormal group from which the majority of them come.' The result of these views, which perhaps it is convenient to forget today, was an increase in the number of places in institutions for people registered under the 1913 Mental Deficiency Act. Between 1918 and 1931 the numbers of admissions tripled and between 1931 and 1939 they doubled again until they reached 32,000 (Ryan and Thomas 1980).

This biased legislation continued to be the mechanism of admission to institutional care until the 1959 Mental Health Act. This Act was a result of a Royal Commission in 1954–57 which began to place emphasis on community care and an end to segregation. It was this Commission that began to state that hospitals should be an appropriate placement only for those requiring specialist medical treatment, training, or continual nursing supervision. It stressed that mentally handicapped people should not be isolated but should be cared for in centres of population and residents should take part in the life of the local community. However, as previously indicated, it took public concern over conditions in long-stay hospitals, and official enquiries, to create a climate of opinion that would allow for the implementation of these ideals.

The direction, therefore, is clearly signposted; community care will, in the future, be the answer for the majority of mentally handicapped people. Official figures give some indication that this change is taking place: in 1969 there was a total of 4,200 places in residential homes, by 1977 there were 11,700 (DHSS 1980).

In order to monitor these developments, the Government has taken several initiatives intended to strengthen the drive towards building up the pattern of services described in the 1971 White Paper. One of these initiatives was the setting-up in 1975 of the National Development Group. This group was charged with providing advice to the Secretary of State on national policy matters. Another initiative was the creation of the Development Team, this body having the task of offering advice as to the actual application of the official policy, translating from philosophy to practical arrangements in the light of local needs and opportunities.

The National Development Group has been disbanded having completed its task by publishing six influential pamphlets. The Development Team has been strengthened and now has the right to visit any health and social service authority to carry out its analysis, whereas formerly it could only do so by invitation. In addition to its reports on individual hospitals and local services, it has produced three important annual reports. The fact that, in all three of these most important and influential documents, there is no mention at all of the creative therapies gives some indication of the difficulties facing developing professions like art, music, and drama therapy.

It could be argued that this is just as much a lack of recognition of those creative aspects of the client group as of any policy decision to exclude minority professions. There is a tendency, particularly with the work of the National Development Group, to concentrate on methods of alleviating the problems of the mentally handicapped people by recommending an approach which seems to indicate that its subjects are a collection of skill deficits rather than a group of people with as full a range of creative, expressive, emotional, and spiritual needs as any other section of the community, as well as with specific skill deficits.

There is one concept that has been gaining ground steadily in the field and that is 'normalization'. A philosophy developed initially in Sweden and Denmark, it concentrates on analysing the needs of the mentally handicapped and on giving them the same rights and obligations in society as other people. Grunwald writing about the development of the Swedish services, states that:

> 'Differences in people's capacity to adjust to society are purely quantitative, and even the most severely handicapped person can be "normalized" in one or more respects.
>
> The validity of this principle is not negated by the fact that the majority of retarded people cannot become fully adjusted to society. The term implies rather a striving in various ways to what is normal. Normalization does not imply any denial of the retarded person's handicap. It involves rather exploiting his other mental and physical capacities, so that his handicap becomes less pronounced.'   (Grunwald 1974)

Nirje (1970) had earlier suggested eight facets of the normalization principle: normalization means a 'normal rhythm of the day', also implies a 'normal weekly rhythm', and experiencing the 'normal rhythm of the year'. It also means an opportunity to undergo the 'normal developmental experience of the life cycle'. This principle also means 'choices, wishes and desires that have to be respected' living in a sexually integrated world with all that implies. It means a respect for the right to have as close as possible 'normal economic standards' and, finally, the right to have appropriate standards of physical facilities, i.e. adapted buildings and equipment.

It seems quite extraordinary to consider that such basic human rights have to be delineated in this manner for a not insignificant number of our community, but such is our inheritance.

Art therapy, with its score of freedoms, self-expressions, and consequent reinforcement of a sense of individuality and self-confidence, would seem to have an important role in creating and supporting such a philosophy.

The role of art therapy in caring for people who are mentally handicapped

With the roots of art therapy firmly based in psychotherapy and with most art therapists working in the field of psychiatry we ask the question, can art therapy be applied to mental handicap?

The main difficulty resulting directly from mental handicap is a limited ability to learn and reason. This leads to problems which are both practical and emotional in nature. The practical problems could include various everyday tasks which cannot be performed satisfactorily. The emotional difficulties stem from the inability to understand and cope with emotional needs. It may be that the full meaning and complexity of speech cannot be understood. Moreover, where physical limitations are a factor, extra frustrations will occur and speech, for example, may be impaired or absent altogether.

Inability to perform practical tasks inevitably leads to a degree of dependence on others. This will range from financial dependence, because a living cannot be earned, to total physical care for the severely handicapped. Constant dependence on others in turn exacerbates emotional difficulties.

When chronic dependence makes excessive demands on the family, the mentally handicapped find themselves transferred to an institution which may be a large hospital or a small hostel. Being separated from family life can lead to emotional deprivation; other secondary difficulties may result, for example, lack of privacy and space and the conformity of institutional life.

How can art therapy help with these difficulties? The generally agreed aim of art therapy is to act as a means of communication and self-expression. Clearly, art therapy can offer an alternative, non-verbal means of communication for those whose use of speech or understanding of words is incomplete or non-existent. In providing a means of communication where one was previously inadequate or lacking the opportunity for self-expression is increased. Through self-expression it may be possible to ease the various difficulties discussed above. For example, a sense of identity – easily lost in an institution – can be re-established.

How will the use of art therapy with the mentally handicapped differ from its use in psychiatry?

Since the psychiatric model predominates in art therapy training courses, art therapists working in the field of mental handicap have a specialist skill to offer when working with those mentally handicapped people who also have psychiatric problems. However, as we have already stated, mentally handicapped people have certain problems as a direct result of mental handicap. It follows that special attention should be given to determine the best approach to use with them: this has led us to do our own research. Let us consider the possible approaches and how they compare with the use of art therapy in psychiatry.

Working with the mentally handicapped has advantages and disadvantages. A particular advantage is outlined by J. Males (1979). She states that mentally handicapped adults may have child-like qualities, but they are rarely childish. She explains by defining these terms as follows:

> child-like – having good qualities of a child, innocence, frankness, spontaneity,* etc.
> childish – of, proper to, a child ... improper for a grown person.

They should not, therefore, be treated like children but we should recognize and use to advantage their child-like qualities.

The quality of spontaneity is especially useful in art therapy. When mentally handicapped people are presented with art media their spontaneity very often prompts them into using these media freely. This is very important as it results in what we term direct therapeutic benefit – that the 'therapy' is happening while working directly with the art media. In contrast, adult people of 'normal' intellect are more likely to have inhibitions. Comments such as 'I can't draw' may be heard as memories of struggling with perspective in the school classroom are recalled. In psychiatry this problem would add to the difficulties already present; part of the therapist's role would then be to overcome any inhibitions and promote spontaneity.

The existence of this 'direct therapeutic benefit' as a direct consequence of spontaneity suggests the appropriateness of a non-directive approach with the mentally handicapped, in which they can work in their own time, setting their own goals and standards. Achievement, confidence, self-awareness, and growth result. In contrast, in a directive approach the therapist intervenes to a greater or lesser extent. This procedure would help for example when spontaneity is lacking and an impasse or *idée fixe* has been reached. A survey (Males and Males 1977) of art therapists working with the mentally handicapped showed that the directive and non-directive approaches are equally used. Clearly both approaches are valid, so it is important to determine when each is most appropriate. The two were compared in a recent research programme, funded by the DHSS and undertaken as a collaboration between Males, Males, and Stott (publication in preparation). We shall return to this discussion later but first we shall conclude the comparison of the uses of art therapy in mental handicap and psychiatry.

Reflection on the content of the art work produced forms an important part of art therapy. The therapist's skills are required to help the client reflect on the content of the art work and thereby gain insight in order to overcome difficulties. An obvious problem arises in the field of mental handicap, where problems of intellect will limit the ability to learn and

---

* In discussion J. Males agreed that spontaneity is an example of a child-like quality, although it is not mentioned in her article.

reason. The therapist must take into special consideration the individual's capabilities including the ability to cope with a discussion about the art work. Reflection by the mentally handicapped person may occur either during or after the production of art work – and discussion with the therapist may be included – but it is less likely to be as prominent as in psychiatry.

It follows that interpretation and diagnosis will be similarly less prominent since, if we consider that a picture should not be discussed out of the context of the person who produced it, then, if the person concerned cannot discuss it for whatever reason, accuracy of interpretation is suspect. The therapist can use his or her knowledge of common symbolism to a certain extent, but there can be no certainties as to individual meaning. For example, the colour black can mean negative things to many people but to an African tribeswoman it can be positive – when the sky is black the rain comes to water the crops.

Other considerations peculiar to working with mentally handicapped people are: (i) they cannot be cured of mental handicap; (ii) they may need therapy for long periods; and (iii) there is more need for involvement from the therapist.

The second point results from the first, although it should be made clear that, as mental handicap is not an illness, many such people will lead content and happy lives without the need for therapy. If they do require therapy, it may be to help them over a short period when they may need support, for instance following a bereavement, or they may need long-term support because the basic problem of mental handicap presents too many subsequent problems which require help. The third point, involvement and hence friendship, represents an important difference from psychiatric practice. Friendship with the mentally handicapped is actually encouraged as part of therapy. To extend the example of bereavement, an art therapist would attend a funeral in support of, and sympathy with, those left behind.

Directive or non-directive art therapy

We now continue the discussion of non-directive and directive approaches, including two examples which illustrate their appropriate use.

Creativity is not essential to art therapy but it is important to understand that mentally handicapped people have the same potential for creativity, and that it is is not impaired by the handicap. In order to illustrate how art media can reflect the thoughts and feelings of the individual we take the example of M. He is particularly creative in a way we can understand; his example helps us gain some insight into those whose work we cannot readily comprehend, such as those who mainly scribble. What they are doing has a particular meaning for them but we may not be able to understand it. (We shall amplify this point when we discuss stages of development.)

M is now forty-three and has lived in an institution since the age of four, when he was abandoned at a railway station. He has Down's Syndrome. He first attended the art therapy department five years ago, as it was discovered by a nurse that giving him drawing was the only way to pacify his difficult moods. There are many interesting examples of his creativity but space limits us to one.

M entered the department one day carrying conkers. He obtained a cardboard box and some clay and proceeded to place a layer of clay on the bottom of the box. On top of this he placed the conkers, evenly distributed, finally covering them with clay to the top of the box. He then said, with his limited speech, 'plant'. During the next few days he watered the planted conkers, after which we went for a walk and returned with lots of twigs. He planted them in the top of the clay and painted the box blue and the twigs multi-coloured. As it was the Christmas season he went on to decorate it. He cut out paper shapes, made a hole in the middle of each, and then secured them to the twigs by passing strips of fabric through the holes. This was M's Christmas tree which he shared with the others in the department. The decorations were removed after Christmas but the box concealing the conkers and decorated twigs remained in the department for over a year.

When the flower festival in the church came near, M joined a group of residents to collect wild flowers. Being dissatisfied with the group flower display he set off again and returned only to make a brighter and hence more attractive display of his own. Both displays were placed in the church. Before the service he took a pair of scissors and, returning to the box, cut off all the twigs. He then took a large sheet of white paper and arranged the twigs inside to make a bouquet. He completed it with a label that had scribble writing on it and added more and more paint to the twigs, saying 'colour'. Finally, M presented the bouquet, still dripping wet, to his favourite retired Nursing Officer at the end of the service. The Nursing Officer in his white linen jacket graciously accepted the gift and M left the church smiling.

M's spontaneous creativity clearly allows him to derive direct therapeutic benefit from his art work; the non-directive approach is appropriate for him. We now discuss some of the factors involved in a directive approach and give an example of its use.

As we have already stated, in a directive approach the therapist intervenes to a greater or lesser extent. For this to be beneficial the intervention must be appropriate; one guide that we have found very useful is the concept of stages of development in comparison with children.

There are similarities between the drawings produced by children of 'normal' intellect and mentally handicapped adults. In both cases, the drawings will reflect the particular stage of development that has been reached. If this is recognized it is possible for the therapist to work in a directive way which brings benefits without detracting from the individual's worth and capabilities.

An analogy with normal child development will make this clear. When a child names a scribble as 'mummy', while to the onlooker it does not resemble the child's mother in any way, praise should nevertheless be given in order not to diminish the child's sense of worth. The child may not have the skills to make a drawing look like its mother, but by naming the scribble it is demonstrating a direct link between thought and the mark made on the paper. Realistic drawing will come at another stage of development, a process which can be encouraged but not rushed beyond the child's abilities.

Similarly, the art therapist can work in a directive way with mentally handicapped adults. The therapist must observe the stage of development that an individual has reached; armed with this knowledge the appropriate intervention can be made. It might be sufficient to guide the individual into using a medium which is appropriate at his stage of development – i.e. one with which achievement is possible. The therapist may choose to intervene more directly by encouraging or participating in the art activity. The therapist's contribution to the activity must always match the individual's stage of development, ensuring that the individual can succeed. The therapist can work towards the next stage (as with the 'normal' child), but not set impossible goals. Unlike the 'normal' child, the mentally handicapped may be unable to reach the next stage.

All the art media should be explored thoroughly in order to find the one best suited to the individual, according to the stage of development. For example, a random scribbler may also respond to finger painting or squeezing clay. The stage of development also affects behaviour, communication, socialization, and skills. For example, the same random scribbler might have limited concentration and find it difficult to relate to others.

Let us now look at an example of the use of a directive approach. A is elderly, has limited speech and, having lived in hospital for many years, has become institutionalized and withdrawn.

A found it difficult to relate to the art material, hesitating, with her hand poised close to the paper. Following a great deal of encouragement she suddenly made the positive gesture of writing some of the letters from her first name – particularly the 'A'. It was as if she felt secure in something familiar, even though she had probably not taken pen to paper for many years. The clear way in which she drew the letters suggested a stage of development at which she should be able to do more – she clearly had the necessary control. She was restricted by her own hesitancy.

In order to help her explore the medium and achieve her full potential, the therapist intervened by drawing the letters upside-down beneath her originals, and by extracting the underlying patterns such as the arch in the capital 'A'. The therapist thus responded exactly to A's stage of development by repeating the letters, communicated with her within the safety and familiarity of her visual world, yet directed her towards seeing them as patterns and shapes. A responded by joining in this variation process. Further progress in her use of the material in response to intervention by the therapist has been slow but steady, accompanied by her being more communicative.

It is ultimately for the therapist to decide in the light of experience whether intervention in this way is the most appropriate approach. We consider that both non-directive and directive methods of art therapy can be used.

The practical application of art therapy with mentally handicapped people

In this section we examine the various practical aspects of using art therapy with mentally handicapped people, referred to here as residents since the context of a residential hospital is assumed. However, several of the points covered will also apply to other situations.

The organization of an art therapy programme includes several stages:

1 identifying those residents for whom art therapy can be of most benefit;
2 finding the art medium of most use to each resident, bearing in mind any physical handicaps;
3 the therapy sessions themselves;
4 recording and reporting the results of sessions.

In addition there are day-to-day chores not directly related to the therapy programme, for example, maintaining supplies of materials. Stages 1 and 4 involve communication with other professions, which is the topic we now address.

Communications with other professions

Art therapy will not be appropriate for all residents. Some will not need it; others, who need therapy, may not respond to art media but might respond better to something else, say music or drama. Furthermore, art therapy resources may in practice be limited. We must, therefore, identify those residents who will benefit most from art therapy.

Since residents spend most of their time in the care of other professions, it is important to recognize that the selection of residents to be referred to art therapy is made by these same professions; a multi-disciplinary team approach is thus required. Two things are needed to make this work.

First, the other professions must have a clear understanding of what art therapy is and what it can achieve. Without it, referrals for art therapy will be made for the wrong reasons. Any efforts the art therapist devotes to fostering understanding will ease the job of the art therapist and that of the team as a whole. The use of formally structured occasions such as lectures to other professions as part of their training is obvious, but other opportunities can be taken as they present themselves, for instance when meeting other professionals to discuss a case.

Second, any communication between professions specific to a resident (for example at the referral stage, or as a report on progress during therapy) must be in an easily understood 'common language'. This may be helped by use of carefully worded standard forms. With all forms it is important to remember that they are there to serve a purpose – to ensure that all necessary information is recorded in a way that is easy to comprehend. The forms are 'tools' whose sole function is to aid those who use them. They eliminate needless tasks and repetitive information and thereby afford the therapist more time to spend with the residents. By way of example, let us consider the forms used for referral for art therapy and for subsequent assessment.

The Referral Form should be kept simple so that referrals are indeed made and staff are not put off by complicated details. Further pertinent information can always be sought later. Art therapists will always receive referrals describing the reason for referral such as 'likes art', 'to keep occupied', 'to get off the ward', and so on. However, with continued effort in creating good working relations and mutual understanding of how the different professions can best help each other, more appropriate referrals will be made. These take the form of describing the resident's symptoms, such as depression, behaviour problems, changes in mood or circumstances, or communication problems generally, in the hope that art therapy may help to clarify and to heal the areas of difficulty. (We chose 'heal' to describe what therapy means when talking of mental handicap as it is less appropriate to talk of treatment or cure.)

All newly referred residents should be seen for an initial assessment. A period of 6–10 sessions is suggested, during which they should be offered a wide range of materials and given every opportunity to explore the media. After this, the therapist completes an Initial Art Therapy Assessment Report. Two possible presentations may be considered. The first comprises a written summary of the art work produced and the accompanying behaviour. In the second a tabular form is used to describe the art work and behaviour with a space following for the therapist's comments and recommendations (see *Sample 1*). This tabular form has the advantage of allowing the reader to scan the results, easily finding a summary of the information required. This may be of particular value when comparing it with subsequent reports.

Name:	Date:
Ward:	Consultant:
Date of birth:	

This report is made when a resident has attended Art Therapy for 6–10 sessions. The art work produced and the accompanying behaviour are summarized in the tables below: a tick indicates the best description of each aspect in the range from A to B.

Art work produced

A	*A applies*	*Inclines to A*	*Neither A nor B applies*	*Inclines to B*	*B applies*	B
Variety of work		✓				No variety
Monochrome			✓			Colourful
Well-developed images		✓				Poorly-developed images
Does not develop own ideas		✓				Develops own ideas
Good observational skills			✓			No observational skills
Well motivated			✓			Poorly motivated
No concentration				✓		Good concentration

Behaviour

A	*A applies*	*Inclines to A*	*Neither A nor B applies*	*Inclines to B*	*B applies*	B
Settled well	✓					Did not settle
Demanding		✓				Undemanding
Quiet				✓		Noisy
Dependent		✓				Independent
Undisturbed behaviour		✓				Disturbed behaviour
Relates well to staff	✓					Does not relate well to staff
Does not relate well to residents			✓			Relates well to residents

Benefits

A	*A applies*	*Inclines to A*	*Neither A nor B applies*	*Inclines to B*	*B applies*	B
Benefits greatly		✓				No benefit

Therapist's comments see over

Any subsequent reports could be done with the same form as a basis, but changing the title to Art Therapy Report. The first sentence which explains the number of sessions in the initial assessment, would then be omitted. These Reports would be sent as appropriate to all professions involved throughout therapy and at its completion.

These other professions, some of whom may have been involved in the initial referral, will want to know the answers to the following questions:

1 Does this person benefit from art therapy?
2 If so, in what way?
3 What are the results of art therapy for this person?
4 What are the recommendations for the future?

Every resident is unique but the questions as outlined above will apply to everyone attending art therapy. The answers to them will vary accordingly and may or may not include details of the content of the work produced.

Regular observations of a resident's behaviour, activities, and concentration during therapy sessions will assist the preparation of therapy reports. For example, the following questions might be noted:

— is the resident easily distracted, or totally involved in his activity?
— does he talk to other residents or only to staff?
— what is the stretch of arm movement when there is physical handicap?
— does the resident collect his own materials, or wait for staff to provide them?

A 'common language' is essential when communicating with other professions and if, as Ulman says, 'therapy should outlast the session itself' then the best common language will place the emphasis on the effects of therapy rather than on the therapy itself (Ulman 1975:3–13).

Art therapy sessions

Central to the application of art therapy is the way the therapy sessions themselves are conducted. The right materials, environment and, above all, support must be provided by the therapist.

A range of art materials is necessary in order to match the residents' mental and physical capabilities, as well as their psychological needs. Consider the properties of common two-dimensional media:

1 a thick wax crayon is easy to hold and use, and is unlikely to wear out during a session;

2 a thick felt-tipped pen has the advantages of 1 but will not withstand great pressure and requires the removal of a cap;

3 chalks, usually thinner, are less easy to hold and are easily broken;

4 a pencil has the disadvantage of wearing down, thus requiring sharpening or replacing, and, like the felt-tipped pen and chalk, cannot withstand great pressure;

5 finger paints have the advantage of being easy to use but they do not lend themselves to detail and need frequent replenishment;

6 conventional liquid paints (for use with brushes) require many stages, e.g. pick up brush; if necessary, put it into water; put it in the paint; make mark on paper; repeat the process. There is less control than with drawing, and accidents such as spillage and blobs can occur.

Most residents work readily with drawing materials. Some, usually the more able, paint as well as draw; very few only paint. More skills are needed for painting by brush. It demands physical dexterity and the mental ability to link a series of operations in order to make a mark on the paper. To a lesser degree, the same differences are present between the easier drawing media, for example crayon, and the more difficult ones such as pencil. A similar argument applies when comparing two- and three-dimensional media. Exclusive use of three-dimensional media is rare.

In summary, the media that are most appropriate when the degree of handicap is relatively severe are those, such as the wax crayon, which require minimal mental and physical skill. For residents with a lesser degree of handicap the use of those media which require greater skill becomes feasible and may offer more satisfaction. This does not preclude their appreciation of the simpler media as well. In every case the material must match the residents' needs at the time.

We have already noted that physical handicap may limit the choice of media. This restriction can often be eased by the use of aids. These range from simply securing the paper to the table, through the provision of angled or free-standing drawing boards, to the construction of special tools for particular handicaps. Someone who cannot shape clay directly with the fingers may still be able to grip, and have greater control of, a suitable tool. A small collection of basic woodworking implements will suffice to make most aids.

The environment in which art therapy takes place – that is 'the surrounding conditions that influence development or growth' – is very important. It can be asylum within an asylum. If residents are permitted a degree of freedom to influence their environment they can then identify with it, making an investment and a commitment. They can choose a place to work, which may be isolated in a corner or integrated on a large shared table. They can establish their own territory by putting their work on the walls around them. They can bring materials to work with and possessions, such as radios, to share. They can also share practical jobs such as unloading supplies of materials. This process of identification can be encouraged by the therapist who must also ensure that freedom for one individual does not threaten the safety and sanctuary of another.

By promoting a low-stress environment the therapist will help the residents to relax and develop their creativity and self-expression. The therapist can provide encouragement, friendship, and positive reinforcement, so that the residents can achieve the objectives of therapy. The subconscious way that residents relate to their own art work, communicating with themselves as they produce it, is unique to their understanding and may or may not be shared with the therapist. In any discussions of the art work produced the therapist must remember the limitations of speech and understanding which the residents may have.

We have discussed several practical aspects of art therapy, mainly drawing on our experience of working in a large hospital. We hope that they can be used as the basis for developing the new skills required in the future, as the emphasis of care for mentally handicapped people moves from institutions to the community.

The way forward

Most art therapists working with mentally handicapped people function from hospital bases. The move towards a system of care based in the community can, therefore, be viewed as threatening for art therapy. This need not be so any more than for any other professional groups.

One method of employing therapists outside institutions is joint funding. This is the method of financing projects which divides the cost between the health and social services. The aim is to move the funding of services on a tapering principle from the health to social services, so that in the future, the majority of care can be provided by local social services and not by the National Health Service.

This model for employing therapists and other specialists should be explored, to ensure the development of a balanced service. In one London borough using the joint funding principle, agreement has been reached for the appointment of a Community Art Therapist (Mental Handicap), with the aim of supporting mentally handicapped clients and their families – here the experience of art therapists in family therapy should find appropriate use.

To summarize, we feel that the emphasis now placed on individual development and the greater integration of mentally handicapped people matches the philosophy of art therapists in such a way as to ensure a long and interesting relationship.

References

Department of Health and Social Security (DHSS) (1971) *Better Services for the Mentally Handicapped* (Cmnd. 4638). London: HMSO.
— (1980) *Mental Handicap: Progress, Problems and Priorities.* London: HMSO.
Grunwald, K. (1974) *The Mentally Retarded in Sweden.* The Swedish Institute, Stockholm.
Heaton-Ward, W. A. (1977) *Left Behind: A Study of Mental Handicap.* London: Macdonald & Evans.
Males, B. (1981) 'Public Attitudes to Mental Handicap as Reflected in the Opinions of Schoolchildren'. Unpublished MA thesis, Keele University.
Males, J. (1979) The Mentally Handicapped Child – A Plan for Action. *Royal Society of Health Journal* 99(2), 79–81.
Males, J. and Males, B. (1977) Unpublished Survey. Psychology Department, St Lawrence's Hospital, Caterham, Surrey.
Nirje, B. (1970) Symposium on Normalization: The Normalization Principle – Implications and Comments. *Journal of Mental Subnormality* 16 pt 2(31): 62–70.
Ryan, J. and Thomas, F. (1980) *The Politics of Mental Handicap.* Harmondsworth: Penguin.
Ulman, E. (1975) *Art Therapy: Problem of Definition.* In Ulman, E. and Dachinger, P. (eds) *Art Therapy in Theory and Practice.* New York: Shocken.

Biographical notes

Janie Stott   Diploma in Art Therapy, Herts College of Art and Design, St Albans, 1978. Since then, she has worked in a large hospital for mentally handicapped people, where she is now Head Art Therapist. Prior to this appointment, she was engaged in a two-year programme of research, funded by the DHSS, which studied the use of art therapy with the mentally handicapped. She is an Officer and Council Member of BAAT.

Bruce Males   Diploma in Art Therapy, Herts College of Art and Design, St Albans, 1972. Subsequently, worked as Head of Art Therapy in a large hospital for mentally handicapped people. He obtained an MA in Psychology of Mental Handicap at Keele University in 1981, and is presently working as Co-ordinator of Social Education and Training in the same hospital. He is currently an external examiner for the Diploma in Art Therapy and has served as an Officer and Council member of BAAT.

9 | Art therapy with the elderly and the terminally ill

Bruce Miller

The scope that the title of this chapter implies is enormous, and could not be dealt with in any depth in the space available. I intend therefore to limit the area of discussion to a particular group, within the client group specified, and to a specific area of concern with these people. Everyone just over retirement age could be elderly, and there are many young people who are terminally ill. I shall not be addressing myself to the particular problems of either of these groups, although I hope much of what I have to say will have a wider implication. The client group with whom I have had the most experience, and who are the particular concern of this chapter, are those people, usually living in institutions, who are very old (in their eighties or nineties), perhaps suffering from a terminal condition, and yet who are not senile, and who could be aware that their life might be soon coming to an end.

These people living in the geriatric wards of large hospitals, old people's homes, hospices, and the like, can be as prone to the gamut of neuroses and psychoses that affect the rest of society, but they are more vulnerable to, and less able to defend themselves against, those fears that a close proximity to death can bring. Although we in the west have an incredible ability to deny our mortality, even in the most extreme conditions, the people that are my concern here may have seen their friends and loved ones die, the person in the bed or armchair next to them could have changed several times, they might be in pain, and they will certainly be aware of their physical decline. Many of their colleagues or fellow residents will have senile dementia or Alzheimer's disease (premature senile dementia) and this also could contribute to their discomfort.

The conditions that I have described seem grim and there can be little hope that the future will improve the circumstances of the group I have defined. Inevitably one of their principal areas of concern is likely to be the approach of death. It will be the thesis of this chapter that working towards death in an open constructive way, as the important conclusion of the growth process, but still part of growing, is a crucial area of work that is sometimes neglected and for which art therapy is uniquely suited. It might seem dismissive, or even callous to place such an emphasis on the acceptance of death with this group. I hope to show that it is neither of these things, and that understanding death is a vital ingredient in the enjoyment of life; an enjoyment of which the elderly and terminally ill are still capable, despite some of the conditions our society compels them to accept. Death is one ol the most difficult subjects to talk about in contemporary western society and there are many people whose reluctance to discuss or in any way confront this subject gives death some of the qualities of a taboo.

Art therapy has developed, in part at least, as a result of the need to find alternatives to verbal forms of communication, to allow people who have difficulty with words to express themselves, and to enable the unsayable to be said. It follows therefore that art therapy can be of great service to workers with the elderly and the terminally ill and I shall be looking at some of the ways this service might be rendered and also at some of the background to this subject.

To say that our society avoids the subject of death is to state the obvious. It is now possible to lead one's life without ever having to see a dead body or even having the subject of death brought sharply into focus, until someone close to you dies and by then it can be difficult to have a healthy attitude towards the event. This denial is often in the guise of protecting people from distress and can take many forms. Children are sometimes excluded from having anything to do with death, they may be sent away to relatives or friends when someone in the house is dying. Euphemisms designed to avoid the explicit statement of death abound in our society. Phrases such as 'passed over' and 'laid to rest' are still often used and it is true, as Aries says, that modern society is 'a society where the interdiction of death paralyses and inhibits the reactions of the medical staff and family involved' (Aries 1976:103). This interdiction of death in the name of preventing distress can take extreme forms and I have seen patients who in the event had only a few hours to live told that they would soon be 'up and about'.

It is true that a belief in one's ability to survive can be a crucial factor in overcoming a great illness and the desire to fight can be an important weapon in the physician's armoury. It is also true that people need an element of hope in their lives in order to carry on. The sudden scientific breakthrough that will lead to a miracle cure, or the unexplained remission of their symptoms are important ideas that people need. These ideas need not, however, exclude the possibility of working towards an understanding and acceptance of death, and they should not result in the total denial of death that seems so common in our society.

There is a time, and there are occasions when death can be a natural, even beautiful event. In the foreword by C. Murray Parkes to the book by Elizabeth Kübler-Ross *On Death and Dying* a patient is quoted as saying 'I *wish* I could tell people how nice it can be to die of cancer' (Kübler-Ross 1970: vii). I have also heard people say similar, if not quite so extreme, things and I feel that it is our life task to work towards death as an acceptable occurrence, the consummation of life rather than its negation.

The reasons for this denial of death in our society could have their foundations in some of our religious, philosophical, and psychological thinking and seem to stem from our predilection for one of the two, seemingly polar, ways of understanding the human psyche. It could be that the emphasis western society places on biology and the empiricism of natural science makes the concept of death threatening and alien. The antithesis of this empirical approach is the gnostic religious view of the world, that in its extreme form is blind faith, and which even the spiritual institutions of the west tend to reject. These two philosophies, one inward and one outward looking, have become mutually exclusive. Jung's view of the world seems to agree with this when he remarks:

> 'In my picture of the world there is a vast outer realm and an equally vast inner realm; between these two stands man, facing now one and now the other, and, according to his mood or disposition, taking the one for the absolute truth by denying or sacrificing the other.'   (Jung 1933:137)

The society in which we live appears to have a preference towards a scientific, or outward view of the world and seems to have 'sacrificed' the inner or mystical aspects of life.

It is this rejection that I feel causes many of the problems related to death that we experience in our society. Why this denial of mysticism should create these problems can perhaps be explained by the multiplicity of mental life, and the fact that the part of the psyche most affronted by death is the ego which is shaped by the reality principle, and which is also the place of fears. An understanding of death, however, must be an instinctive acquisition as we can have no conscious knowledge of what it is like to die, or what happens afterwards. Science, reason, and consciousness then, are not able to contribute a great deal to any understanding of death. If the light of reason cannot illuminate the questions posed by death, and yet reason is considered the only valid source of illumination, dark areas are created into which people choose not to look.

Fortunately reason and intellectual thought are not the only ways of understanding we have at our disposal. There is also a way of thinking in primordial images which Jung explains as a way of thinking in 'symbols which are older than historic man; which have been ingrained in him from earliest times, and, eternally living, outlasting generations, still make up the groundwork of the human psyche' (Jung 1933:130). It is the light of these symbols that I feel is necessary in order to contemplate and understand an eternal theme such as death, and I think art therapy can provide a natural venue for these symbols. The visual arts are one of the best vehicles for discussing recurrent themes that man has invented, and they have been since pre-historic times. It is no coincidence that the arts have often found themselves in the service of a religion, or that death has been one of the principal subjects it has dealt with.

Examples of this preoccupation with death and dying in the arts are not hard to find, and they cut across temporal and cultural boundaries. The Egyptian pyramids, the Taj-Mahal, and medieval manuscripts such as the Winchester psalter with its gruesome depictions of hell, are illustrations from the past. Closer to our own time there are painters such as Mark Rothko, whose work especially in the latter part of his life had a preoccupation with nothingness and non-being, which although abstract seems to be a meditation on the same theme. Fuller writes of Rothko's work: 'Sensuous pleasure is not all there is to a Rothko. Soon there enters in to that subtle drama within the boundaries of his canvases deep black spaces of beckoning nothingness which seem to invite you, the viewer, to annihilate yourself in them' (Fuller 1980:222). For Rothko the result of this medita-tion was his suicide in 1970 after completing a series of paintings in browns, blacks, and greys, that were the epitome of emptiness. Every work of art is, as Kandinsky begins *Concerning the Spiritual in Art*, 'a child of its age, and in many cases the mother of our emotions' (Kandinsky 1914:1). Rothko's work is all of this, and in being a child of its age I believe it reflects our society's difficulty in understanding death and the death drive, Thanatos.

It seems that for Rothko the existence of death eventually made life superfluous, and yet he was a man who had the courage and imagination to confront this problem head on. For other people, living in different societies and times, however, this confrontation had quite an opposite effect on their lives. The ancient Egyptians, for example, devoted much of their cultural activity to the question of death, and yet, unlike Rothko, they seem to have found this life affirming. Dunne (1974) attributes the stability of Egyptian culture for the best part of two millennia to their ability to face death squarely, and to face it with hope, and not need to repress the thought of death in order to be happy. Egyptian art was a way of thinking in primordial images, and was also a function of a religion that embraced death in a positive way.

Tibetan culture also preoccupied itself with death in this confident way, and in the Tibetan Book of the Dead the travels of the spirit during and after death are depicted as a journey through a series of planes of existence or Bardos. The central plane or Bardo is described as a place of positive non-existence. This plane is similar to, and perhaps is the forerunner of, the psychoanalytic notion of a differentiated union at death, as opposed to the chaotic, undifferentiated union of the child at birth. The Tibetans saw this plane of existence as something to work towards, and not a threatening void to be ignored or resisted at all costs.

That some societies have managed to perceive death in this non-threatening way, and yet our society has created the interdict of which I have already spoken, could be part of a more general difference in the way that we see ourselves, that is demonstrated in the analogies that we use to describe our mental and physical processes. The metaphors that ancient man used to describe the world and his journey through it were derived from his immediate surroundings: birds, flowers, trees, and the celestial bodies seen in the sky. The Egyptians said that death was like 'passing through a field of reeds'. With the advent of technology, people began to use the language of objects they had made and the processes that they instigated to understand their existence. The Romans, for example, likened the workings of the heart to a metal refiner's fire. They saw that in each case a liquid entered, underwent a change, and emerged brighter. The refiner's fire was also a popular symbol of purity and the purifying process and is used in the Old Testament in *Malachi* to describe the coming of the Messiah 'But who may abide the day of his coming? and who shall stand when he appeareth? for he is like a refiner's fire' (*Malachi* 3, v.2).

From these simple beginnings a way of perceiving ourselves in terms of the machines we make and the processes we induce developed. This symbolic language is gaining a new vocabulary, and there is an increased momentum to use mechanistic metaphors to describe the lives of human beings. The brain is often compared to a computer, the nervous system to electrical circuits, and the eyes to television cameras. Phrases such as 'electronic eye' and 'artificial intelligence' have become part of our everyday usage. The accuracy of these comparisons is irrelevant, the important fact is that they are made, and made with enough frequency to become an integral part of the way in which we see ourselves. The importance of this imagery must not be underestimated, as it is through symbols such as these that we comprehend all that is most meaningful and tangible to us. Gordon (1978) makes the point that, as it is through images and symbols that we commune with ourselves and each other, the complexion of these images and symbols is of great significance.

These mechanical symbols, as useful as they sometimes are, cannot always illuminate the complex range of situations that constitute human existence. A machine is either on or off, and as a symbol, therefore, it can throw little light on the subtle cycle of birth, differentiation, and death. Also, a machine merely ceases to function, it does not die, and it cannot be aware of its impending demise. It could be that one of the results, or functions, of perceiving ourselves with mechanical symbols is to distance and defend ourselves from death.

Actual mechanical devices can sometimes be used in this way in hospitals. Most modern hospitals contain vast arrays of technical equipment, and it can sometimes seem that patients are treated through the intermediary of this machinery. In the case of the terminally ill patient this situation can become exaggerated, as the staff might feel that they have in some way failed. It can become more emotionally comfortable for the staff to devote their time to the drip or the ECG machine (where they might feel they can have some control, and, even if the patient dies, at least the equipment is working properly) than to become involved with the patient as a human being. The dying patient can therefore become isolated, reduced to the status of a component of the apparatus they are supposed to be served by. In these circumstances it is also possible for the people who visit the terminally ill person to keep their own fears of death in some sort of quarantine as there is an emphasis placed on cure and no need to confront death.

What then can art therapy contribute to this situation of people living in institutions, approaching their demise, and facing the denial of death that seems inherent in our society? First I feel that visual communication can, if not altogether avoid, then circumnavigate the interdict, and allow people to express their anger, acceptance, or fear of death in a way that allows this expression to be acceptable. I have known many people who could not talk about death at all, paint pictures which were overtly concerned with this subject. There are many reasons to explain this, one of which is the fact that paintings are not usually addressed to one particular person, and therefore a statement made in a painting is more likely to be left to stand. One of the results of the repression of the subject of death, is that when people are confronted by its verbal expression they construct a barrier of desensitizing remarks around it. The example that I gave at the beginning of this chapter, where dying patients are told that they will soon be all right, is an example of this. That most people do not feel that they have to react to a painting in this way encourages the dying person to feel freer to express his or her feelings. A second virtue that that visual expression has over other forms of communication is that the painted image can cope with the expression of the infinite and the oblique, in ways that language cannot. As has already been mentioned, expression of the infinite has been one of the principal concerns of the visual arts in many societies. Third, visual images are capable of working on many levels and of expressing seemingly contradictory ideas and feelings simultaneously.

This facility can be vital for the terminally ill patient who may have ambivalent feelings about his or her condition, and need to express anger and depression, or acceptance and fear, in the same image. This duality of feeling is common amongst dying patients; they will sometimes talk quite openly about death in a way that seems accepting, and yet in the next instant make remarks that appear defensive. I feel that it is vital that they are able to fluctuate in this way, and that they are also able to come to terms with death in their own way and in their own time. The many levels on which a visual statement is able to work can allow this ambivalence to be expressed with great ease and fluidity. I have seen people paint pictures depicting their own funeral, perhaps as a way of mourning for themselves and therefore seemingly working towards an acceptance of death, and combining this with images of their anger, clenched fists, and screaming heads, etc.

The visual arts are also able to express abstract qualities and feelings with great precision, and one of the most common feelings, and one of the hardest to describe, is that of physical pain. I remember a patient suffering from rheumatoid arthritis who painted a picture of a flower, and then covered the whole page with thin green lines about one inch apart with a felt-tip pen. The lines were sometimes straight, and sometimes undulating, and were mostly vertical in orientation. She said that they represented the background pain that she always felt, and that this was the best explanation she had ever been able to make of how the pain felt. I said that the effect was rather cage-like, and she agreed saying that being in pain all the time was just like being in prison. This patient was obviously relieved to have externalized her feelings and to have found an equivalent to the way she felt, and she showed the painting to the doctors to help explain her symptoms. The flower in her painting seemed to be a representation of herself, a living thing caged by pain.

Another feature of art therapy that can be important to the elderly and terminally ill patient is that paintings can have a sequential, or cumulative effect, and are therefore capable of depicting change over a period of time. Kübler-Ross has defined a sequence that dying people go through once they are told, or become aware that they are dying. This sequence is denial and isolation, anger, bargaining, depression, and acceptance (Kübler-Ross 1970). I shall use this terminology as I have found it to be accurate, although I have found in my own experience that people often oscillate between two or more of these stages. An example of how a number of paintings can illustrate, and perhaps encourage, the passage of an individual through these stages, is given by the case of an elderly Indian man. This gentleman was attending a day centre for the physically handicapped where I ran an art group. He was suffering from the after effects of a very severe stroke, and had considerable difficulty in moving one side of his body. His first paintings were of a variety of subjects such as animals, people, and landscapes, and he often used photographs to work from. He then had another heart attack and was away from the centre for some time, and his condition was reported to be grave.

When he returned to the centre he was obviously very seriously ill, and his speech had been seriously impaired, a fact which embarrassed him greatly. His painting underwent a change at this point, and although he had far less control, his work became more intense. He embarked on a series of paintings which were all of sunsets. The first of these had, what only can be described as, angry skies. They consisted of bright blues changing to purples and reds, the colours often meeting each other abruptly. The foreground of these paintings frequently had bare trees painted in silhouette probing across the sky, and the overall effect of these paintings was one of emotional disturbance and rage.

Gradually in painting after painting, all of sunsets, the imagery changed. The skies became predominantly red, and the colours began to merge in gentle gradations. The trees in the foreground disappeared and in their place he painted clumps of grass with wild flowers in between, illuminated by the soft glow of the sky behind. This change in his art work corresponded, not surprisingly, with a change in his general demeanour. He became more relaxed, and more prepared to talk despite his speech difficulties, about which he was less embarrassed. It really did seem that he was painting out his acceptance with this series of pictures, and that he was using archetypal imagery. Jung uses the metaphor of the sun's cycle to illustrate the stages of life, and suggests that the duty of ageing people is to use their energy to illuminate themselves. He points out some of the dangers of not doing so when he says:

> 'After having lavished its light upon the world, the sun withdraws its rays in order to illumine itself. Instead of doing likewise, many old people prefer to be hypochondriacs, niggards, doctrinaires, applauders of the past or eternal adolescents – all lamentable substitutes for the illumination of the self, but inevitable consequences of the delusion that the second half of life must be governed by the principles of the first.'
>
> (Jung 1933:125)

It seems to me that the man I have just mentioned was able to use his art work as a way of thinking in primordial images, and was therefore able to come to terms with his situation in a way that conscious thought might not have facilitated.

Another patient who used archetypal imagery in this way was an eighty-year-old Polish woman who attended the art group on the ward of a geriatric hospital. She had lived in this country for the past twenty years and had learnt to speak fluent English. She had been placed on the ward because of her inability to cope with the problems of a stroke she had suffered. This stroke had not only paralysed one side of her body but had also had the unusual effect of making her forget all the English that she had learnt. She could still speak Polish, although this was not a great deal of use on the ward. Her attitude on the ward was often cheerful, and she was always pleased to see visitors, although she would sometimes have spells of uncontrollable weeping.

She painted with great enthusiasm and was always the first to arrive to the group and the last to leave. Her paintings, two of which are reproduced here (see *Illustrations 9.1* and *9.2*) were freely painted and always from her imagination. These two paintings were both painted in the same session and have similar subject content. The first (*Illustration 9.1*) is painted in bright colours and represents the painter sitting on a swing seen through an open door (this is the rectangular shape just below centre). The shapes inside and outside the circular arena were very difficult to understand at first until she mentioned the word 'bacterialogia', and then it became clear that these were different forms of bacteria. It seems then that this picture represents the artist surrounded by a whole host of threatening creatures. She is protected by the door frame, but the door is open and she looks small and rather defenceless compared to her surroundings. The scale inversion of this

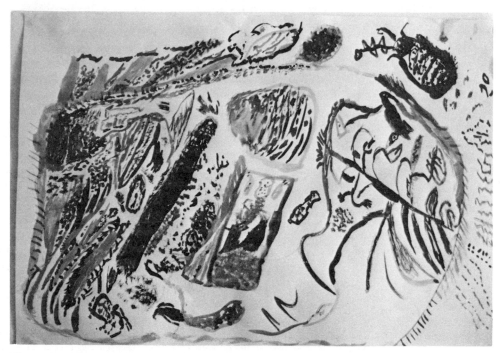

Illustration 9.1

picture, where microscopic animals are made larger than the figure, contribute to the menacing nature of this juxtaposition, and give it an almost science fiction quality. This image works on many levels, but it is as a picture of her in the ward that I feel it is most succinct. For one thing she is both isolated and surrounded, just as she is in the ward sitting-room and in the sleeping area. The circular area that encompasses both the image of the figure and most of the bacteria could be a metaphor for the hospital which contains most of her worries, but there is at least one major area of concern outside the hospital perimeter (she was very worried as to what would happen to her flat now that she was in hospital).

On one level I believe this picture to be about institutionalization, and the concerns of the individual to retain an individuality despite the forces that would destroy this identity. On another level this picture could illustrate some transcendant symbols of the collective unconscious. Bacteria seem to me to be an ideal way of describing unseen yet potentially powerful entities, and as animals I feel they fit Joseph L. Henderson's definition of animals as symbols of transcendence as given in *Man and his Symbols* where he says, 'These creatures, figuratively coming from the depths of the ancient Earth Mother, are symbolic denizens of the collective unconscious. They bring into the field of consciousness a special chthonic (underworld) message' (Jung 1964: 153). One of the chthonic messages that seems to be presented in this image seems to be the painter's concern about death. The large cigar shape to the left of centre has a phallic form, and this effect is increased by the brown and flesh colours in which it is painted. The relationship between the phallus symbol and death is well known, and is personified in the Greek god Hermes. This god who was called 'psycho-pomp' (soul-guide), was represented with an erect phallus, and he had the job of guiding the dead to the underworld. His roles were, according to Henderson, to be a 'messenger, a god of the cross-roads, and finally the leader of souls to and from the underworld. His phallus therefore penetrates from the known into the unknown world, seeking a spiritual message of deliverance and healing' (Jung 1964: 155).

The sexual nature of this client's work could seem overstated were it not for the second painting illustrated here (*Illustration 9.2*). This image, painted on a torn scrap of paper that she found, depicts two bacteria in sexual union. It was painted immediately after the first picture and is one foot by four inches at its widest. The male bacteria (the long thin shape) is open one end and is joined to an open section of the female (the larger heart-shaped form). This could demonstrate that life is flowing from one to the other, and that a significant change is taking place. The female is already pregnant, and the artist made it clear that the three dots in the right hand side of the female would grow into new bacteria.

It could be that these two bacteria are a version of that important symbol

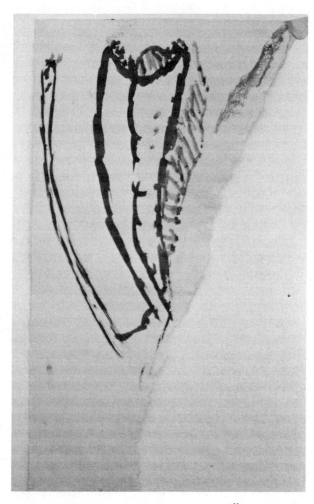

Illustration 9.2

of chthonic transcendence, the two entwined serpents. These serpents are represented in the act of sexual union and are also found in connection with the god Hermes, and in Indian mythology as the Naga serpents. Hermes became the Roman god Mercury, who acquired wings that further reinforced him as a symbol of spiritual transcendence. It seems that in these two related images the idea of personal death and spiritual transcendence are discussed, and that primordial images have been used. I feel that an attempt has been made here to use visual images as a way of uniting the opposing, yet complementary forces of Eros and Thanatos, and that this unity is a goal towards which we all should work.

I feel that I cannot conclude this chapter without saying something about the organization of art groups for the elderly and the terminally ill. Questions such as whether it is preferable to work in groups or in individual sessions, and if a directive or non-directive approach is the best, are issues that all workers in this field must address themselves to. Also the area of recruitment must be considered and the possibility of a formal or informal referral system involving other disciplines should be examined. The answers to these questions cannot exist in a theoretical vacuum, but must take into account the external practical constraints that exist in all areas of work, and which seem especially numerous with this client group. I have often found myself working in corridors, or in screened-off corners of wards with insufficient or inferior materials, and this must affect the way in which one works. However impoverished the environment, I feel that it is possible to find a way of working that is meaningful and it is surprising how things can improve when one has a 'foot in the door'. With the great number of variables affecting work in this area, it is impossible to make any definitive remarks concerning organization, so it must be borne in mind that everything I have to say relates to myself and the situations that I have encountered.

One of the most important elements is, of course, the therapist himself and it is important to devise a way of working in which one feels relaxed and in control. I have a personal preference for working with individuals though I appreciate the value of the group experience. I often see people individually either side of their membership of a group. When clients first find themselves admitted to a ward, an individual session can be extremely useful in getting to know them and in breaking down the inevitable 'I can't paint' feelings. These sessions can be used to develop trust and to make it clear that art is being used as an alternative to verbal forms of expression. The selection of people for these sessions is best done with the consultation of an interdisciplinary team and good relationships with such a team is essential. Individual sessions are also useful when people are no longer able to come to a group because they are too ill. These are perhaps the most important as people often become isolated from human contact just when they need it most. These sessions, sometimes held at the bedside, can be beautiful though traumatic experiences and one should have a good understanding of one's own attitude towards death before undertaking them. The groups themselves I feel should be working towards self-development and illumination through the expressive medium of the visual arts. The function of art therapy with this client group should be to help people towards the realization that different periods of life require different objectives, and what might be right for one period could be wrong for another. The role of the therapist should be to be someone who accepts whatever the patient has to say and who does not 'run a mile' when the topic of death enters the arena.

References

Aries, P. (1976) *Western Attitudes To Death*. London: Marion Boyars.

Dunne, J. (1974) *The City of the Gods*. London: Sheldon Press.

Fuller, P. (1980) *Art and Psychoanalysis*. London: Writers and Readers Cooperative.

Gordon, R. (1978) *Dying and Creating*. The Library of Analytical Psychology, vol. 4. London: The Society of Analytical Psychology.

Kandinsky, W. (1914) *Concerning the Spiritual in Art*. Trans. M. T. H. Sadler. London: Constable.

Kübler-Ross, E. (1970) *On Death and Dying*. London: Tavistock.

Jung, C. G. (1933) *Modern Man in Search of a Soul*. London: Routledge & Kegan Paul.

— (1964) *Man and his Symbols*. London: Aldus.

Biographical note

Bruce Miller Born Liverpool 1947. Studied Graphic Design at Ravensbourne College of Art and Design (1965–66), Painting at Hammersmith College of Art (1966–69), and Art Therapy at Goldsmiths' College of Art (1980–82).

In 1971 I was employed by an analyst to use art with his deaf son. I became an art tutor for an adult education institute in 1973 and in that same year I was given two classes in the Special Education Needs section of the institute. The number of classes grew and in 1981 I was made full-time Lecturer in Art, with half my allocation of hours in the Special Education Needs department. Currently I work with the terminally ill in a day centre and a home for the elderly.

10 | Art therapy in prisons

Joyce Laing

You have to be something of an opportunist to get the arts established in a therapeutic way in prison. Prisons are such jungles. Any well-planned scheme in art therapy, admirably suitable for a hospital or special school, would disappear in the undergrowth of the prison system.

Most prisons are housed in gigantic architectural monstrosities quite out of proportion to our concept of human accommodation needs. Inside, they are densely populated places, often with three men confined in the space of a single cell. The buildings constantly echo with a metal sound, the clanging of keys, and the repetitive slamming of heavy metal doors. Areas are either crowded with prisoners, in their ill-fitting denim uniforms, and with uniformed officers positioned at brief intervals, or at other times the area will be quite deserted. As one penetrates further into the life of the prison one encounters the long history of a haphazard coming together of multitudinous rules and regulations which control those committed to prison.

The prisons and their problems

The history of penology makes fearful reading. Man's inhumanity to man, it seems, has known no bounds. Physical torture, the pillory, banishment, the burning of witches, corporal punishment, and hanging make a heinous catalogue of punishments. Over the centuries prison reformers can take some comfort that these acts have, one by one, been abolished, although the speed at which betterment has come about has been, and still is, painfully slow. Imprisonment is as old as mankind. The powerful held the power of punishment. With no code of justice, enemies or inadequate servants could be thrown into the dungeons. As commercialism grew in the eighteenth century, debtors were sent to jail and their possessions taken. The jails solved nothing, for the debtors could no longer earn to repay their debts.

In the nineteenth century, until 1877, prisons had been the responsibility of local authorities. Attempts, which had been made shortly before this, to bring about a uniformity in the prisons had not succeeded. It was a further effort to impose a uniformity which led to prisons coming under the state. In England and Wales, the prisons became the responsibility of the Home Secretary and in Scotland a separate but parallel scheme was introduced. During this century, small material advances have been made towards improvement of conditions, such as nutrition, education, and recreation. In the Prison Scotland Rules of 1952, Rule 5 states 'The purposes of the training and treatment of convicted prisoners shall be to establish in them the will to lead a good and useful life on discharge, and to fit them to do so.'

However lofty these sentiments, somehow the accent of what goes on within the prisons has remained custodial. The implementation of education facilities, libraries, a work routine, and leisure pursuits has been kept very secondary to containment and the continuance of the militarist regime of instant obedience to the prison officer.

It is interesting to read that in 1895, the then Home Secretary, Asquith, set up a committee to look at prison conditions, which commented, 'few inmates left prison better than they came in'.

Today, prisons are an emotive subject. So why after all the years of enquiries and successive governments is there so little change in the situation? Scarcely a day goes by without the press or media warning of the potentially explosive and violent situation which may erupt at any time in our overcrowded prisons. Perhaps it is the public polarization of opinion which has brought about the present stalemate. There are probably as many 'bring back hanging' lobbyists as there are penal reformers in our society.

Somewhere in between this debate are the people who run the prisons and those who are closely involved with the inmates. There are the politicians who are responsible for the Prison Service. Then there are the civil servants of the Prisons Department, who are responsible to the politicians. There are the prison governors who are responsible to the officials at the Department and there are the prison staff who are, hierarchically, responsible to the governor – to say nothing of the judiciary, the sheriffs, the victims of crime, and the prisoners' families, all clamouring for contradictory retribution or treatment of the offender. It has become an Uncle Tom Cobley and all affair.

In the context of this historical tradition of imprisonment, it is hardly surprising there is conflict about the purpose of prisons. The aims of each prison are decided in a rigidly hierarchical management structure. Strict adherence to the rules fills the void where no internal debate or discussion is permitted. The prisoners are never consulted even on small internal decisions. The daily routine of feeding, exercising, working (if available), recreation, and lock-ups never alters. With so many penal establishments vastly overcrowded, it takes the prison staff all their time just getting through the locking and unlocking routine. For the prisoner, the frustration of the futility of prison existence simmers and bubbles continuously in his mind. Great energy is being spent by the governors immediately responsible in many institutions, at present, just to hold the lid on the bubbling cauldron.

Added to the difficulties and conflicts of aim is the unsuitability of the prison buildings. Most prisons were built in the Victorian era when the concept of mad and bad overlapped. Both categories were determinedly restrained and silenced from public view. The Victorians placed lunatics and criminals ouside their city boundaries, hidden from public scrutiny. While the lunatic asylums were surrounded by rambling woodland parks which served further to screen the patients from pubic awareness, there was also the slender hope that the beauties of nature might alleviate the madness. For the bad, the prisoners were to be encompassed by concrete courtyards and high brick walls. Prison buildings are of considerable ugliness and are mostly constructed on a similar plan of an internal tier system, the cells made accessible by metal stairways and galleries linked by catwalks.

Punitive as the prisons were in Victorian times, they held only a fraction of the number of inmates who, today, are locked in them. The inferior sanitation of that era has in many cases not been improved, in spite of the increase in prisoners, thus imposing a disgraceful state of hygiene which both offenders and staff have to tolerate each day.

In the present system there are various categories of prison; local, training, long-term, open, and so on, designed to meet the sentences imposed by the courts. Just as the legal system is traditionally separate in Scotland from England and Wales, the types and uses of the various prisons also differ and blur. The different types of prison and categories of prisoner throughout the United Kingdom read like a catalogue list. Rules and regulations have been compiled (albeit that the implementation often varies in different establishments) for every possible sentence or category of prisoner.

For the safety and protection of the public, imprisonment of certain offenders is an obvious necessity. While imprisonment can be viewed as a punishment for those convicted of offences, there is no evidence it acts as a deterrent. So unless the prisoner undergoes an experience in prison which will alter his pattern of previous behaviour against society, an experience in which he reviews his standpoint as a member of a social group, imprisonment can only be seen as a futile exercise and a constant strain on the tax-payer.

Art therapy in prisons

What can art therapy offer in this strange, debilitating, and unreal environment? Therapy, usually an integral part of a treatment plan where the patient's relationships with family and friends are strengthened and supported, is expected to take place where family visits, at least in the crucial first stages of a sentence, are limited to a few hours a year.

And how can the art therapist practise his profession, when so often the internal rules of a prison militate against it? Art therapy is about the thoughts, the feelings, and the psyche of the individual, so it is to the recipient (in this case the prisoner) to whom we must first look.

What shall we call the recipient? Patient, client, pupil, or prisoner – does it really matter? Labels do matter; not only are they convenient tags for administrative purposes, they also affect the way the person is perceived. And indeed, the way in which the person perceives the self.

The therapist is not a moralist and while it would not be helpful to discard knowledge of the prisoner's past record, the person in therapy, whatever term is used, is first and foremost a fellow human being. And the prisoner, coming into a therapy situation, seeks after change in some way. Whatever nature this quest for change takes, it cannot be enforced and so the art therapist working in prison has to create an environment in which the therapy aspect of art therapy becomes more or less invisible. Fortunately, the arts are an acceptable shop window in prisons and it is the skill of the therapist to mould the use of the arts for the therapeutic benefit of each individual he or she seeks to help.

The patient, with the exception of a few severely mentally ill, has an overwhelming desire to get well, to restore, or to improve his health. The client, with social difficulties, seeks to alter the environment or transient circumstances which are proving a strain for himself and his family. In such cases the therapist can readily share compassionately and join in a partnership to unravel the origins of the problem and set in motion healing energies. It is much more difficult to identify with the prisoner who may have committed some terrible crime; yet it is the crime which is evil. The prisoner is a fellow human being.

Once the criminal is in prison, his outlook is a bleak one. First, he will experience the instinctive drive to escape from incarceration. Like all species of animal, humans have a primal need for freedom. Enforced imprisonment touches the deepest psychological forces of the mind, although it is unlikely the prisoner will think of it in these terms. More likely, he will rationalize his situation, blaming the judge, the witnesses, his co-accused, and maybe friends and family. Loss of liberty may in itself be the punishment for the crime, unfortunately it seldom brings with it repentance. Nor does it appear to have much deterrent effect judging by the number of recidivists in our prisons.

In the unreal environment of the prison, the art therapist must not lose sight of his goals. Somehow he has to work through the mind of the prisoner, which can always remain free. Art therapy has to release within the prisoner the ability to pour on to paper or canvas the pent-up emotions and the deeper images of the unconscious. The therapist has to establish a relationship with the prisoner in which, together, they can explore the underlying motives or attitudes which cause his anti-social activities. Surprisingly, of all the professionals – the doctors, the social workers, the psychologists, or the teachers – who work in a supportive role with the prisoners, it is the artist who may have the closest personality traits. For it seems there may be underlying links in the drive of certain offenders and that of the creative artist.

While labelled as deviants, many offenders are inventive, ingenious, quick-witted and have great vitality. It may be that the creative aspects of the criminal have, for reasons of background experience or psychological make-up, been misdirected towards destructive ends. If the art therapist can channel these talents in a positive, creative direction, the offender will experience a new perception of the self and where he belongs in society. Over the weeks in which the art work is being produced, step by step, an alteration in his previous thinking pattern will take place. The more he becomes engrossed in art, the less likely will he be content to see himself just as a criminal who is destroying his own potential prospects and the lives of his family, as well as being a menace to everyone else. Art opens so many doors in life. By studying the history of fine art, which is a social document about people and the history of mankind, the prisoner extends his understanding of his own background and that of others, and is thus helped to see himself more objectively. Most likely the prisoner will have rejected a formal education in his childhood or youth. Or maybe one could view it as the educational system which has failed to meet his needs. What is apparent in so many young adult prisoners is the avid thirst for knowledge. Art therapy then has to provide a true educational gateway where the prisoner can become genuinely curious and keen to learn.

Each art work produced, in any medium, is more than just a statement; it is also a mirror of the person's thinking at that point of time. Each week will lead to further research of the way artists and poets in the past have portrayed that theme and of how the prisoner may set about subsequent art works. In the Barlinnie Special Unit (Carrell and Laing 1982), where so much art work is created, it can be seen how the prisoners who have produced many works, have gone on to study allied subjects at university level. It was their own involvement in creativity which directed them on the journey of discovery.

Art therapy and art education

There is in the prison service a network of education units. Prisoners are usually allowed, subject of course to numerous conditions, to attend certain day classes for a few hours a week. Most prisoners are entitled to enrol for one or two evening classes to be attended weekly. The subjects and courses offered are very varied, ranging from classes in remedial education to Open University study. Education is defined by the Prisons Department as being a privilege, not a right, for prisoners, consequently the participation in a course of studies can be suspended at the discretion of the governor.

The arts are here defined as any original creative work, however unskilled, in the media of painting, sculpture, music, creative writing, poetry, film-making, play-writing, theatre, and any of the art crafts, provided that each work is the spontaneous venture of the producer. Crafts such as rug-making, weaving, or painting to a given pattern, copying, etc., are not regarded as art forms.

The arts then can encompass any creative medium provided the works express the prisoner's thoughts, feelings, or ideas in his own way. Essentially, the arts are communication. The educational and therapeutic aspects of the arts are not separate entities but rather points on a continuum, both being complementary to the other. From the educational end of the spectrum towards the therapeutic, the arts include technical skills, craftsmanship, experimentation of media, study of the history of art, art appreciation, self-expression, spontaneous image-making, psychotherapeutic art. While this definition may be obvious in theory, it has become blurred in practice with, only too often, emphasis and encouragement being given in prisons, under the label of art, to slick copy-productions.

One of the first experiences the newly appointed artist to the prison is likely to encounter is to be shown the many paintings and drawings which the inmates have already produced; and there will be a great many. Commercialized art is one of the ongoing businesses in prisons. There will be numerous examples of 'Constables' and 'Van Goghs', a smattering of 'Raphael' religious works, not to mention the plethora of nudes, poodle dogs, and wee girls crying. Some will have been executed with remarkable skill, the producer having spent many hours on the detail and lifelikeness of his paintings. The market seems always to be there – visitors, cell-mates, and staff are all good customers for this superficial, 'best-seller' type of picture. The art therapist or art teacher will have to encounter this anti-art movement in his own way. Once art of authentic and genuine merit is established, the copyists' work seems to fade away.

Group therapy or individual therapy

The prison governor is most likely to expect the art therapist to take groups of prisoners. Simple arithmetic dictates this will offer better value for money and unless the therapist puts forward a good case to see individuals, groups may be programmed in for hourly, or two-hourly, sessions. Even more likely is that the prison staff will call the groups 'classes', thus implying that they will be seen as teaching sessions in the scholastic sense. The therapist must work out very carefully how he wants to practise before having preconceived notions foisted on him. There are also the expectations of the prisoners to be considered. Many who would be quite enthusiastic about attending art classes may be wary of attending an art group, with its possible connotations of a 'psyche' group meeting. Much of the art therapist's initial work is in breaking down these false notions and this is not an easy task when he will probably be the only artist, and his ideas may compete, or conflict, with the traditionally instilled beliefs of hundreds of prison staff. As well as the concept of an art group being established in the institution, it is also vital to discuss the selection of prisoners to be allocated to the groups. To overcome it being seen, in the inmates' eyes, as a 'cissy' option or a group for the 'mad', there is much to be said for including one or two 'hard men'. It can be seen that the art therapist is initially dependent on the assistance of senior staff in selecting workable groups. Further, there is the psychologically disturbed inmate to consider and in what setting he can best be supported.

Many prisons operate an assessment period for newly admitted young prisoners and, if it is possible for the art therapist to take on an assessment group, it will provide an opportunity to get to know all the inmates. Thereafter, the therapist will be in a position to join in staff discussion about selection and to recognize the individual needs of each inmate.

Few prisons will have had a previous art therapist, so the initial phase is also a critical stage. It is on the first few weeks of art therapy being established that its reputation will be based.

Prior to commencing, an area in the prison will have been designated for art therapy. The image of art is more important than the practical issues of good light and running water and it will be fortunate indeed if the selected space offers these commodities. The image however will to some extent be dictated by the area of the prison in which art therapy is established. For example, if the room is near the chapel, it will carry an aura of religion, the spiritual, the serious. If it is in an educational venue, it will be seen as another academic class. If in the hospital wing, it will gain the 'psyche', but perhaps also the healing, label. As it is almost certain that HM prisons will not have a purpose-built space for art therapy, the therapist will have to choose with care, considering all the merits, the drawbacks, and the implications of suggested spaces. Most likely, it will be an area of corridor or extended storage space which is offered. It would be well worth the artist taking his time to walk through the institution and when some area appeals, putting in a request for it. Art of a therapeutic nature will be a new venture for most prison governors, so it may be that the end of a corridor sealed off by fire doors, would make a good art therapy studio but would not have been thought of by the governor or staff as being suitable or even possible. Once the space has been agreed upon, then the art therapist enters a public relations or image selling stage. If the space can be made colourful, lively and inviting, many barriers and apprehensions will be broken down.

As the concept of an art studio being open during the day is established, prisoners will become curious. Few prisoners are mentally ill and understandably will resent the idea that they need therapy. As the concept of the artist seems readily acceptable, it may be worth while simply being considered as the artist who visits the prison. It seems that as long as no great emphasis is laid on the term 'therapy', the actual art activities, run on psychotherapeutic lines, are received agreeably.

If a prisoner is referred for individual therapy by the psychiatrist or the governor, the therapist must make it quite clear to everyone involved that the decision must be that of the prisoner to accept or reject individual sessions. Usually referred prisoners have been having a hard time emotionally for whatever reason, and will welcome the opportunity to be seen regularly.

The prisoner has the stress of the prison environment twenty-four hours a day and it would be no kindness to work too deeply or too quickly into psychological problems, leaving him to bear the memories or guilt until the next session. Nor would it be deserved by the prison staff who have enough to do without picking up the pieces resulting from a therapy session. Further, there are the fellow inmates to consider, who may have to share a cell many hours of the day and night, and who will have enough problems of their own.

Some prisoners, who are not allowed to mix freely with the others for security reasons, albeit temporarily, will have to be seen in their cells, or maybe in a punishment cell. In these cases it is important to inform prison staff of the exact nature of the art materials to be taken into the cell. The very basic materials are all that are required – paper, pencil, non-toxic crayons. Paints, or other materials, are unlikely to be allowed and, frustrating as this may be for the artistically skilled inmate, it should not hamper his self-expression.

As there are few provisions available for the prisoner to store or display his art, the art therapist may need to take on the responsibility of looking after work. Many therapists prefer to keep the art work, dated and documented, for their own reference. It is usually a matter for discussion between prisoner and art therapist as to the safekeeping of poems and writing, as well as paintings and craft.

Women in prison

The whole concept of women being imprisoned is, in this day and age, a questionable one. Few women offenders constitute a public danger and most could be dealt with in outside residential accommodation, if needed, or given non-custodial sentences. More and more, psychologists and criminologists are further suggesting that the present system of incarcerating women in prison, who have alcohol related problems, are homeless, or psychologically unstable, is making matters worse for them. Separated from their children and homes, women's imprisonment adds great hardships on the family and may put the marriage in jeopardy.

Criminologist Pat Carlen argues that women's imprisonment 'has traditionally been characterized by its invisibility, its domesticity and its infantilisation' (Carlen 1983:18). Certainly, judges and sheriffs often refer to women's prisons as being like places of domestic education. Thus the prisoners are seen as inadequate, rather than in need of imprisonment. Prison staff claim they have to look after disturbed women, again suggesting they are seen as unstable or ill, rather than just criminal. Nevertheless, women's prisons are run on full prison regulations and the prisoners are not only treated as subordinates, but often thought of as like children. In this situation of contradictions, of infantilization, of rewards for conforming and punishment for individuality, the art therapist faces a difficult role of identity. Therapy has to be supportive rather than analytic. It has to be a comfort and can do little by opening up past wounds. The contradictory world of prison, mocked up in a home style, makes it too distant for the women to remember with clarity their outside difficulties. Mostly, the women, only too conscious of their children and family left outside, learn to slide through, as quietly and hopefully as quickly as possible, the time of their sentence.

Participation in the arts and fine art crafts can be cheering and also of consolation to many women. Apart from those genuinely enthusiastic about art, some women prisoners choose to retreat to their cells and engross themselves in a piece of craft work, in preference to being under constant staff surveillance and the pressure of fellow inmates in a common room. If a prisoner becomes disturbed, either as a reaction to a situation or as a result of an underlying psychological state, art materials may be withdrawn from her use. Again, art is seen as a privilege, and there is evidence that therapy from whichever specialist, is also considered to be a luxury and something to be given as a reward for good behaviour. The therapist once more must turn his energies to communicating with staff and helping them to see that the use of art may well alleviate, rather than aggravate tension.

For the longer-term prisoner, one-to-one therapy sessions have some hope of success. If it is possible, a wide range of art materials makes participation more exciting and also helps to extend the range of skills which can be learned.

Women prisoners seem much less concerned about the 'psyche' label on art therapy sessions than the male prisoners and often request to be seen, as a form of treatment. A good therapeutic relationship can also result from a woman inmate seeing the artist each week with her paintings or embroidery. It makes for a relaxed atmosphere for the prisoner and little by little emotional difficulties will emerge and can be discussed without strain. Art sessions are viewed as less threatening than therapy sessions, by the staff. Needlework still retains something of a socially acceptable Victorian-lady image and it is the prisoner rather than the artist who is quick to capitalize on this acceptable guise.

The content of the art productions is similar to that in any woman's setting. There does seem to be emphasis on scenes with cottages, animals, children, trees, and flowers. The pictures are often portrayals of the idyllic, the peaceful. Occasionally, turbulent, violent, and aggressive images appear indicating the underlying stress of the inmate. Poems take a very personal note and the women, understandably, are at pains to keep them private. It is important to protect this need for privacy. A wrong word or criticism, whether by fellow inmate or prison officer, may mean an end to the women using this means of expression.

If a prison officer is instructed to sit in on therapy sessions, whether in a women's or a men's prison, it poses a multitude of hazards for the art therapist. Immediately, it negates individual therapy sessions; however, it may be possible to work out a staff training programme in which a selected member of staff can attend group sessions on a regular basis. The art therapist in this situation will also be training the prison officer in group therapy techniques. Staff, denied access to all art therapy sessions will, naturally, become suspicious of them. Staff, on the other hand, who attend art therapy sessions as part of the training in caring for inmates, may help to improve relationships for everyone involved. It is something which requires serious thought and detailed discussion with senior staff.

The Special Unit, Barlinnie Prison, Glasgow

Following the abolition of capital punishment in 1965, concern began to grow within the prison system about the life sentence prisoner. With very long sentences and consequently little to lose, it was feared some might become uncontainably disruptive. By the late 1960s, there was growing evidence of violence by a few prisoners against prison staff, although the prisoners were already in conditions of the strictest security, solitary confinement, and segregation.

In 1970 a Working Party was set up by the Scottish Prisons Department to consider 'The Treatment of Certain Male Long-Term Prisoners and Potentially Violent Prisoners'. This Working Party recommended the setting-up of a special unit which opened in 1973, segregated from the main prison, but within the confines of HM Prison, Barlinnie, Glasgow. Based on the concept of the therapeutic community, the Special Unit operates by the mutual trust of prisoner and prison officer. Each prisoner not only has to work out his own life-style and behaviour within the Unit, but also is responsible for helping his fellow inmates. Prisoners and prison officers have an equal say in the day-to-day running of the Unit and all the internal decision-making. As it was not possible to offer a work scheme for inmates, each one has to decide on his own routine. They wear their own clothes, decorate their cells, cook their meals, and together work out the daily living. Each member of the community is accountable to a weekly community meeting.

Shortly after the opening of the Special Unit, I was asked by the governor if I would consider trying to interest the prisoners in art. There were, at that time, five inmates, all recently transferred from solitary confinement in other prisons, where they had been placed because of their repeated violent and disruptive behaviour. In the first few weeks I found it impossible even to get the inmates to touch the art materials. All were in something of a state of shock at the extreme polarization of their transfer. They would sit suspiciously watching me as I chatted about art and tried in vain to encourage them to participate. Eventually I decided just to work on some art piece of my own and, that day, one of the prisoners asked if I would leave some clay for him. By my next visit he had made a few small works. One entitled 'Solitary' was a striking piece evoking all the isolation and despair of solitary confinement. That inmate, Jimmy Boyle, later went on to write *A Sense of Freedom*, in which he described his first experience with art materials.

> 'I began to pour all my energies into this new means of expression and was knocked out by the depth of feeling when I completed a piece of sculpture. . . . I worked at a prolific rate with most of the work based on the expressions of my soul with pain/anger/hate/love/despair and fears embodied in it. This was very important for me as a person because it allowed me to retain all these very deep emotional feelings but to channel them in another way – sculpture.'   (Boyle 1977:251)

From these first tentative pieces of sculpture, the arts took off in the Unit. Now, ten years later, most inmates who have been in the Unit involve themselves in some art or craft form. Furthermore, the concept of creativity permeated through the daily living. The concrete courtyard is transformed into a garden. The walls are hung with paintings, pieces of sculpture are displayed through the main hallway, ceramics and crafts fill every shelf. Each inmate has to find his own space in which to work. They have access at all times to any type of tool they need for their art or craftwork. On no occasion have these tools been misused. These men with the most serious records of violence in former prisons, now peaceably spend their time involved creatively.

In this unique experiment in penology in world terms, the community has grown in maturity. The Special Unit is about living creatively and positively to the mutual benefit of everyone involved. After ten years, it can no longer be regarded simply as an experiment. Its success raises very real questions for the prison system. It further reveals how the arts can be used as an integral part of a rehabilitative approach.

Art is not a privilege or a luxury, it is an essential part of life. Art in prisons, by releasing tension, aggression, hatred, and violence into a meaningful form of expression offers a basis for building relationships. The art therapist working in prisons has to use every opportunity to ignite the creativity which lies dormant in the prisoners. It will be through their own journey in the arts that the prisoners will rebuild their lives in an intelligent way, which society can accept.

Illustration 10.1   'Christ' (pen and ink drawing; knife-slashed paper at top left)

One of the first drawings by a young man transferred to the Barlinnie Special Unit because of violent behaviour in a previous prison.

Still angry and suspicious, he was initially confused by the sudden transformation of his new environment. He found the relaxation of constant supervision, the friendliness of the staff, and the access to tools and art materials difficult to accept.

Having drawn the Christ, he slashed the paper with a knife and discarded the drawing on the floor.

He has gone on to painting, sculpting, and studying most of the time.

Illustration 10.2 Solitary confinement (gouache colours)

The despair, anguish, and utter loneliness of solitary confinement are portrayed in this painting by a youth on borstal training. Although unskilled as an artist, he has conveyed his emotional state quite vividly and without glamorizing the experience.

Illustration 10.3   Pierrot (fabric scraps and embroidery)

A pierrot doll was designed and made by a seventeen-year-old inmate of a women's prison. It was constructed out of pipe-cleaners, fabric scraps, and embroidered. The prisoner became enchanted by the theme of the pierrot, producing numerous paintings about them, collecting pictures of pierrots out of magazines, and making this doll. At first the paintings portrayed a very tearful figure, bravely trying to smile through the adversity. As her date of liberation drew near, she began to ask for 'artistic' advice to make the pierrot portraits appear to smile more. The traditional tear continued to be given prominence.

The clown image is frequently portrayed in the paintings by women in prison. The funny and stupid circus clown, the stylish harlequin, the sad and foolish clown, the witty jester, and the ever beautiful, young and asexual pierrot mirror the perception the women have of themselves.

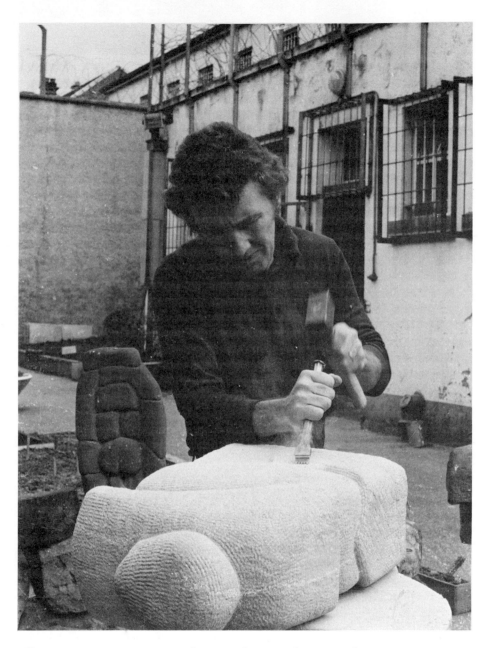

Illustration 10.4   Inmate sculpting (The Special Unit, Barlinnie Prison, Glasgow)

Early in the history of the Special Unit, sandstone from old buildings was formed by the inmates into a circle. Within the circle, like a miniature Stonehenge, the stone to be sculpted was set on an old cable drum. It is unlikely, at that stage, that the inmates were aware of the ancient stone circles. To them it represented the group.

References

Babington, A. (1968) *The Power to Silence: A History of Punishment in Britain.* London: Robert Maxwell.
Boyle, J. (1977) *A Sense of Freedom.* Edinburgh: Canongate.
Carlen, P. (1983) *Women's Imprisonment: A Study in Social Control.* London: Routledge & Kegan Paul.
Carrell, C. and Laing, J. (1982) *The Special Unit, Barlinnie Prison: Its Evolution through its Art.* Glasgow: Third Eye Centre.
Fitzgerald, M. and Sim, J. (1979) *British Prisons.* Oxford: Basil Blackwell.
Laing, J. (1975) Recurring Fantasies in the Paintings and Writings by Sadomasochists. In I. Jakab and S. Karger (eds) *Transcultural Aspects of Psychiatric Art.* Basle: S. Karger.

Biographical note

Joyce Laing Following Fine Art Studies at Gray's School of Art, Aberdeen, Joyce Laing became Art Therapist to the Deeside Sanatoria. She studied psychotherapy and established the first Art Therapy department in Scotland at the Ross Clinic, Aberdeen. Following a Nuffield Fellowship in Art and Psychopathology, she worked with patients in general and psychiatric hospitals, in child and adolescent psychiatry, and with young persons and adults in prison.

Founder member of the British Association of Art Therapists (BAAT) and the Scottish Association of Art Therapists, from 1970–80 Joyce Laing was Chairwoman of the Scottish Society of Art and Psychology. She is a council member of the Société Internationale de Psychopathologie de l'Expression and a member of the Scottish Committee for Arts and Disability.

11 | *Art games and group structures*

Marian Liebmann

Introduction

Art therapy originated with the general practice of one therapist working with a number of clients but the therapist's interaction with each was on a one-to-one basis. More recently the use of structured group interaction in art therapy has become quite widespread. Most art therapy groups use some kind of theme, game, or structure to stimulate group learning and discussion, and a group setting is useful for teaching purposes as well. Very little has so far been written about how the particular choice of activity may influence the experience of the group and the individuals in it (Denny 1975:132).

In this chapter, I shall be looking at the use of games or structured activities in some art therapy groups. Some of the material will be based on a survey of forty art therapists (all working with groups), whom I interviewed as part of my MA dissertation for Birmingham Polytechnic in 1979, and some will be drawn from the subsequently published compendium of art games and structures for groups (Liebmann 1982). Finally I shall give some detailed examples of art therapy in different group settings, to show the wide variety of experiences which may occur.

Groupwork and art therapy

In common with many other disciplines, art therapy has moved from depending on an 'individual casework' approach to including a groupwork approach where suitable. It seems worth looking at the general reasons for using groupwork rather than individual therapy (Brown 1979). These may be summarized as follows:

1 Much of social learning is done in groups; therefore groupwork provides a relevant context in which to practise.
2 People with similar needs can provide mutual support for each other, and help with mutual problem-solving.
3 Group members can learn from the feedback from other members; 'It takes two to see one' (Culbert 1967).
4 Group members can try new roles, from seeing how others react (role-modelling), and can be supported and reinforced in this.
5 Groups can be catalysts for developing latent resources and abilities.
6 Groups are more suitable for certain individuals, e.g. those who find the intimacy of individual work too intense.
7 Groups can be more democratic, sharing the power and responsibility.
8 Some therapists/groupworkers find groupwork more satisfying than individual work.
9 Groups can be an economical way of using expertise to help several people at the same time.

However there are also some disadvantages:

1 Confidentiality is more difficult because more people are involved.
2 Groups need resources and can be difficult to organize.
3 Less individual attention is available to members of a group.
4 A group may be 'labelled' or acquire a stigma.   (Brown 1979:11–12)

Many of these points are relevant to groups working with art, and there are some further aspects specifically related to art therapy groups. In my survey, I interviewed art therapists working in a wide variety of treatment and educational settings: general psychiatric and day hospitals, probation and social services day-centres, schools, adolescents units, art therapy colleges, adult education institutes. They were working with an even wider cross section of the community: long-stay and geriatric patients, acute psychiatric patients, mentally handicapped, ex-offenders, social work clients, alcoholics, families, children, art therapists, and social workers in training.

I asked all the therapists what purposes their groups had, and the answers seemed to fall into two clusters, personal and social. The purposes mentioned are summarized in *Tables 11.1* and *11.2*.

Table 11.1	*Table* 11.2
General personal purposes (not in any order)	*General social purposes (not in any order)*
1 Creativity and spontaneity.	1 Awareness, recognition, and appreciation of others.
2 Confidence-building, self-validation, realization of own potential.	2 Co-operation, involvement in group activity.
3 Increase personal autonomy and motivation, develop as individual.	3 Communication.
4 Freedom to make decisions, experiment, test out ideas.	4 Sharing of problems, experiences, and insights.
5 Express feelings, emotions, conflicts.	5 Discovery of universality of experience/uniqueness of individual.
6 Work with fantasy and unconscious.	
7 Insight, self-awareness, reflection.	6 Relate to others in a group, understanding of effect of self on others, and relationships.
8 Ordering of experience visually and verbally.	
9 Relaxation.	7 Social support and trust.
	8 Cohesion of group.
	9 Examine group issues.

Source: Liebmann (1981:27).

As the tables show, art therapists saw their groups as aiming to enhance and sometimes change the personal and social functioning of the group members, rather than as a specific treatment for a particular disease. This ties in with the fact that many art therapists run workshops of a similar kind for people in the wider community.

It is probably worth drawing out the aspects of groupwork which are enhanced by using art as the group activity:

1 Everyone can join in at the same time, at their own level. The process of the activity is important, and a scribble can be as much of a contribution as a finished painting.
2 Art can be another important avenue of communication and expression, especially when words fail.
3 Art facilitates creativity.
4 Art is useful in working with fantasy and unconscious.
5 Art products are tangible and can be examined at a later time.

To summarize, art therapy groups can provide a combination of individual and group experiences which draw on the traditions of both groupwork and art therapy.

Structured art therapy groups

Most art therapy groups, in common with other 'small groups', have a membership of between six and twelve, although larger groups are occasionally manageable. This size is important to ensure the following factors:

1 Members can maintain visual and verbal contact with all other members.
2 Group cohesiveness can be achieved.
3 There is an opportunity for each person to have an adequate share of time in discussion.
4 There are enough people to encourage interaction and a free flow of ideas, and to undertake group projects.   (Douglas 1976: 85–6)

Some art therapists work non-directively using a non-theme centred approach which McNeilly (1983) suggests amounts to 'group analytic art therapy'. However, my concern here is with directive group techniques, with those groups which undertake a particular task to do together. Working in a 'structured' way can include using just a simple boundary rule (e.g. paint what you like, but use only three colours); or more prescribed activities (e.g. choose one crayon and have a non-verbal conversation with one other person on the same sheet of paper). Whatever structures are used, they can usually be interpreted on many levels, and can act as a stimulus to creativity or to exploring certain areas of human conduct.

Most art therapy groups have a similar format: (1) introduction; (2) activity; and (3) discussion (Liebmann 1979: 51–6). It is worth looking at each of these in turn.

1 *Introduction*   This might include a welcome to the group if it is a new activity, introductions if there are new members, and explanation of the purpose of the group, any specific boundary rules (e.g. no smoking, feel free not to join in, etc.), a 're-cap' of previous sessions if part of a series. Some therapists include a physical movement or relaxation 'warm-up' at this stage, or check out how people are feeling (verbally or using paints).

The main activity or theme for the session is then introduced. Usually the therapist chooses the activity, according to what has gone on in previous sessions, or the issues that are important at that time. Groups which have been together for some time often play a significant part in choosing the activity for a particular session, and also take on more responsibility in others ways, helping new members for example.

2 *Activity*   This usually takes about half the available time. In institutions this often amounts to 30–45 mins, as the timetable usually allows for $1\frac{1}{2}$–2 hours for the whole session. For community groups and art therapy students, sessions can be longer.

Art therapists have to decide to what extent they will participate at this stage. This decision depends on several factors, such as personal philosophy and orientation of the therapist, the kind of group, and the particular activity. Some therapists do join in, because it helps to break down barriers – if they are asking group members to reveal themselves, then participation by the therapist facilitates this process within the group.

3 *Discussion* This usually takes the second half of the session, and can take many forms. Sometimes each person has a share of the time available; sometimes everyone contributes to the discussion of one or two paintings; sometimes everyone relates how he or she felt during a group painting; sometimes the therapist takes charge of the discussion. There are many ways of discussing the art products, according to the philosophy and theoretical orientation of the therapist, the setting, and the particular group.

There are of course other formats for structured art therapy groups, for instance discussion followed by painting (geriatric group needing time to bring back memories), or inclusion of social time (group for mentally handicapped living in the community).

Many sessions form part of a larger programme (e.g. therapeutic community, alcoholics' day hospital) which influences what goes on. Some are closed groups running for, say, six sessions; others are open groups (e.g. many acute ward groups in psychiatric hospitals) with a constantly changing membership; and in between these extremes there are groups with some continuity, but fresh members may join if they wish (many probation and social services day-centres).

In the wider community many people take part in such groups on an occasional basis, for instance at a conference on creative therapies, or church gatherings, but it must be emphasized that the participants attend for other reasons, such as learning new techniques and to experience personally their effects within a group.

I have described some of the usual formats for structured art therapy groups, but what actually happens in the group is influenced by many other factors. The group membership, different leaders, and settings have a strong influence; the support of other staff in an institution can be crucial. The way the art group complements or contrasts with the rest of the programme plays its part. Different therapists have different styles and lay emphasis on different things and an obvious factor is the space and materials available.

A practical example will illustrate some of the different outcomes of one particular exercise. The following extract gives the comments of three art therapists who have all used the same exercise with groups, 'Draw an advertisement for yourself'. (The first two therapists work with psychiatric inpatients and day-patients in a hospital, the third works in a social services day-centre for ex-psychiatric patients.)

Therapist 1: 'The purpose of this is to look at positive self-image. It is useful with a particularly depressed group – lots of positive feedback from group members to other individuals.'

Therapist 2: 'A difficult theme which needs careful introduction, but can become very negative, I've found.'

Therapist 3: 'I usually suggest that people consider not only those aspects of themselves which are worthwhile but also what kind of people they wish to attract.... Becoming conscious of how one presents oneself publicly is a difficult enterprise and people often present their disabilities and uncertainties rather than their abilities and good points.'   (Liebmann 1979: 127–28)

In therapy, many difficulties are confronted, but it is important to keep the amount of stress in groups within the bounds of what the group can cope with. Some art therapists have found the concept of 'games' helpful here, and I shall explore this in the next section.

Games and play

To some art therapists the words 'game' and 'play' are inappropriate words because they suggest a frivolous activity, or an activity which ought always to be fun; and therapy on the other hand is a serious business. In some hospitals art therapists feel the use of 'games' or 'play' would undermine the value of their work in other staff's eyes.

However there is a burgeoning literature on games of all sorts, mostly for groups, and mostly concerned with enhancing people's experience of themselves and others. There are manuals of 'growth games', 'movement games', 'drama games', 'new games', to mention but a few (Brandes and Phillips 1979; Butler and Allison 1978; Fluegelman 1978; Höper *et al.* 1975; Lewis and Streitfeld 1970; and Orlick 1982). They are used with children and with adults, with special groups and with community groups. Many art therapists use them alongside art activities. In what sense is the word 'games' used?

In the sphere of 'personal growth', a game is any activity which is based on rules which define the framework of that activity and can be used to play. In a worthwhile game, these rules are flexible enough to be interpreted in different ways to allow for many levels of response, and the rules can also be changed by agreement of the participants. A definition of play which underlines many of the manuals is the one given by Huizinga: 'Play is an activity which proceeds within certain limits of time and space, in a visible order, according to rules freely accepted, and outside the sphere of necessity or material utility' (Huizinga 1970: 47).

Any game constitutes a 'real life' situation in microcosm. This provides one of the most significant qualities for therapy: a parallel frame of reference which operates alongside 'real life' but does not become confused with it. Games can also provide indirect approaches to matters of moment which may be difficult to confront directly. In this way, they can be used as experimental learning processes. Because there are no real life consequences of a game, or there should not be, it may be possible to try out new aspects of oneself without excessive risk.

The opposite of 'play' is not seriousness, but 'non-play' (Huizinga 1970: 10, 47). Sometimes maximum enjoyment is only achieved by playing seriously; there is no game at all if people refuse to play.

In my survey, about two-thirds of the art therapists I interviewed referred to at least some of their structured activities with groups as 'games'. I would like to include three of these therapists' comments:

> Therapist A: 'A game is a collection of loosely bound rules with a light-hearted feel, which can lead unwittingly into pertinent areas – though it needn't do that.'
> Therapist B: 'Like play, games reflect individual inner experience plus the interaction of the group on these.'
> Therapist C: 'Games relax people, give them confidence and enjoyment, and can also be revealing.' (Liebmann 1979: 70)

These comments show another important aspect of games, their ability to be taken on many levels, according to individual needs or wishes. Since art shares this capacity, 'art games' should be very flexible tools!

Most games need at least two players, some of them need a group to be really enjoyable. Thus the group activities which come nearest to 'art games' are those which (as well as being played with the attitude outlined above) require a group as an integral part of the game, as well as for the discussion. (I have included a special section of these in my collection of Art Games, compiled from the art therapists I interviewed (Liebmann 1982: 43–53).)

How does the 'games attitude' help us with the problems involved in using the exercise 'Draw an advertisement for yourself'? If we regard this exercise as a game whose outcome does not quite satisfy us, then we are free to change or add to the rules. Below are three modifications invented by different art therapists:

1 After each person has drawn a self-advertisement, others in the group add qualities they think have been missed.
2 Imagine you are the owner of a department store, displaying your personal qualities. Others in the group can then select, from the wares on display, things they find particularly attractive.
3 Paint a badge to advertise yourself, and when you have finished, wear it. Then everyone in the group paints badges for everyone else, so that you can compare how you see yourself and how others see you.

(Liebmann 1979: 128)

This section can do no more than point the way to a concept of 'art games' which draws on the traditions of individual art therapy, groupwork, and the newer developments in group games. The rest of this chapter will be devoted to accounts of different art therapy groups, compiled from interviews with the art therapists leading them. All groups are different, and I would not claim that the selection which follows is 'typical' or 'comprehensive', rather it demonstrates the wide range of possibilities.

Examples of art therapy groups

Three groups are described in detail, and then a brief summary given of others. The first example is of a new group using a theme related to issues relevant to the group.

New group at an alcoholics unit

The alcoholics unit is a day hospital accommodated in a converted Georgian house. Recovering alcoholics attend daily for an average of six weeks for an intensive programme of group therapy and educational sessions. They are encouraged to express their feelings and work through them in a variety of ways, such as verbal discussion groups and role plays, which can be quite direct and confrontative.

Most of the art therapy sessions so far have provided an intentional contrast to the rest of the programme, with clients pursuing their own work (although meeting as a group), under the guidance of the art therapist at the unit. Recently however the art therapist invited a colleague from a neighbouring hospital to come and lead a structured art therapy group at the unit, to see if it might be of value to the clients.

At the first of these fortnightly groups, there were 12 members of the group: 3 staff (2 male art therapists, 1 male nurse) and 9 patients (5 men, 4 women, all ages). After a brief introduction, the visiting art therapist introduced the task of the group:

'Warm-ups': (1) Draw yourself as an animal.
            (2) Draw yourself as a form of transport.

Main theme: (3) Yourself – physically, mentally, and spiritually.

The two art therapists had chosen this theme to help clients explore the spiritual aspect of their lives and the part this played in their recovery from alcoholism. It also tied in with the tenets of Alcoholics Anonymous, which encourages people to overcome powerlessness in the face of alcohol by handing over to a 'higher power'.

The next three-quarters of an hour was spent painting, using PVA paints. The staff all joined in, trying to be as open in their work as they expected the clients to be. Most people managed to finish the three parts, and there was a further three-quarters of an hour left for discussion, which followed up each exercise in turn.

In the first exercise, people drew a wide variety of animals: a mouse, a rabbit, a horse, a stag, a fox, and several cats and dogs. These images gave rise to an interesting discussion of how different animals were seen by the group. Cats, for instance, were seen as having the best of all possible worlds, being given food, yet being able to retain their independence and live their own lives. Rabbits were seen as soft, cuddly, unaggressive, and possibly sexual ('breed like rabbits'). Most of the domestic animals were seen as offering their owners uncritical affection, and the group members acknowledged this as a general need experienced by them.

The largest (and best executed) drawing was of a fox, which was seen as sly, cunning, predatory, and untrusting. The artist readily admitted to these as his own personal characteristics, but claimed they were necessary to his survival. The art therapist noticed that the fox seemed to be looking over his shoulder, and asked its owner if he wanted to continue his life with these characteristics. He said 'No' and when invited to choose another image, he replied 'a horse', which suggested quite a change of direction.

As time was fairly short, the group moved on to the forms of transport, which introduced aeroplanes, cars, and several sailing vessels, some quite vast and splendidly rigged. These led to a general discussion of freedom, independence, and power. There were also some individual associations with particular memories which they chose to concentrate on and develop further. One woman had painted an E-type Jaguar in a rather depressing grey. She had been a prostitute, and the powerful car seemed to remind her of memories of good times, by contrast with her present situation where she was struggling to face life without alcohol or drugs.

When the discussion moved on to the main theme, the 'physical' aspect was represented by images of sport, walking, gardening, sailing, the earth, and so on. The 'spiritual aspect' appeared mostly in images of various kinds of churches, and everyone had included something spiritual.

The way people had combined the different aspects in their pictures was of great interest. The ex-prostitute had painted the religious aspect centrally in her picture, as something she held on to. One of the staff painted a complicated picture indicating the importance of religion to him, and felt it had been helpful clarifying this for himself.

Some clients' paintings seemed to be linked to their general progress at the unit. One man covered his piece of paper with red and yellow, and then surrounded this with a shapeless blue area, which he came to see as his brain. He associated this with the fact that he was beginning to distrust his intellect. The therapist interpreted this (in the context of the unit) as his previously hidden feelings starting to disturb his equilibrium, and took this as a hopeful sign of a change in attitude taking place.

The overall effect of the group had been to talk about personal matters in an oblique way and to draw out spiritual issues that rarely get discussed in institutions. The staff of the unit were impressed at the range and depth of the group; the clients had valued sharing their experience, and were keen to continue using a group theme in the art therapy sessions.

In the group just described, the images are all personal ones, leading to possibilities for personal learning. The sharing of experience facilitates this, and the therapist takes a leading role in managing the discussion, as it is a new group. The next account concerns an established group which has been running for some months, and has acquired a mode of working together.

Established women's group at a day hospital

This session was one of a series of eight closed sessions, after which the group would re-form for the next series. It had a membership of six women and two therapists, one of whom was the art therapist, Karen. The women were referred from the out-patient clinic as likely to benefit from the group, and had problems of depression, low self-image, pending divorce, violent husband, etc. Many techniques were being used, for example psychodrama, role play, Gestalt therapy, interwoven with art therapy, which occupied about every third session. Body tracings, childhood memories, and lists of 'male' and 'female' qualities had been part of this group's previous sessions. It was the penultimate session of the series, and several women who had been coming for about seven months were about to leave. This core group had become very close.

Before the session Karen had put out paints and made a huge sheet of paper which covered the floor of the large room. She introduced the theme by asking the group to imagine going in a spaceship which landed on a far-away planet, providing an opportunity for the group to make a new start and create its own environment away from base (an obvious parallel to the ending of the group and the new start all its members would need to make).

Karen asked if the group wanted to plan the joint project, but got no response, as no one seemed to know how to start. Then she suggested they might think of their basic needs first. This immediately sparked off a chord, and all the women drew themselves individual houses as starting points, from which they then emerged. (For most of them, their houses were their lives, away from the hospital.) The houses they drew demonstrated some of the progress they had made in the group over the months.

One woman, who had a violent husband, had initially just sat and cried in the group. She painted her house with fruit, vegetables, and a bike outside, things she thought people might need, and it looked an inviting and welcoming house. She had discovered during the group that she was a very providing person, and was about to move out to her own flat to give herself space to do this.

Another depicted a tree-house, indicating a wish for independence and privacy, with no demands. The group was a bit concerned that there was not even a rope or ladder for anyone to visit her, but she was adamant that was how she wanted it.

The one most anxious about the group finishing put herself in the corner, with a telephone as a link to the rest of the world. She also brought her whole family with her, whereas most of the other women had just brought their children but not their husbands!

Others drew very conventional houses, but all expressed interest in the nurse's drawing of a gypsy caravan, with wares to sell. They had not even conceived of such a nomadic existence being possible for them, and admired her courage.

When the individual houses were finished, the women made paths from one to another to open up communication, and also painted a communal playground (for their children, not themselves). Meanwhile Karen put in a centre for people to meet, seeing herself as an organizer who got people together, while still sharing their problems.

It was a very comfortable group, the women working together and sharing space very easily. The main issues which seemed to emerge were the ending of the group and the independence felt by several of the women as they prepared to move forward.

Karen felt she would probably suggest a continuation of this idea for the last week: perhaps some kind of summary of the group's experience, and a projection forward to 'Where next? My situation in five years' time' or a similar theme.

Both the accounts so far concern groups of clients with defined problems attending a centre for regular sessions of treatment. However, there are many ordinary people who are interested in experiencing new ways of learning about themselves and others, and the next account is of a one-day workshop for a group of students and families with no previous experience of art therapy (and who would probably not even use the word 'therapy').

One-day workshop with a community group

This was a workshop I had been asked to run by a student friend of mine, to be suitable mainly for students just after their final exams, but also for families (and their children) associated with the Catholic chaplaincy. There would be some people who could stay all day, and some who could come only for the morning or the afternoon.

And so it proved to be. There were ten people to begin with, but eighteen by the end of the morning, including three children. Quite a few left at lunchtime, and one family was replaced by another with very young children. Meanwhile I myself had a small baby who needed occasional attention. About eight people were constant throughout the day. (This did not matter too much because they knew each other to a certain extent and this gave a feeling of 'basic trust' to the group.)

Some therapists would hold up their hands in horror at the inconstancy and disparity of the group members, but work in the wider community is bound to be fairly unpredictable if it is to include all those who want to come. It is important to keep the level fairly light in a one-day event with no follow-up, and to remember that most people come to be interested and stimulated rather than to engage in serious personal therapy. It is fine to leave people with some thought-provoking experiences to mull over; not so fine to leave people realizing they have a big problem and no support to tackle it.

So I introduced the workshop by explaining it as an opportunity to use art as a means of communication, creativity, and enjoyment, for which no previous experience was needed. A neat phrase used by one art therapist is 'no special ability or disability needed'. Anyone should feel free not to join in at any point, and could choose their own level of response. The group met in a large carpeted room, over which my friend had spread newspapers. She had mixed up powder paints beforehand to save time, and we did most of the exercises with these paints. The summary of the day's programme was as follows:

1. Introductions: name and a personal interest outside one's main occupation, and any expectations of the workshop.
2. Passing paintings round. Everyone numbered their sheet (1–13), and started on their own sheet. Every minute they passed their sheet on, and contributed to the next one until everyone had their own back. People appreciated this exercise as it was a good ice-breaker.
3. Conversation in paint, with one partner. Everyone found this very interesting and enjoyable. Much of the lunchtime conversation came back to it as having made quite an impact.
4. Paint yourself as a kind of food, then join up with another food that goes well with it, and converse as if you were that food. The previous exercise was still in people's minds, as they assumed that all conversations henceforth were to be in paint only. It seemed to be a good lead-up to lunch, which was how I had intended it.
5. Lunch, shared, upstairs in another room, as the weather was bad.
6. Group story. On a long sheet of paper, the group created a story together in silence. We had previously agreed the starting point on the paper (one end) and which way up (one side). Some people worked at

one point on the paper, some moved around, and of course they had to take into account all the aspects of other people's contributions as it grew. When it was finished, I asked people to write a story from the picture, then we read them out. Some amazing stories came out of this, and there was a very real depth to the experience. (Endless exploration of these is possible, but in a group of this nature, I felt it best simply to listen to each others' stories and accept them.)

7 Group collage. This was designed to be a rounding-off experience to sum up the day, but several people had to go early, leaving the rest of us with an over-large prepared sheet of paper, and too little energy after the last one, to do very much.

Those who stayed the full length shared experiences and had found it interesting and enjoyable. They were however surprised to find themselves so exhausted after an ostensibly relaxing day. I suggested that maybe they had been using some unusual parts of themselves.

I want to finish with short accounts of how art techniques in three different groups led to experiences that provided valuable insights into the groups' interaction.

Group painting at a day centre for ex-offenders

This was a group of four young men. I asked them to start with a doodle in their own space on a large sheet, then to fill in the spaces with a limited selection of oil pastel colours.

All went well until one person started treading rapidly and clumsily on others' territories, and then the destruction escalated to the point of being symbolized by a mushroom cloud! They had clearly experienced the opportunity for legitimate destruction, and bore the painting off to put up on the lounge wall for all to see; it remained a topic of conversation for the rest of the day.

Group painting at a peace conference

The theme of this half-day event was 'Conflict and Resolution' and the painting group had twelve members, mostly young and middle-aged adults. On this occasion I asked them to start by painting (using powder paints) something to represent themselves in their space round the edge of a large sheet, then to move outwards towards their neighbours and the middle, resolving any conflicts with paint rather than words.

I had hardly completed the introduction when one man plunged into the picture with a thick black line to demarcate 'his' area. This provoked

Illustration 11.1　The photograph shows the general 'atmosphere' of working in a group, taken at the Peace Conference, by Maurice Benington, who participated in the group painting. The photograph was developed and printed by Michael Masheder.

hostility from others who challenged these barriers, resulting in an endemic 'guerrilla warfare' in one corner.

For a group committed to pacifist solutions to world problems, the mess they had produced came as quite a shock. However it led to a very useful discussion on the nature of boundaries, and whether they should be firm and clear, or open and negotiable. We were also able to look at the painting and see how we had misinterpreted each other's messages.

Non-verbal conversation in pairs on art therapists' training course

This session was one of a weekly series of workshops for art therapy students, who were expected to experience many of the techniques they would themselves be using later on. There were twelve mature students in the group.

After a warm-up, the therapist asked each person to select one colour (oil, pastel, crayon) different from their partner's. Each pair was to have a conversation (in silence) on the shared paper, with each person carrying on their own line where it had been left off, and being aware of any feelings in response to what happened. Like an ordinary conversation, it would have a natural ending. These 'conversations' took only about ten minutes, then each pair discussed what had happened and traced the course of the interaction. Some pairs had interpreted each other correctly, some had reacted to mistaken perceptions, for example had experienced gestures intended as 'friendly' as intrusive, and then responded inappropriately.

Finally the results were shared in the large group, and the different patterns of communication noted. Some conversations had been uneventful, some angry confrontations, some like ritual dances, some like 'follow-my-leader', and so on. The students reflected on their personal patterns and found themselves thinking about the implications for several days afterwards.

The great strength of these interactive paintings is their potential for mirroring the group in a tangible way which can be inspected and discussed after the event, and thus used for insight and learning. They may easily 'get out of hand' as interpersonal issues are explored within the group but it is important that some learning is achieved from the experience by the individuals and group as a whole.

Conclusion

I hope that these accounts of particular art therapy groups give some indication of the variety of experience available in such groups, although it is generally recognized that there is no substitute for the actual experience of group interaction.

Using art therapy games and structured activities draws on expertise in art therapy, groups, and games, and it remains the responsibility of the therapist to make the right choices for the particular group and context, and to learn with the group.

There is still a lot to be done in the way of research into art therapy groups of different kinds and their effectiveness in therapeutic terms. Nevertheless, I hope I have shown that they can provide a context in which to explore aspects of social and personal behaviour of interest to everyone, both in therapeutic institutions and in the wider community.

References

Brandes, D. and Phillips, H. (1979) *Gamesters Handbook*. London: Hutchinson.

Brown, A. (1979) *Groupwork*. London: Heinemann.

Butler, L. and Allison, L. (1978) *Games, Games*. London: Playspace.

Culbert, S. A. (1967) *The Interpersonal Process of Self-Disclosure: It Takes Two to See One*. Explorations in Applied Behavioral Science no. 3. New York: Renaissance Editions.

Denny, J. (1975) Techniques for Individual and Group Art Therapy. In E. Ulman and P. Dachinger (eds) *Art Therapy in Theory and Practice*. New York: Schocken.

Douglas, T. (1976) *Groupwork Practice*. London: Tavistock.

Fluegelman, A. (ed.) (1978) *The New Games Book*. London: Sidgwick & Jackson.

Höper, C., Kutzleb, U., Stobbe, A., and Weber, B. (1975) *Awareness Games*. London: St James Press.

Huizinga, J. (1970) *Homo Ludens*. London: Temple-Smith.

Lewis, H. and Streitfeld, H. (1970) *Growth Games*. London: Souvenir Press.

Liebmann, M. (1979) 'A Study of Structured Art Therapy Groups'. Unpublished thesis, Birmingham Polytechnic.

— (1981) The Many Purposes of Art Therapy. *Inscape* 5(1): 26–8.

— (1982) *Art Games and Structures for Groups*. Bristol: Bristol Art Therapy Group.

McNeilly, G. (1984) Directive and Non-Directive Approaches in Art Therapy. *Journal of Group Analysis* (in press).

Orlick, T. (1982) *The Co-operative Sports and Games Book*. London: Writers and Readers Publishing Co-operative.

Acknowledgements

I would like to thank Roy Thornton and Paul Curtis (Alcoholic Unit), Karen Lee Drucker (Psychiatric Day Hospital), and Patsy Nowell-Hall (Art Therapy courses at Herts College of Art and Design and Goldsmiths' College) – all fellow art therapists who have provided invaluable material and personal support for the writing of this chapter.

Biographical note

Marian Liebmann   Has always had an interest in art, but took a degree in Physics at Oxford, during which she took up painting seriously. After a varied career of teaching and educational writing, and two exhibitions of paintings, she became involved in using art with community groups. For several years she worked at a day centre for adult ex-offenders and others with social problems, and was responsible for education and art. This led her to the MA in Art Therapy, School of Art Education, Birmingham Polytechnic, 1979. Since then she has compiled the collection 'Art Games and Structures for Groups', published by Bristol Art Therapy Group in 1982, and used these with a variety of community groups in Bristol.

12 Art therapy with long-stay residents of psychiatric hospitals

Suzanne Charlton

The long-stay population

An art therapy department can play a unique part in improving the quality of life of people who live in large psychiatric hospitals. This chapter hopes to convey aspects of what is involved when working with long-stay residents; it is derived from practice at Glenside Hospital, Bristol and from an awareness of established departments in the south west. Before discussing the specific contribution of art therapy, it is necessary to understand something of the background and the day-to-day living conditions of this population.

Most have spent a large proportion of their lives in overcrowded wards, where the basic needs for food, clothing, and shelter have been met, where they have received an extraordinary range of 'treatments', but where life has been culturally impoverished. Current trends in therapeutic practice aim to make amends for this by providing a variety of activities and developing a less restricted lifestyle within the hospital. However, most of the longer-term residents have experienced years of institutional care, they have been isolated from the culture of the outside world, and do not know how to handle the exchanges involved in daily living. Much of their time still seems to be spent in pacing the corridors of the backwards and if they wander beyond the hospital into local streets and shopping centres, they are stigmatized by their strange mannerisms and posturings, their ill-fitting clothing, their mutterings, and their aura of isolation. Is it surprising that in this context many have maintained a rich inner-life, a personal culture, where they have restructured a reality that provides a significant place for themselves?

There are over 70,000 long-stay psychiatric hospital residents in England alone (DHSS 1978). Most were admitted for psychotic disorders, others for what has been described in retrospect as social dissidence. The majority are from the working class and there are more women than men. The symptoms occur in widely different combinations and with varying intensity; among them are deep disturbances or distortions of feeling, thinking, perception, and conduct which lead to a kind of withdrawal from the outside world. About two-thirds of this population are currently diagnosed as chronic schizophrenic but most of these people also have problems that have been accrued from prolonged stays in hospital. These problems can be as debilitating as the disturbances with which they were originally admitted. Institutionalization manifests itself in a variety of ways: low self-esteem, fear of failure, repetitive and apparently meaningless behaviour, profound insecurity, and difficulties in communication. These characteristics which have traditionally been seen as symptoms of insanity can also be understood as adaptations to survive an authoritarian system. As Goodwin states:

'After half a lifetime of being treated as sick, helpless, and unable to behave in socially acceptable ways, patients may conclude that they are indeed helpless, not responsible for their actions, incapable of changing anything, and a failure at whatever they do.'   (Goodwin 1978: 3–9)

Any therapeutic approach must take into account residents' rights and the specific needs of each individual. Many hospitals subdivide the long-stay population into three groups, each of which has its own requirements. The three groups are described as: 'rehabilitation', 'chronic' or residential, and 'psycho-geriatric' or elderly. The rehabilitation group is comprised of the shorter-term long-stay residents for whom it is hoped that there will be an eventual move back into the community. Their main needs are to recover a realistic self-image and to acquire the social skills necessary to become an integrated member of society outside the hospital. For the residential group there is little hope for a return to a society in which many had only a very tenuous position before admission. Their needs include personal validation and an improvement of their position in the hospital community which has become their 'home'. The elderly group have the added problems of dementia, physical illness, and immobility. The main aims of therapy are to arrest rapid deterioration and to develop a better quality of life on the wards. There are attempts at rehabilitation for all these people but the lack of appropriate accommodation and support services outside the hospital results in a restriction of the numbers who could be discharged. Unfortunately, it is realistic to expect that the majority will remain in institutional care for the rest of their lives.

In these circumstances, resignation into the 'patient role' can lead to a vicious circle of dependency: the more she or he is treated as incapable, the more passive the resident becomes. The art therapist aims at breaking this pattern by assisting the resident to develop a means of self-expression and to cultivate some independence within the hospital setting. Art therapy aims to change the circumstances which lead to residents becoming so dependent by providing the arena in which actions can be taken to bring about change. It can also help residents to focus upon their positive abilities and their potential for taking responsibility for their own lives. The art room provides a setting where residents can experience trust, experiment with different behaviour, exercise choice, and feel a sense of competence. When working with this resident group art activities have certain advantages over other approaches in that picture-making is defined by the resident's own inventiveness and level of ability. As Donnelly states:

'There are clearly defined limits of successful or unsuccessful behaviour in many of the other activities that a long-stay patient may be invited to take part in. In picture making the client can often start at his own level with very few imposed limits or directives as to what he should do or how he should perform. I see this as a vital advantage of picture making that we are not in a position to impose our values or standards of behaviour on the client in order then to be able to help them but in many ways the act of picture making enables us to join the client where they are and not where we would like them to be!' (Donnelly 1983)

Art therapy differs from many other activities because it is not, in fact, 'product-orientated'; that is to say, the primary interest is not in technical skill, but in ways of perceiving, in ways of concentrating, ways of working together, ways of interpreting mark-making and constructing, and the 'finished product' is useful in reflecting or illuminating these aspects. Fundamental to most therapies are the principles of understanding oneself and one's situation better and the fostering of an ability to make change. As this group in general have a poor or unconventional facility with words, and do not generally base their understanding on intellectual rationalizations, image-making can be a most suitable medium as it is a pre-verbal communication system, and as such is more basic and direct. The art therapist aims at making contact on this level. It is found that obscure, verbally mediated therapies can intimidate and mystify and residents usually do not participate.

Many residents have lost touch with their feelings and their experiences have led them to project themselves in stylized and often ambiguous ways, peculiar to themselves. Painting and drawing, the use of shape, colour, and symbol can be powerful communicators and can provide a more direct link with the individual's state of being.

Therapeutic objectives

Encouragement of a positive self-image

If the 'illness' or the process of institutionalization has caused residents to change their attitude towards themselves, one aim of art therapy is to challenge these negative self-concepts by demonstrating the residents' possession of certain capabilities. A painting is a tangible achievement and is the evidence of organizational skills, manual competence, imagination, and motivation – the qualities required for its creation. Paintings reflect aspects of the painter and a series of pictures can be a visual record of change. Residents can feel a sense of personal validation when their work is received with serious interest and understanding.

There is a close connection between confidence and competence such that the development of one can further the development of the other. Confidence can stem from the acknowledgement of abilities while competence is more closely associated with the resident's familiarity with the art materials. Although there is generally a high premium put on 'spontaneous creative expression', a low level of confidence will inhibit spontaneity. Many of this client group tend to respond with indifference, compliance, or caution, and so the resident/therapist relationship is important in providing the support and encouragement necessary to make the initial steps into picture-making. Residents who say 'I can't do it' may well be looking for reassurance, whilst others may attend for weeks before attempting to participate. After such initial resistance, many find substantial rewards in art activities which keep them coming back.

This can be illustrated by Joan, a woman in her late sixties who had been hospitalized since her mid-twenties, and who had attended the art therapy department every day for several months. She always sat in the same place and always proceeded to do her knitting, quietly and in a withdrawn manner, never making contact with other residents. She responded to friendly overtures with a stiff politeness but would allow me to spend some ten minutes each day to sit and talk with her. She would tell me about the 'progress' of her knitting, she was always knitting a scarf, and how every day her knitting was unravelled by the staff as it was never good enough. If I so much as mentioned 'drawing' to her, she would look in alarm, say 'Oh no, I can't do it dear', bundle up her knitting, and leave. I began to arrange a small assortment of pictures and stencils on her table in the hope that one day she may be attracted to one of them. This continued for some weeks until the morning came when Joan picked up a small stencil of a flower. This time she replied 'Yes, alright dear!' to my suggestion that she might draw round the stencil! She took a pencil and a ruler and carefully constructed a border of flowers around the edge of the paper.

Joan received much praise for this picture and over the course of the next week produced many pictures. They were all the same. All started and finished at the same point on the paper and all were shaded with pencil. It was clear that Joan was methodically reproducing that first picture that I had praised. As she seemed happy now for me to spend more time with her, I made available other media, such as coloured crayons and paints that she could try if she wished. When she chose wax crayons, the flowers in the border became larger, were drawn freehand, and filled more of the page. She told me she loved flowers and had used them to decorate the hats she had made when she was a milliner before her marriage. She began to talk to me a lot about her life in the past. Joan found a stencil of a horse and painted two horses, one brown and one black and white. Then she painted in fields, flowers, trees, and sky. Her pictures no longer had a vacant space in the centre. The painting now occupied the whole page, the imagery was representational and the pictures had content. She talked about her childhood; of her and her sister visiting their aunt on the farm. Joan was emerging as a person. Her contacts with others in the art room developed, although on a polite level, and she would still suddenly get up and leave when she felt she had had enough.

After the period of 'going back' and reclaiming her identity before admission, Joan moved towards taking a more active role in the art room. She would request to take around tea to the other residents and to water the plants and her picture-making took a further development. She began to draw objects in the room and she drew them in the round. She had moved from flat pattern-making borders to bold and expressive imagery. To us in the art room, the change had been concurrent with Joan emerging as a full personality and sharing everyday experiences with us.

Residents often return to their wards with splendid paintings that surprise the staff. Some can hardly believe that the residents have painted them; such is their low expectation of their abilities. The concept of self-image seems dependent on the reactions and opinions of others as well as the individual's own judgement. Displays of paintings on the wards can help keep staff in touch with the residents, can re-affirm the residents' competence, and enchance their status.

Promoting social interaction

Although long-stay residents live communally, spending much of their time sitting in day rooms with ten or twenty others, there is rarely any obvious interaction between them. Where they do make contact with each other or with staff, exchanges can be inappropriate, exaggerated, or sometimes threatening – usually when the staff are 'overworked' and when the residents are more concerned with their own preoccupations than with shared experience. To counteract estranged behaviour, the art therapy room provides an environment where sincere attention is given to the products of their invention and where it is made clear that to gain recognition they need not contrive 'acts of craziness'.

Initially, some residents choose to attend the art room for a variety of reasons other than to paint and draw; to escape the ward, because of a lack of options for other activities, to get a cup of tea, because people are nice to them. New attenders to the art room often have an ambivalent attitude to being with others and feel understandably nervous at joining in with structured group work. They are often happier to draw on their own and perhaps join in the general care and routine of the department. Therapists can facilitate some social interaction by making opportunities for new residents to share in tasks such as distributing art materials, making tea, or processing clay.

Group painting provides a more structured arena for developing communication skills and introducing methods of working co-operatively. Creative tasks for groups of people furnish a safe environment to experiment with interactions which would normally be too hazardous. For example, where six people are involved in making a collage together, there has to be a lot of negotiation concerning who does what. This can be a valuable situation for relearning a variety of social skills.

Development of concentration and dexterity

Many residents have a very short concentration span, sometimes only a few minutes at a stretch. Lack of concentration is associated with lack of purpose, interest, and security, and any programme designed to extend it needs to take all of these into consideration. People who find concentration difficult are often agitated and fear failure in tasks that they feel are beyond their capabilities. For this reason, activities should be mutually constructed by the resident and therapist, the sessions kept short or with the inclusion of frequent breaks. The completion of a simple exercise at the beginning of therapy may provide the resident with the needed confidence to try more difficult things later on.

Amongst older residents there are also those whose manual dexterity is severely limited. They can find great difficulty in handling art materials especially fluid media such as paint and inks. If appropriate techniques are selected these people can experience a sense of achievement despite their handicaps. A therapist may even need to guide the drawing hand of a resident with very poor motor control with her or his own.

Techniques for use with groups

Most structured art work is done in groups in order to promote shared experience. Each of the three sections of the long-stay population require appropriate methods to meet their specific needs. Not many of these residents paint spontaneously nor do they readily respond to insight or analytic therapy. Because of this a more directive approach to group work can be appropriate, where themes and structures are chosen to suit the particular group. The theme can relate to group concerns and the structures should be as democratic as possible, according to the level of residents' abilities. It is important to establish co-operative agreement of basic group rules and objectives by taking some time to discuss them from the outset. Each member's contribution is significant but the therapist will generally take responsibility for encouraging participation, facilitating interaction, 're-framing' when necessary, protecting submissive residents, and helping the group to deal with domineering characters.

An art group can work within one of several formats. For example, each member participates on one large picture, members work on individual pictures in a group setting, each member contributes to a communal product, or members pair up, as in body-tracing. The effect of these group techniques must be considered and applied appropriately to fit the needs of a particular group. The processes that operate within the group should be discussed at the end of each session.

Rehabilitation group

Most psychiatric hospitals have designated 'rehabilitation' wards which are populated by younger residents, many of whom have recurring psychotic episodes or else have entrenched 'personality disorders'. They have generally spent a shorter time in hospital and are less institutionalized than the other two groups mentioned, and so can cope with techniques that are more demanding on all levels.

Making murals can be an effective way of working together. The principal advantages of large pictures that are communally created are that they promote interaction, negotiation, and responsibility. There are several ways of organizing groups to work on murals but for this population the more straightforward methods work best. I have adapted a co-operative team game from Pavey's *Art-Based Games* (Pavey 1979) which, as it stands with its numerous directions, is too confusing for this client group.

Basically, the object of the game is to create a mural, by the contribution of two groups of two to four members. A theme for the mural is selected – for a simple example 'a pattern'. Both groups choose what colours and shapes will represent them and proceed by drawing and painting their images on individual sheets of paper. The images are cut out and both groups, working on separate tables, arrange a layout for their design. The mural will be a combination of these two designs. The next stage is the transfer of both designs onto the mural. Two members, one from each group, transfer a cut-out shape onto the mural and so on until the mural is complete. At this stage there may be overlaps of shapes and changes of composition. The groups are encouraged to negotiate how best to merge the designs.

When the mural is finished, there is a period for contemplating the picture and discussing the session as a whole. Ideally, the painting is viewed as reflecting the interaction within the group and is used as an aid to understand where these work well and where there are problems. Aspects that can be discussed are: the overall effect of the finished work; is it balanced or discordant? Was the overall game enjoyable or stressful – why? How well did people get on with each other – were there problems?

Providing a comments book can reveal ideas and attitudes that some members are either not prepared or unable to voice within the group. This book can be incorporated into 'the game' and comments reviewed at the beginning of the next session.

The structure of this group involves members in their own assessment. They are encouraged to identify their own areas of difficulty and view them in the context of others. An individual making a change requires everyone else in that situation to make some change also. For example, if the peripheral, overlapped shapes in the mural are identified as belonging to Bill and the bold, central shapes as belonging to Muriel, Muriel will need to take less responsibility to allow Bill to take a more active part.

Another way of working as a group is again to provide a large sheet of paper which is shared between the members. A theme is selected, for example 'the South Pacific'. Everyone is asked to imagine that the paper is the ocean onto which they can paint an island, complete with details such as vegetation, animal life, shelter, and so on. When this has been done, members choose an island and illustrate a means of getting there.

Members are invited to tell the group which island they chose to visit and why. As people are found to reflect aspects of themselves in what they draw, a picture of an island can become analogous with personal attributes. Residents often find that they can give and receive compliments and criticisms in this situation that would be too threatening to make direct.

A similar projective technique can be used for portraits. Group members are asked to think of one group member as: an animal, a building, a piece of food, etc., and to paint them as such. Each portrait is considered in terms of its qualities and the identity guessed.

As these residents often have very poor self-concepts, self-portraits can make these feelings explicit and discussion can provide a forum for testing them out. Portraits of each other can reinforce mutual recognition. 'Body-tracing' brings people into physical contact with each other, much like a 'trust exercise' with results particularly valuable for those who experience great disturbances of body-image. Large sheets of paper are pinned to the wall and in pairs people trace around each other's body outline. The figure is then completed as the resident wishes.

Group members may work on individual paintings in a group setting. Fantasy themes are generally welcomed as they draw from the imagination and can legitimize fantastic ideas. They can provide a channel for otherwise private preoccupations and may be a metaphor for feelings and aspirations. Themes are inexhaustible but can include: three wishes, a magic garden, life on another planet, a hiding place.

In contrast, themes related to 'daily living' can provide valuable material for understanding how the resident sees her or his position within the hospital and exemplify the specific problem areas. Themes can include: ward life, the weekend, going shopping, a typical day.

Residential group

The majority of long-stay residents are in this group. Because they have spent such a long time in hospital they are often the most institutionalized, but in spite of this they tend to value the opportunity to participate in art therapy as long as they are relatively free to work as they wish. They sometimes produce stylized or stereotyped imagery with a tendency towards repetition and embellishment of forms. They usually find it difficult to talk about their work in terms of feelings although their mood of the moment is often reflected in the work they produce.

People who go about picture-making in an almost ritualistic way, always selecting the same materials, methodically plotting out the same imagery, using the same colours, seem to be striving to construct for themselves something which is safe, known, and controlled. It requires intuitiveness on the part of the therapist to know when to attempt to break this pattern and when to condone it.

James, a residential client, attended the art room regularly and generally painted bright pictures of people and places. James was allergic to psychotropic drugs, so lived through his distraught periods without drug control. During these phases he was more eager to maintain his daily routine of attending the art room. If he was so distressed that it was felt best for him not to leave the ward, I would take his art materials to him. His drawing would revert to rigid, geometric pattern-making, lining-up the paper with a ruler, and blocking in the shapes row by row. This style of drawing would continue throughout this phase. James was not accessible to any kind of dialogue about his work or about anything else, but would occasionally grunt or exclaim in a breathless voice something incoherent. His drawings appeared to be his way of controlling the inner chaos he seemed to be experiencing.

At other times repetitive picture-making can reflect a kind of vacancy – the lack of variety in hospital life supplies little inspiration for new material and this has led many art therapy departments to include outings and day-trips as part of their therapeutic programme. Morning sessions are usually more lively and productive than the afternoons when residents are often drowsy from lunchtime medication. The major tranquillizers used to control psychotic symptoms can also give the residents blurry vision, tremors, and cause the loss of fine manual control.

As many people from long-term wards are stiff-limbed and slowed-down, some structured ways of working have been found to be appreciated. For example, copying a picture is a safe activity which can be helpful to encourage more inhibited people. Pictures are often copied in a very individualistic and even original style which makes room for self-expression and personal interpretation. Similarly, stencils can be used to advantage when someone has poor manual dexterity, or with people who continually 'scrub' over the same line. Making murals can become highly structured by drawing out designs which are then filled in, or by using agreed themes of animals, plants, household items, to which each person can contribute their own design.

Collage is an interesting means of incorporating several different skills. Various tasks can be negotiated and shared amongst the group. It provides an opportunity for the use of multi-media; bits of scrap, small objects, and pictures can all contribute to an effective collage. The request for found items allows for the inevitable wandering around the room that the long-stay folk are so fond of!

For the more cohesive group there are 'awareness exercises'. These are exercises which aim at improving awareness of the environment and drawing attention to sensory experience. This is the 'Denner's Technique' (Denner 1967) which is based on the theory that emotional tensions block perception. Objects are provided that can be looked at, smelt, listened to, and touched, then the rhythms of the curves and other impressions are transferred onto paper to become the drawing. These pictures can be done on huge sheets of paper attached to the wall or on the floor, where the large space allows for more free-flowing expression.

The elderly

Older people often develop fixed thought processes with a deterioration in their ability for abstraction and expression. There is a range of abilities within this group but some may have little control over materials and their pictures may take the form of scribbles and marks. When they attempt to use paints they can feel dissatisfaction at having 'made a mess'. In this situation the use of paint would be inappropriate and coloured paper, torn into shapes and stuck onto card can be a more successful way to construct a picture.

The therapist needs to empathize with individuals who have lived in a different generation, have unique personal histories, and who may hold quite different values. These people may feel that their lives are now redundant and that they are a burden. One basic aim of therapy is to promote a sense of personal worth. Art therapy may focus on past events, problems inherent in old age, or how to deal with loss. The elderly are often frustrated by their awareness that they are no longer able to function as they used to. Creative therapy hopes to demonstrate to them what they are still able to achieve in spite of their handicaps, with well-devised sessions providing some assurance of success.

Sessions can start with introductions to remind everyone of everyone else's name. An array of too many art materials can add to the confusion of older residents and it is better to limit the media to easy-to-use ones, such as oil pastels or felt-tip markers. The difficulty that many of these people have with short-term recall requires therapists to explain things clearly, repeat them thoroughly, and keep the length of the session short.

Art therapy with the elderly, then, aims to provide an activity which allows members to project their feelings, which matches their ability level, but which is not so simple that it is demoralizing: the elderly are very well aware when the activities are childlike and the therapist patronizing. Structures and themes need to cover these three aspects, and one that I have found to work well for initial sessions is the theme of 'National Flags'. Flags are flat, geometric designs with distinctive colours and emblems. These designs can be transferred as bold outlines onto individual sheets of paper for group members to colour in. The task of selecting a flag and colouring-in broad areas is usually within the ability range of this group and the subject can provide a stimulus for memories of the past. I have found that for this client group, flag images prompt memories particularly of the war era. In one particular session several members of the group chose flags of countries in which they were stationed during the war. A discussion emerged on where they were and what they were doing: Bill was in the postal service in India, Gladys in a munitions factory, Arthur did not speak but listened, bright-eyed and attentive.

Long-term memory can be surprisingly clear and the recreation of a shared experience can consolidate a group. People tend to look forward to group sessions when there is both meaning and security. A productive art session can be the basis for future ones, with the therapist providing material that will possibly extend the themes that have been brought up by the group.

Elderly residents suffering from dementia will have a poor short-term memory, sometimes forgetting what they are doing in a group session. It is important that the art therapist is always available to give assistance and to encourage members to help each other. Dementing residents' long-term memory is usually better than recall of recent events and older people tend to enjoy recounting things that have long since passed. Butler (1963) interpreted reminiscing as a 'life review process' which reflects the old person's need to make sense out of all her or his previous experiences when confronted with impending death. If this is so, then it is possible to give assistance to these people in constructing such a meaning. There are several ways of drawing upon experiences of early adult life. For example, (a) household items, tools, and various objects from the era of their youth can be provided to look at, touch, pass around, draw, and talk about. Such items can stimulate memories and function to connect past with present; (b) available photographs, cut-out pictures, and free-hand drawing can be used to represent aspects of the individual's life. Family, friends, jobs, and places where they have lived can all be portrayed in a picture, to form a sort of autobiography.

With a cohesive and trusting group it can be found that relatively simple subjects for drawing can provoke quite a serious session. For example, the taboo subjects of death, dying, and bereavement were raised in a session that was overtly concerned with 'picture completion'. Picture completion is where an outline drawing of, say, a shop front, tool cupboard, the ward, etc., is provided for residents to complete in their own way. In this particular session the outline drawing was of a house. At first people drew in flowers around the house, the doors, and the colour of the curtains. Then quietly and respectfully, figures of people were included in the pictures. Some by choosing pictures of people who resembled their relatives and some by drawing figures that represented their husband, wife, or friend. Most of these relatives had died, and the group talked about living with illness, about life, and about their own death. Most of these people have lost their families and friends and feel alone. It is vital that they have an opportunity to think about, express, and share these experiences.

During these sessions not everyone participates verbally, and some members interject with what might seem to be irrelevant comments; nevertheless, group members can extend a lot of care and understanding to these individuals and they become valued and indispensable members of the group.

Art media

There is great advantage in making a wide range of materials available as the nature of the media plays an important part in the therapeutic process.

Paint lends itself more to fluid, emotional expression whilst marks made by pencils are generally more controlled. A development of ideas and feelings can result from the creative encounter with the materials. With some groups it is important that a variety of materials is readily accessible so that they can make their own choices.

With the elderly especially, success can depend on choosing the right medium and it is sometimes necessary for a therapist to help the resident select the appropriate materials. Felt-tip marker pens are easy to handle and produce clear, bright colours, which makes them particularly suitable for use by older residents with impaired vision or poor motor control.

The art room

Many visitors to psychiatric hospitals remark on their impression of the art therapy room as 'an asylum within the asylum'. This refers to the aspect of the art room which functions as a refuge, with a relaxed atmosphere that is often unavailable elsewhere. Although many wards are breaking down rigid routines and are developing activities, most lack space and facilities for creative work. Certain restrictions that are necessary for an efficiently run ward do not apply to an art room. Residents do not have to eat, sleep, wash, dress, see the doctor or take medication there, so the art therapist is in the advantageous position of rarely being in confrontation with residents over these issues.

By contrast to the ward the art room is a place where residents can make their own choices, within the sphere of creative activity, without fear of the consequences. Implicit in the art-making process is permission to get messy, to experiment, to ponder, or to invent. In this situation creative behaviour is condoned, which in other areas may be seen as unacceptable. The accessibility of books, pictures, and interesting objects can prove to be stimulating and the room can also become a home for residents' *'objets trouvés'* which are not always appreciated elsewhere! The relative freedom associated with the art room can bring about marked changes in behaviour; it is not unusual for residents with a reputation for aggression to be approachable and co-operative over years of attendance.

The organization of the department will be affected both by the therapeutic orientation of the staff and the nature of the facilities. Some hospitals provide purpose-built departments whilst others offer inappropriate and cramped premises. The type and size of room significantly affects the way a department functions. A room large enough to take one-to-one work and structured groupwork simultaneously will have a less confidential atmosphere than a room housing just one activity. It is possible to partition very large rooms into specific areas so that (a) several groups can be run concurrently; (b) individuals do not feel 'exposed'; (c) specialized activities can be accommodated such as pottery, weaving, and printmaking; and (d) individuals can identify with a particular area.

An art therapy department generally serves the whole hospital and consequently competing demands are made on the space available. This problem can be resolved by doing a small proportion of sessions on the wards. This policy is appropriate in the case of non-ambulant or elderly residents, who would not otherwise attend, or when other activities in the art room would detract from groupwork and a more confidential atmosphere is required. Therapists who make use of available ward space have to limit the variety of techniques employed and need to construct a portable 'art-kit' with materials that are compact and not too messy. However, this situation does have the advantage of directly involving ward staff in the art sessions and results in a prompt display of pictures in the ward.

Supporting creativity

Picture-making gives some people an alternative language to examine and re-order a confused view of the world. It can bring to awareness the significance of their present actions and feelings without the intrusive negotiation required in verbally mediated therapy. It can become a powerful medium for self-definition. Amongst this population there are some who seem to experience catharsis through picture-making, whilst a number of others derive an unspecific satisfaction from being absorbed in the creative process.

Creativity is an experience which could be available to everyone, but because in western society it has largely been the province of 'the expert', few people feel that they have access. Art therapy aims at breaking down these barriers, so that there is no monopoly over art. Pictures can make profound statements about oneself, one's perceptions and experiences, and art therapy hopes to contribute to opening up these creative possibilities.

Individual work with the long-stay resident

There are many long-stay residents who enjoy and benefit more from an individual relationship with the therapist, than with joining structured groupwork. Whilst therapy with people from acute admission wards is usually more insight-orientated and done intensively over a few weeks or months, with long-stay residents it is an open-ended process. The goals of therapy are less specific in terms of time but possibly more directly concerned with personal fulfilment and self-enhancement within the limitations of the hospital setting.

There are a number of residents who do not want therapeutic intervention but simply require the necessary resources to get on with picture-making. Using a non-directive approach, the therapist's role is to provide these resources to allow this creativity to flourish. When left to work on their own, some residents can use the space to create pictures which are rich and fluid expressions of their inner world. They seem to have few barriers when it comes to picture-making and are often unconcerned with the traditional western conventions of art, such as proportion and perspective. Thus unlimited, their creative expressions become direct and basic. These pictures in particular can display a wealth of images and symbolism, and because of this, it might be tempting to use this material for purposes of analysis, but therapeutic interpretations are neither appropriate nor beneficial. Rather the therapist's attitude can be non-judgemental: a recipient and a listener, where the art product has a mediating role, providing a bridge for therapist and resident. These people proceed best at their own pace, with the due acknowledgement for their skill and creativity. In itself this may serve to stabilize or even re-integrate a fragmented personality, but the resulting pictures certainly can give other people some understanding of their subjective world.

This is the stuff that art collections are made of. The 'Prinzhorn Collection' (1880–1920) and Jean Dubuffet's 'Collection de l'Art Brut' (1945–71) both contain the work of long-term patients from mental institutions, collected in the main before the extensive use of drug therapy. Both Prinzhorn and Dubuffet felt that the most direct and original art, the art with the most 'raw purity' was born of people who were outside the influences of the prevailing culture. However, although these paintings can be appreciated for their 'primitive' qualities, they may also be seen as testimonies full of anguish and oppression.

Summary

Psychiatric hospitals still accommodate large numbers of people who are likely to live out their lives in institutions. I have described some of the theoretical and practical aspects of art therapy in this setting. The ideal of creating an atmosphere of trust where people can emerge from years of withdrawal has to meet the all too obvious constraints of existing in a large, hierarchically-organized institution.

In comparison to other client groups long-stay residents change at a slower pace, and one works with them in an open-ended way, without criteria for cure or cessation of attendance. They bring with them a different attitude to the art-making process, being less inhibited by the influence of an artistic tradition and the prevailing culture. Like everyone else they have their daily interests and concerns, but are only likely to share these with people who are respectful of them and value their work. So the art room at its best becomes a 'micro-culture' where everyone is taken seriously and is as far as possible, free from the stigma which has systematically invalidated their contribution in the past. The challenge is to achieve this in practice and to develop ways of working which prevent people from getting stuck in self-defeating patterns but which avoid imposing unnecessarily patronizing structures on them. Art therapy can have much to contribute to a new sort of environment that facilitates social and cultural life rather than denying it.

Illustrations

12.1   Pencil drawing by long-stay resident of a female ward. It was drawn in response to the theme 'Life on the ward'. Although she did not discuss the picture in terms of how she felt, the picture conveys a strong sense of women confined.

12.2 Long-stay resident working on a group portrait. One project at Glenside involved residents painting a large mural to be fixed to the outside of the art therapy building, to identify the department and to welcome others. This mixed group of long-stay residents painted a life-size group portrait as their 'welcome sign'. It was painted on hardboard with household paints and varnished to be weatherproof.

References

Butler, R. N. (1963) The Life Review: An Interpretation of Reminiscence of the Aged. *Psychiatry* **26**: 65–76.

Denner, A. (1967) *L'Expression plastique, pathologie, et rééducation des schizo-phrènes*. Paris: Les Editions Sociales Françaises.

DHSS (1978) *In-Patient Statistics from the Mental Health Enquiry for England*. London: HMSO.

Donnelly, M. (1983) Personal correspondence, in response to a survey carried out by S.W. Regional Group of BAAT.

Goodwin, M. (1978) Art Therapy with the Institutionalized Patient. *American Journal of Art Therapy* **18** (October): 3–9.

Pavey, D. (1979) *Art-Based Games*. London: Methuen.

Biographical note

Suzanne Charlton trained at Canterbury College of Art and Newcastle-upon-Tyne Polytechnic, where she received her BA Hons in Fine Art. Following this she worked in community arts in Northumberland, mask-making for a theatre group. She did an 'in-service' training at Glenside Hospital, Bristol, where she then worked as Art Therapist for five years; the latter two years as Head of Department. After travelling abroad for a year she is now concentrating on screen-printing and her own art work.

13 | *Training in art therapy*

Diane Waller and Kim James

Art therapy is a term which has existed since the 1940s in Britain, and has been used to cover activities which could be classified as non-directive art teaching on the one hand and psychotherapy through art on the other, and which has taken place in institutions treating mentally ill and mentally handicapped children and adults.

The question of what constitutes a suitable training for such a practice has been perplexing various committees since the days when art therapy was simply a way of encouraging patients to paint, to the present time, when there is a considerable interest in the philosophical problems which underlie the use of the creative process in therapy.

In 1949, Adrian Hill was invited to become Chairman of the Art Therapy Committee set up by the South-West Metropolitan Regional Hospital Board. In order to find out to what extent art therapy was already being used in the south west, and if its introduction would be welcome in general and mental hospitals, a questionnaire was sent out to all hospitals in the region. The resulting replies gave a great deal of encouragement to the Committee, except those from geriatric hospitals which implied that art therapy would be too difficult to implement. On analysis of the results, the Committee found that there were three different concepts of the function of art therapy; in sanatoria, where the patients were mostly long-stay and the emphasis was on the relief of boredom; in mental hospitals, and in consulting rooms, where art therapy could be used in co-operation with a doctor or a psychotherapist, often for diagnostic purposes or for 'free association'; in general hospitals where two aspects of art were seen as important – the activity itself was found to release tension and the product provided a variety of pictures to decorate the walls. The 'art classes' were generally held by an art teacher or an occupational therapist.

In December 1949, a meeting was held at the National Association for Mental Health, attended by John Trevelyan (one-time film censor but then Director of Research into hospital administration), Gilbert and Irene Champernowne (Directors of the Withymead Centre for Psychotherapy through the Arts), Rudolf Laban (dancer and choreographer), a psychiatrist, a psychotherapist, two occupational therapists, and a music therapist. Interestingly, no artists or art teachers were present.

One of the main topics of debate was whether or not occupational therapy could cover the field of art therapy. There was no agreement on this, but Irene Champernowne, a Jungian analyst, stated that art therapy could release a terrific force from the unconscious and that the personality of the art therapist was supremely important in the receiving and containing of this force. Trevelyan felt that the 'real' educationalist would be in complete sympathy with the patient and that it would be possible for him or her to be both educator and healer. He suggested that a multi-disciplinary centre, rather like the one at Withymead, be established, where various professions could be represented and work closely together. One of the psychiatrists, was in favour of analysis for the art therapist, and described the analysand as 'someone who has experienced his own unadapted inner energy – that energy by which the artist groans and suffers to express himself'.[1] He believed that this experience could not be 'taught' in the ordinary sense. No conclusions were reached at that meeting, but in 1950, Trevelyan chaired a Conference of Art Therapists in Hospitals and Clinics and received suggestions about standards and training for art therapy, which were subsequently discussed at a Working Party which met at the National Association for Mental Health (NAMH) in 1951, chaired by Adrian Hill.

It is interesting to note that at this time, art training was not necessarily considered to be a good foundation for art therapy, since many believed art students to lack the necessary personality and experience of human relationships to make good therapists! Why this view was so strongly held is not clear from the minutes of these committees, but could stem from the stereotype of the Bohemian artist who preferred to work in isolation, was prone to neurosis, and was irresponsible as well…. Again, nobody was clear about what qualities were needed for an art therapist, but suggestions ranged from 'having insight' and a 'good knowledge of psychology', to 'a wide knowledge of art history'.[2]

The Working Party concluded that an Art Therapy Panel should be set up to assist those hospitals wishing to employ art therapists. This Panel included Adrian Hill, Irene Champernowne, and Edward Adamson. It was convinced that art therapy was a discipline separate from occupational therapy and play therapy, but despite the fact that the Panel did much to encourage the use of art in hospitals, no training scheme emerged other than that in the private Withymead Centre, which supplied many of the founder members of BAAT (The British Association of Art Therapists). When BAAT was formed in 1964, one of its briefs was to investigate the possibilities of training along with standards of professional practice and conditions of service.

A training sub-committee began negotiations with the University of London in 1965, and by 1967 it seemed as if a course could be started in the Institute of Education. Entrants to the course would require graduate or equivalent qualifications in visual, dramatic, or musical arts plus five years of teaching or related experience. The course would last for one year full-time, after which a diploma would be awarded. The proposal had been given a boost by the fact that homes and hostels for the mentally and physically handicapped, once the province of the DHSS, were to come under the DES, and that staff within them were to be teacher-trained in future. It was thought that art therapy could develop well within these areas. Unfortunately, however, the unfavourable economic climate of the late 1960s prevented this new venture from starting, complicated as it was by its intention to cover not only art but also music and drama therapy too.

In 1970, negotiations were also taking place to start some art therapy training at the University of Birmingham in the School of Art Education (now within the Polytechnic of Birmingham). In 1971, a quarter of the students on the Art Teacher's Diploma course chose an option led by Michael Edwards, which then came under a section of 'informal teaching activities' covering work in youth clubs, community projects, hospitals, and clinics. The option developed from these modest beginnings to become a training in art therapy which was recognized by the BAAT Registration and Training Sub-Committee in 1976. An MA in Art Education later included a Mode in Art Therapy. This programme thus followed very closely that historical root of art therapy which stemmed from art education.

At St Albans College of Art in 1969, a pilot scheme emerged which later became a course entitled the Certificate in Remedial Art. The art college at St Albans, surrounded as it was by several large mental handicap and psychiatric hospitals seemed a logical place to develop a course which was clearly aimed at training art therapists who wished to work in the health service and who were not teachers. The course admitted occupational therapists, nurses, and other health service personnel, as well as art graduates, provided the former could demonstrate a commitment to art. The Certificate developed to become the Postgraduate Diploma in Art Therapy, validated by the CNAA, and in 1981, the college introduced an MA in Art Therapy.

The third course to emerge was within the University of London, but at

Goldsmiths' College, not the Institute as before. It began as an option in 1974 within the Art Teacher's Certificate course, but the intention was to mount a separate Diploma in Art Therapy at the earliest opportunity. However, this proposal hit the same economic difficulties as the one previously discussed at the Institute and was trying to develop at a time when the DHSS had still not stated categorically that training was needed for art therapy, making the DES reluctant to approve a second course. Therefore the course went through several stages of existence as an in-service course, as part of the post-graduate Diploma in Art and Design structure, before eventually being approved as a separate Diploma in Art Therapy with two Modes: Clinical and Educational.

So although there is a strong involvement in art therapy training at Birmingham, dating from the early 1970s, there are still only two colleges, Goldsmiths' and Herts College of Art, St Albans, where separate diploma courses exist.

In November 1964 the then Ministry of Health wrote to the Secretary of BAAT as follows: 'Teachers give instruction in recognised courses many of which lead to some qualification while art therapists necessarily work along with other members of the hospital staff, all of whom are contributing in their various ways towards the patients' recovery.' This statement was, it appears, meant to justify why art therapists received under half of the salary of an art teacher. If we consider that, at the time, the Ministry only required two years post A-level study of art as an art therapy qualification and thought that occupational therapists could encompass art therapy anyway, it is not surprising that it took from then until 1980 to convince the DHSS that art therapists required training that involved some knowledge of patient treatment.

In January 1977, the DHSS issued a document on 'Art as a therapeutic activity for physically handicaped, mentally ill or mentally handicapped people'. This document suggested that one of the aims of art was

'to achieve specific remedial results - for example, improved dexterity following trauma or disease, a means of expression, communication and satisfaction for people unable to express themselves through the written or spoken word; an acceptable means of non-verbal expression for aggressive, frustrated or withdrawn patients.'

The skills required by 'the provider' were listed as: 'training and understanding the cause and results of the patients' illnesses and disabilities in order to set appropriate goals and deal with emotional responses.' Artistic ability was considered 'an asset'. It was acknowledged that artists could contribute, with training, but the document recommended that such a service be part of the general occupational therapy provision. In challenging this document, the then Chairman and Secretary of BAAT (D. Waller and A.

Gilroy) wrote to the DHSS putting forward the case for art therapists to be art graduates trained specifically in the practice of art therapy:

'The post-graduate year should enable those with a degree in art to combine their proven ability and understanding of art with basic therapy techniques. This may be achieved through a balance of clinical, theoretical and practical work, including a period of supervised art therapy placements. The clinical and theoretical sections of the course should give students the opportunity to consider important issues in disciplines related to art therapy, e.g. psychiatry, psychology and special education as well as to raise questions about the scope of art therapy and its future development. The practical section of the course which should include workshops and individual art therapy would give students the opportunity to experience and understand art therapeutic processes. We feel such experience at first hand is very necessary, given that the great majority of art therapists work single handed and unsupervised. This being the case, we feel that basic training at post-graduate level is essential to safeguard patients' interests and to give the best possible service.'

(Gilroy and Waller 21.10.77)

There followed a meeting at the DHSS in October 1978 at which the BAAT officers put their case, but were told that to look in detail at ideas for training and qualifications for art therapy was 'putting the cart before the horse'. This seemed to ignore the fact that there were, by this time, three programmes of art therapy training already in existence!

It would not be appropriate here to go into the long and difficult campaign by BAAT and representatives from the three courses which eventually led to the famous PM(80)35, September 1980, in which for the first time the DHSS stated that

'officers responsible for organising appropriate programmes of art activities of a therapeutic application with patients must possess a formal qualification in art which follows at least two years of full-time study beyond A level and a qualification in art therapy following a full-time course of at least one year at a recognised institution of higher or further education.'

As is often the case, practice had informed theory and those pioneers who had struggled to define a very definition-resistant activity to the point where training was actually taking place were boosted by the acceptance of their cause. The introduction of a new career and salary structure for art therapists which took them out of the *ad hoc* position and placed them under the Whitley Council gave impetus to the courses to consider critically their current practice and future plans, and to think about areas other than the health service where art therapists might be employed.[3]

Although there is much agreement within the existing courses about structuring, content, and standards, there are healthy differences which reflect the growing profession. Some of these relate to the demands of different employment situations. For instance, it may be necessary to train art therapy students who wish to work with, say, young children, the mentally handicapped, the elderly infirm, in specialized ways. Courses have developed expertise in certain areas, and will therefore attract students who see their future employed therein.

The colleges are, however, faced with a dauting task of having only one year full-time or two years part-time to train an artist in 'the therapeutic application of their art skills'. It must be stressed, though, that this year is not simply 'tacked on' to the first degree but is an integral part of the whole education of the art therapist. Failure to perceive this means that the one year is dismissed as being impossibly inadequate by all concerned, not least by students and staff, and by other professionals. The difficulty lies in finding a means of using this year to its best advantage, to enable students to acquire the basic 'therapeutic attitude', from which they may develop afterwards and at least be aware of what they do not know. The problem has to be lived with until such time as improvements in the economic climate and a greater acceptance of the value of art therapy lead to a longer course being possible. Such a course may well have as its emphasis the development of art therapy as a new form of non-verbal psychotherapy. It follows that art therapy students face a role in which they are pioneers in a new profession and have to live comfortably with this fact, while bringing together the areas of art and psychotherapy.

The Diploma courses are as a result rigorous in their selection process. Applicants for training should normally have qualifications of the following kind: a first degree, usually in art and design, although graduates from psychology, sociology, or the history of art, and other related areas may be considered if they can demonstrate some ability in and commitment to the practice of the visual arts. The entrance policy for the diploma courses may be summed up as seeking applicants who have realized in practical terms the worth of art activity in their own personal development. It is not so much that they have achieved high degrees of technical skill (although this is the expectation) but that through art they have come to be more aware and in touch with themselves and their environment. This is vital if, as therapists, they are to communicate the worth of art expression to their clients as a process of release, communication, growth, and self-discovery.

In addition to these requirements, applicants are required to have some experience of work in the health or social services or special education before commencing the course. This period ranges from a minimum of six months (Herts College, St Albans) to one year (Goldsmith's College) and is seen as a necessary opportunity for applicants to sample the kind of work and style of institution that they are likely to encounter as qualified therapists. It is also an indication of the motivation of would-be applicants.

As the courses are post-graduate, students will be in their early twenties as a minimum. However, it is recognized that a therapist requires maturity and developed self-awareness and applications are encouraged from mature persons. The usual age range of students is from 24 to 55 years or over, with 30 being an average.

In selecting candidates, courses look for the following characteristics: an understanding of the kind of course he or she is undertaking, including recognition of the emotionally taxing nature of the work involved – this will be particularly important in relation to the inclusion in the course of a training experience in psychotherapy and practical art therapy – a commitment to undertake study at the level required and to participate in the demands of clinical placement. Taking an art therapy course is one of the most demanding, in terms of time and emotional and professional commitment, of any post-graduate training schemes.

In looking for students, priority is given to those who show understanding of the young and still developing nature of the profession of art therapy and the effect of this on future career prospects (which, incidentally, are surprisingly good). Students must possess the basic skills and attitudes necessary for the course – a degree of creativity and openness, ability to express ideas well, personality characteristics such as warmth, flexibility, tolerance; emotional toughness and sensitivity to others combined in a stable personality. These minimum characteristics are what is normally taken as evidence that an applicant is likely to benefit from a course, that they can cope with the practical, academic, and psychological demands of courses, and that they show evidence of the character required of therapists.

As the courses are designed to equip students with basic theoretical knowledge and practical experience of work in a variety of situations, students are made aware of the administrative structure of the health and social services, the education system, and the relationships between them. Students are trained to make effective contact with permanent teams and be active in discussions at case conferences and higher policy levels. Good working relations with colleagues and co-operation with other members of staff who may hold views opposed to art therapy are stressed and the student is expected to be aware of the difference between his or her self-perceived role and that expected of him or her within the formal structure of the hospital and to explore ways of achieving greater congruency between the two.

The difficulty for staff involved in training is how to enable the student to acquire the 'therapeutic attitude' and to be able to communicate adequately within a staff team that is likely to be primarily non-visually trained. Art therapy students have to be rather exceptional people in that, on the one hand, they need to be deeply in touch with their own non-verbal creative processes and those of the patient, and, on the other, they have to be able to transpose this into a mode of communication with others which will ultimately be beneficial to the patients in their care.

A central aspect of the training is the concept of the growth of the student as a whole person, developing the intellectual and practical skills required, but also, and perhaps more important, developing emotional growth and self-awareness. This concept recognizes the fact that therapy involves a developing relationship that must work at the non-verbal affective level, as much as at a verbal and cognitive level. An awareness of this dynamic is essential for the therapist to function effectively.

The courses seek to link theoretical studies with practical application throughout, for a separation of theory and practice could lead to the student seeing his education as consisting of a number of theoretical items to be stored in readiness for the final assessment, and practical items which may come in useful during his career as a therapist. Therefore, the academic and practical units in the courses are arranged so that within a comparatively short period of time, theory and practice are brought together in clinical work. By alternating periods of clinical activity with academic study, students are required at all times to relate the two aspects of course content. On placement, then, the student is constantly encouraged to operate with respect to both these aspects, and to pass flexibly from one to the other. In this way he or she cannot avoid querying abstract formulations in the light of practical outcomes.

The focus of any course, is, however, art therapy theory. The courses are designed so that other elements, theoretical, practical, and exploratory, feed into it while it, in turn, feeds back. In the past, art therapy has lacked a coherent theoretical background; like other forms of psychotherapy its practical applications have often embodied speculative explanations offered in advance of the evidence. The history, development, and interconnection of the ideas and practices from which art therapy derives are presented to students so that they can relate their increasing understanding to a clear conceptual scheme. Consequently, art therapy is seen as a vital part of a whole body of ideas and techniques. As the training period progresses, methodological issues arising from the practice of art therapy are examined in detail so that students can develop a rationale for their subsequent work in a chosen field.

Usually the teaching takes the form of a combination of lectures and seminars provided by members of the course staff and a range of visiting specialists, including practising art therapists. Seminars relate to lectures, but are also developed as an investigative process with an emphasis on participation by students. As the lecture programme covers areas related to art therapy, the students also gain an understanding and ability to use the basic terminology current in psychiatry and to be aware of the current theories regarding the causes of mental illness and handicap and their treatment; or at least should be in a position to consult appropriate sources of reference. Also, as the art therapist will often function closely with psychologists, social workers, and psychotherapists, the courses aim to develop a basic appreciation of psychology as a science of human behaviour. The student will then be aware of psychological theories of personality and develop a basic knowledge of the main psychological treatments in psychotherapy and their relationship to the theories on which they are based.

The range of problems presented in mental illness and mental handicap is vast, and therefore no single art medium could be considered as an appropriate tool for treatment in all circumstances. Students are therefore encouraged to explore the emotional, physical, and intellectual experiences involved in using a wide range of media and processes and special attention is given to those which are usually available in hospitals and other centres.

Art therapy workshops provide the student with an opportunity to use these art materials within the framework of an experiential group where they are 'as if' patient but also trainee therapists. This is a difficult area of the course for students to negotiate, as are the psychotherapy groups, for the student is expected to participate fully and experience the process for himself, yet at the same time, he is required to assess and analyse his performance and to understand the role he plays within the group dynamics. Through such workshops, students can establish a sensitivity to the development of their personality (and the corresponding hindrances to this) and acquire an increased understanding into the workings of such processes within themselves. This conscious link between self and art expression should help in discriminating between nominal 'achievement' in art and important personal discoveries expressed even in the most rudimentary form. This self-awareness provides a confident base for 'mirroring' back a patient's discoveries to him in verbal form, and for communicating verbally with colleagues, untrained in art, the result of sessions with patients. The nature of a therapeutic relationship is therefore experienced and considered in discussion.

As previously mentioned, a large part of the teaching programme involves a clinical placement where students carry out periods of art therapy practice under the guidance of placement supervisors and college tutors. Placements used by the courses may be in psychiatric hospitals, psychiatric wings of general hospitals, hospitals for the mentally handicapped, adult training centres, day centres, reception and assessment centres, and special schools. The clinical placement ensures that students are exposed to the real working situation and it is a vital part of the course. Selection of placement normally takes into account the student's career interest and previous work experience. Normally, by the end of the course, each student will have had the experience of working in at least one and possibly two institutions. Placement provides the students with opportunities to relate the theoretical knowledge and practical skills gained during course work to the clinical setting. It provides the opportunity for teaching staff to supervise the · student in conjunction with the placement clinical supervisor in a highly structured way.

Given the demanding nature of this one-year full-time course, or the slightly less pressured two-year part-time one, it is a credit to the graduates that they have made such a strong commitment and have gone on to establish new posts and to contribute energetically to the new profession through part-time teaching on courses, research, and further training. There is, however, a temptation when students are on such an intense one-year programme, trying to come to terms with unfamiliar disciplines, concepts, and ways of working, to jettison their previous involvement with their own art work. Even though in the art therapy workshops they are involved as individuals within a group in the process of making and exploration, they may, in their enthusiasm to acquire the 'new language' feel inadequate and even reject their artist selves. This is a danger which must be overcome, otherwise art therapy will lose that ingredient which makes it powerful and effective in treatment – namely the non-verbal, expressive, integrating, communicative, and liberating aspect of the art-making process.

Notes

1 A full account of the early professional development of art therapy, including accounts of the committee meetings mentioned here may be found in: Waller, D. (1972) 'A Personal Appraisal of Art Therapy in Britain'. MA thesis, Royal College of Art, London.
2 As above.
3 Full information on the courses approved by the British Association of Art Therapists may be obtained from BAAT, 13C Northwood Road, London, N6 5TL or from the colleges themselves:
The Division of Art and Psychology, Herts College of Art and Design, 7, Hatfield Road, St Albans, Herts. AL1 3RS. Tel: 0727 64414.
Art Therapy Unit, Goldsmith's College, 27, Albury St, London SE8 3PT. Tel: 01-692 1424.
City of Birmingham Polytechnic, Faculty of Art and Design, Corporation St, Gosta Green, Birmingham, B4 7DX. Tel: 021-359 6721.
The American Association of Art Therapy publishes a list of available courses in the USA and Europe:
American Association of Art Therapists, 37, Pike Hill Rd, West Topsham, Vermont 05086, USA.
American Art Therapy Association, 516, 5th Avenue, Suite 507, New York 10036, USA.

At the time of reprinting there have been various changes in the art therapy training courses in the UK. The course in Birmingham is no longer a qualifying course for art therapists. A new course is being established at the University of Sheffield in the Division of Continuing Education, 156 Broomspring Lane, Sheffield S10 2TN.

Acknowledgements

From Diane Waller to Andrea Gilroy for her support and encouragement.

Biographical note

Kim James MA Royal College of Art; MSC in Neurology and Cybernetics at Brunel University; Member of the Scientific Committee of the International Association of Psychomotricity; and at present course leader of Postgraduate Diploma in Art Therapy (CNAA), Herts College of Art and Design, St Albans.

Diane Waller See note on pp. 13–14.

Name index

Subject index